Y0-CLX-145

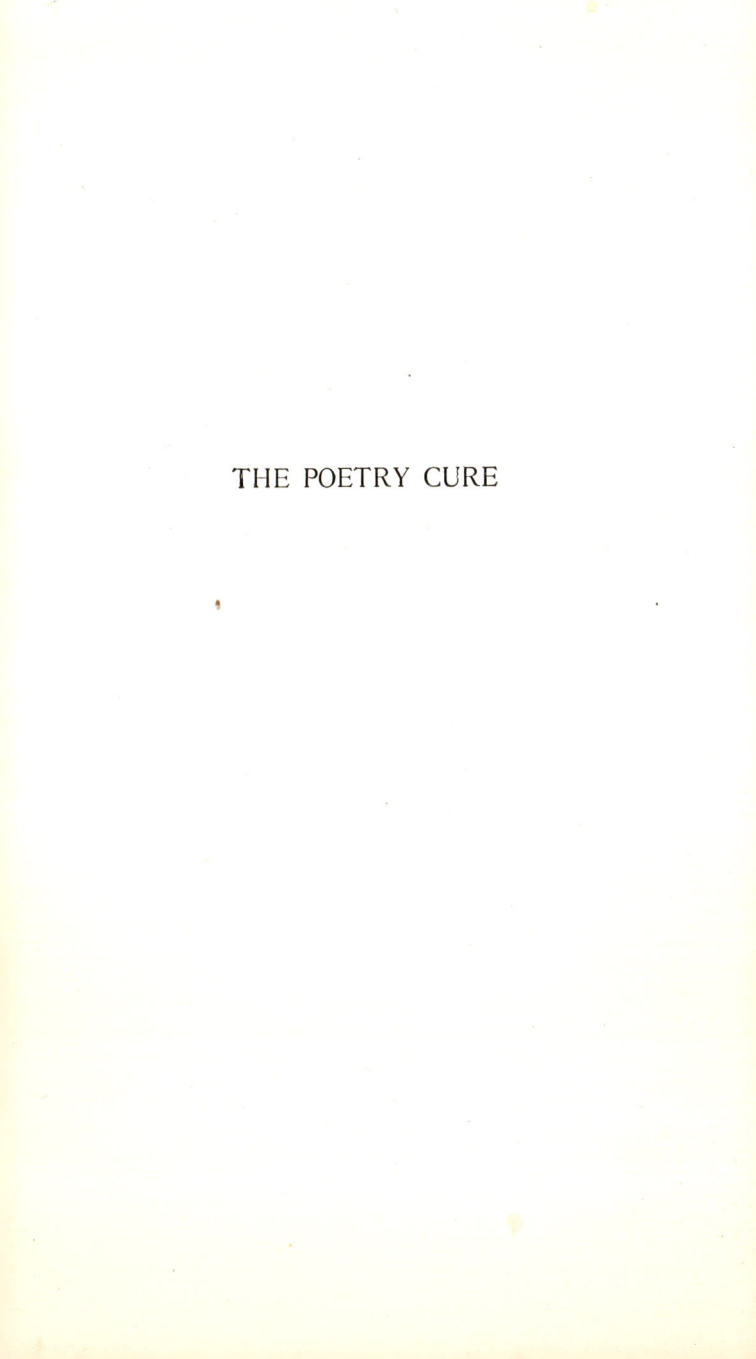

THE POETRY CURE

"Poetry is no more a narcotic than a stimulant; it is a universal bitter-sweet mixture for all possible household emergencies. . . . A well-chosen anthology is a complete dispensary of medicine for the more common mental disorders, and may be used as much for prevention as cure."

ROBERT GRAVES, ON ENGLISH POETRY, 1922.

"O health! health! the blessing of the rich! the riches of the poor! who can buy thee at too dear a rate, since there is no enjoying the world without thee?"

BEN JONSON, VOLPONE. ACT II.

"He ate and drank the precious words,
  His spirit grew robust;
 He knew no more that he was poor,
  Nor that his frame was dust."

EMILY DICKINSON.

THE POETRY CURE

A POCKET MEDICINE CHEST OF VERSE

COMPOUNDED BY

ROBERT HAVEN SCHAUFFLER

Author of "Scum o' the Earth," "Magic Flame," "Fiddler's Luck," "The Joyful Heart," etc. Editor of "Our American Holidays" series, and "Through Italy with the Poets."

NEW YORK
DODD, MEAD AND COMPANY
1932

COPYRIGHT, 1925
BY ROBERT HAVEN SCHAUFFLER

Published, November, 1925
Second Printing, December, 1925
Third Printing, January, 1926
Fourth Printing, March, 1926
Fifth Printing, August, 1926
Sixth Printing, January, 1927
Seventh Printing, February, 1928
Eighth Printing, April, 1929
Ninth Printing, September, 1932

PRINTED IN U. S. A.

THE VAIL-BALLOU PRESS
BINGHAMTON AND NEW YORK

To the noble army of

CREATIVE LIBRARIANS

PRACTITIONERS ALL—

CONSCIOUSLY OR UNCONSCIOUSLY—

OF THE POETRY CURE

THIS BOOK

IS RESPECTFULLY AND CORDIALLY

DEDICATED

ACKNOWLEDGMENTS

For their courteous permission to reprint copyrighted poems included in this volume, thanks are due to the following publishers (alphabetically listed):

D. APPLETON & CO.: "Spring Ode" from NOAH AN' JONAH AN' CAP'N JOHN SMITH, by Don Marquis.

BONI & LIVERIGHT: "The Madman" and "Rufus Prays" from DUBLIN DAYS, by L. A. G. Strong.

BOWES & BOWES: "A Sonnet" from LAPSUS CALAMI AND OTHER VERSES, by James Kenneth Stephen.

PETER G. BOYLE: "A California Vignette," "Not Our Good Luck," "Salmon Fishing," "Suicide's Stone," *"From* Tamar" and "To the Stone Cutters" from TAMAR, by Robinson Jeffers.

JONATHAN CAPE LTD.: "Ale," "Leisure," "Sadness and Joy," and "Songs of Joy" from COLLECTED POEMS, by William H. Davies.

W. B. CONKEY COMPANY: "The World's Need" from PICKED POEMS, by Ella Wheeler Wilcox.

THOMAS Y. CROWELL & CO.: "Communion," "Sleep" and "The Soldier" from COLLECTED POEMS, by Sophie Jewett.

GEORGE H. DORAN CO.: *"From* Sleep" and "Verification" from PARSON'S PLEASURE, by Christopher Morley. "A Prayer for the Old Courage" from A WORLD OF WINDOWS, by Charles Hanson Towne, copyrighted by George H. Doran Company, 1919.

DOUBLEDAY, PAGE & COMPANY: "The Rich Man" and "Villanelle With Stevenson's Assistance" from TOBOGGANING ON PARNASSUS, by Franklin P. Adams. "Flood Tide" and "Ladders Through the Blue" from

ACKNOWLEDGMENTS

LADDERS THROUGH THE BLUE, by Hermann Hagedorn, copyrighted 1925. "The Man With the Hoe" from THE MAN WITH THE HOE, "Outwitted" and "Victory in Defeat" from THE SHOES OF HAPPINESS, by Edwin Markham. "Unrest" by Don Marquis.

DUFFIELD & CO.: "Dedication" from COLLECTED POEMS, by John Erskine. "At the End of the Day" from ALONG THE TRAIL, by Richard Hovey.

E. P. DUTTON & CO.: "The Spark" from THE COAT WITHOUT A SEAM, by Helen Gray Cone. "Measure Me, Sky!" from A CANOPIC JAR, by Leonora Speyer. "Creeds" from LANTERNS IN GETHSEMANE, by Willard Wattles.

FUNK & WAGNALLS CO.: *"From* Town Pictures" from BROAD-CAST, by Ernest Crosby.

PAUL ELDER & CO.: "Sonnet" from SONNETS OF SPINSTERHOOD, by Snow Longley.

HARCOURT, BRACE & CO., INC.: "Spratt vs. Spratt" from "—AND OTHER POEMS," "Prayer" and "Voices" from CHALLENGE, by Louis Untermeyer, by permission of Harcourt, Brace and Company, Inc., holders of the copyright. "The Recompense" from THE CONTEMPLATIVE QUARRY, by Anna Wickham, copyrighted 1921 by Harcourt, Brace and Company, Inc. "Bells in the Rain" from NETS TO CATCH THE WIND, by Elinor Wylie, copyrighted 1921 by Harcourt, Brace and Company, Inc.

HARPER & BROTHERS: "Strictly Germ-Proof" from THE LAUGHING MUSE, by Arthur Guitermann. "First Fig" from A FEW FIGS FROM THISTLES, by Edna St. Vincent Millay, copyrighted 1922 by Edna St. Vincent Millay.

HARR WAGNER PUBLISHING CO.: "Byron" from SONGS OF THE SIERRAS, VOL. II, "Columbus" and "For Those Who Fail" from INTRODUCTION AND AUTOBIOGRAPHY, VOL. I, by Joaquin Miller.

ACKNOWLEDGMENTS

Henry Holt and Company: "An Air of Coolness Plays Upon His Face," "The Anodyne," "For Sleep When Overtired or Worried," "O Altitudo!" and "To Safeguard the Heart from Hardness," from Fellow Captains, by Sarah N. Cleghorn. "A Child's Song Overheard" from Wilderness Songs, by Grace Hazard Conkling. "The Tuft of Flowers" from A Boy's Will, by Robert Frost. "Joy" and "They Will Say" from Chicago Poems, by Carl Sandburg. "The Factories" from The Factories, by Margaret Widdemer.

Houghton Mifflin Company: "Enamoured Architect of Airy Rhyme" from Poems, by Thomas Bailey Aldrich. "The Pool of Sleep" from Poems by Arlo Bates, by Arlo Bates. "Gladness"; and "So I May Feel the Hand of God" from Rose O' the Wind, by Anna Hempstead Branch. "Waiting," by John Burroughs. "The Hill-born" from In the High Hills, by Maxwell Struthers Burt. "The Flower Factory" from The Ride Home, by Florence Wilkinson Evans. "Doves," "The Kings" and "The Wild Ride" from Happy Ending, by Louise Imogen Guiney. "Discovery," by Hermann Hagedorn. "Pandora's Song" from The Fire Bringer, by William Vaughn Moody. "The Riderless Horse" and "Ecstasy" from Mothers and Men, by Harold Trowbridge Pulsifer. "The Secret" from The Lifted Cup and "My Wage" from The Door of Dreams, by Jessie B. Rittenhouse. "Scum o' the Earth" and "Harvest" from Magic Flame, by Robert Haven Schauffler. "Sursum Corda," by Edith M. Thomas.

Mitchell Kennerley: "Compensation" and "One Fight More," from The Earth Cry, by Theodosia Garrison.

Life Publishing Co.: "Advice to Worriers," by George Kaupman; "Epitaph for Any New Yorker," by Christopher Morley; "Song of the Open Country," by

ACKNOWLEDGMENTS

Dorothy Parker; all from POEMS FROM LIFE, 1923.

LITTLE, BROWN AND COMPANY: "My Nosegays are for Captives," "Simplicity," "I'm Nobody!" and "Morning" by Emily Dickinson.

LONGMANS, GREEN & CO.: "The Pillar of Cloud," by John Henry, Cardinal Newman. "One in the Infinite," by George Francis Savage-Armstrong. "The Optimist" from THE BIRD BRIDE, by Graham R. Tomson.

THE MACMILLAN COMPANY: "For Mercy, Courage, Kindness, Mirth," from SELECTED POEMS OF LAWRENCE BINYON, by Lawrence Binyon. *"From* The Deep" from POEMS, by Gladys Cromwell. "God's Pity" from THE GARDEN OF THE WEST, by Louise Driscoll. "Epitaph for a Poet" from SKYLINES AND HORIZONS, by DuBose Heyward. "The Bells of Heaven," by Ralph Hodgson. "Laugh and Be Merry" from COLLECTED POEMS, by John Masefield. "Let me Live Out My Years" from THE QUEST, by John G. Neihardt. *"From* Captain Craig" from COLLECTED POEMS, by Edwin Arlington Robinson. "Lessons" from LOVE SONGS, by Sara Teasdale. "Before Dawn in the Wood," by Marguerite Wilkinson. "Into the Twilight," "The Lake Isle of Innisfree," "An Old Song Resung" and "When You are Old" from COLLECTED POEMS; "To a Friend Whose Work Has Come to Nothing" and "To His Heart, Bidding It Have no Fear" from LATER POEMS; by William Butler Yeats.

ROBERT MCBRIDE & CO.: "The Night," from SONNETS AND VERSE, by Hilaire Belloc.

MCCLELLAND AND STEWART LIMITED: "Idle to Grieve" and "A Road Song," from BEAUTY AND LIFE; "An August Mood," and "Be Strong!" by Duncan Campbell Scott

THOMAS BIRD MOSHER: "Heroism," "A Little Song

ACKNOWLEDGMENTS xi

of Life" and "Tears," from A WAYSIDE HARP, by Lizette Woodworth Reese.

JOHN MURRAY: "Before Action," by William Noel Hodgson.

CHARLES SCRIBNER'S SONS: "A Pitcher of Mignonette" by Henry Cuyler Bunner from POEMS 1899. "Little Boy Blue" and "Wynken Blynken and Nod," from COLLECTED POEMS OF EUGENE FIELD by Eugene Field. "Ballade to Theocritus, In Winter" from BALLADES AND VERSES VAIN; and "The Odyssey," by Andrew Lang. "A Ballad of Trees and the Master" and "The Marshes of Glynn" from POEMS, by Sidney Lanier. "If This Were Faith" and "The Celestial Surgeon" from BALLADS AND OTHER POEMS, by Robert Louis Stevenson. "The Wind of Sorrow" from COLLECTED POEMS, by Henry Van Dyke. "A Lyrical Epigram," by Edith Wharton.

MARTIN SECKER LTD.: "The Old Ships" from COLLECTED POEMS, by James Elroy Flecker.

SIDGWICK & JACKSON LTD.: "From Ducks," reprinted by permission of the author and of the publishers, Sidgwick & Jackson Ltd., from DUCKS AND OTHER VERSES, by F. W. Harvey.

SMALL, MAYNARD & CO.: "Envoy" and "Over the Shoulders and Slopes of the Dune" from SONGS FROM VAGABONDIA; *From* The Word at St. Kavin's" by Bliss Carman. "Comrades," *From* Death Song" from THE MASQUE OF TALIESIN and "Vagabondia" from SONGS FROM VAGABONDIA, by Richard Hovey. Quatrain from THE HOUSE OF A HUNDRED LIGHTS, by Ridgely Torrence.

FREDERICK A. STOKES CO.: "Joy" from SHOES OF THE WIND, by Hilda Conkling.

HAROLD VINAL: "To One With Hands of Sleep," from NOR YOUTH NOR AGE.

ACKNOWLEDGMENTS

YALE UNIVERSITY PRESS: "We" from WAMPUM AND OLD GOLD, by Hervey Allen. "Courage" and "I Love the Friendly Faces of Old Sorrows" from BURNING BUSH, by Karle Wilson Baker. "The Falconer of God" from THE FALCONER OF GOD and "His Ally" from MERCHANTS FROM CATHAY by William Rose Benét. "Portrait of a Boy" from YOUNG ADVENTURE, by Stephen Vincent Benét. "The Escape" from THE MIDDLE MILES, by Lee Wilson Dodd.

Thanks are due to the following magazines:-

ATLANTIC MONTHLY: "On a Subway Express," by Chester Firkins.
THE BOOKMAN: "Epitaph for a Poet" from SKYLINES AND HORIZONS by DuBose Heyward.
CONTEMPORARY VERSE: "The Door," by Mary Carolyn Davies, "The Song of Dark Waters" and "A Street Car Symphony," by Roy Helton; "Comfort," by Margaret French Patton, and "Courage, Mon Ami!", by Willard Wattles.
HARPER'S MAGAZINE: "A Blackbird Suddenly," by Joseph Auslander.
THE LONDON SPECTATOR: "Ode to Discord."

For their kind permissions, thanks are also due to:-

Franklin P. Adams: "The Rich Man" and "Villanelle, with Stevenson's Assistance," from TOBOGGANING ON PARNASSUS; and "Such Stuff as Dreams." Hervey Allen: "We," from WAMPUM AND OLD GOLD. Joseph Auslander: "A Blackbird Suddenly." Katharine Lee Bates: "The Creed of the Wood," from THE RETINUE. William Rose Benét: "The Falconer of God" from THE FALCONER OF GOD and "His Ally" from MERCHANTS FROM CATHAY. E. F. Benson: "Prayer" from THE IMAGE IN THE SAND.

ACKNOWLEDGMENTS

Lawrence Binyon: "For Mercy, Courage, Kindness, Mirth" from SELECTED POEMS OF LAWRENCE BINYON. Anna Hempstead Branch: "Gladness"; and "So I May Feel the Hands of God" from ROSE O' THE WIND. Sarah N. Cleghorn: "An Air of Coolness Plays Upon His Face," "The Anodyne," "For Sleep When Overtired Or Worried," "O Altitudo!" "To Safeguard the Heart from Hardness," from FELLOW CAPTAINS. Isabel Fiske Conant: "Angler" and "Kind Sleep" from FRONTIER. Helen Gray Cone: "The Spark" from THE COAT WITHOUT A SEAM. William H. Davies: "Ale," "Leisure," "Sadness and Joy" and "Songs of Joy" from COLLECTED POEMS. Lee Wilson Dodd: "The Escape"; "More Life. . . . More!" from A MODERN ALCHEMIST. Louise Driscoll: "God's Pity." John Erskine: "Dedication" from COLLECTED POEMS. Florence Wilkinson Evans: "The Flower Factory" from THE RIDE HOME. Arthur Davidson Ficke: "Portrait of an Old Woman" Chester Firkins, by permission of Miss Ina Firkins, holder of the copyright: "On a Subway Express." Hamlin Garland: "Do You Fear the Wind?" Theodosia Garrison: "Compensation" and "One Fight More." "Sleep Sweet," by permission of Mrs. Helen Granville Barker, daughter of Ellen M. Huntington Gates. Arthur Guiterman: "Strictly Germ-Proof" from THE LAUGHING MUSE. Hermann Hagedorn: "Discovery"; "Flood Tide" and "Ladders Through the Blue" from LADDERS THROUGH THE BLUE. F. W. Harvey: *"From* Ducks," Oliver Herford: "The Chimpanzee." DuBose Heyward: "Epitaph for a Poet" from SKYLINES AND HORIZONS. M. A DeWolfe Howe: "At the Heart," "The Helmsman" and "A Treasure House." Robinson Jeffers: "A California Vignette," "Not Our Good Luck," "Salmon Fishing," "Suicide's Stone," "To the Stone Cutters," *"From* Tamar" from TAMAR. Archibald

xiv ACKNOWLEDGMENTS

Lampman, by permission of his literary executor, Duncan Campbell Scott: "Midsummer Night" from POEMS OF ARCHIBALD LAMPMAN. Russell Hillard Loines, by permission of his executor, Mrs. Katharine Loines: "On a Magazine Sonnet." Haniel Long: "Dead Men Tell No Tales." Walter de la Mare: "Tartary." Edwin Markham: "The Man with the Hoe" from THE MAN WITH THE HOE; "Outwitted" and "Victory in Defeat" from THE SHOES OF HAPPINESS. Don Marquis: "Unrest" and "Spring Ode" from NOAH AN' JONAH AN' CAP'N JOHN SMITH. Brander Matthews: "The Ballade of Adaptation." Marjorie Meeker: "Walls." Scudder Middleton: "A Woman." Virginia Moore: "Courage." Shaemas O'Sheel: "Exultation." Lilla Cabot Perry: "Death, Life, Fear" and "Horseman Springing from the Dark: A Dream." Harold Trowbridge Pulsifer: "Ecstasy" and "The Riderless Horse" from MOTHERS AND MEN. Lizette Woodworth Reese: "Heroism," "A Little Song of Life" and "Tears" from A WAYSIDE HARP. Jessie B. Rittenhouse: "My Wage" from THE DOOR OF DREAMS and "The Secret" from THE LIFTED CUP. Charles G. D. Roberts: "All Night the Lone Cicada." Edwin Arlington Robinson: *"From* Captain Craig" from COLLECTED POEMS. James Rorty: "The Bell" and "Escape." George Francis Savage-Armstrong, by permission of Mrs. Savage Armstrong: "One in the Infinite." Duncan Campbell Scott: "An August Mood," "Be Strong!" "Idle to Grieve" and "A Road Song." Leonora Speyer: "Measure Me, Sky!" from A CANOPIC JAR; *"From* Of Mountains," "Protest in Passing" and "Duet." George Sterling: "The Balance." Sara Teasdale: "In the Wood"; "Lessons" from LOVE SONGS. The late Edith M. Thomas: SURSUM CORDA. Wilfrid Thorley: "Buttercups." Nancy Byrd Turner: "Concerning Brownie," "Going

ACKNOWLEDGMENTS

up to London" and "To a Staring Baby in a Perambulator." Jean Starr Untermeyer: "Nature Cure." Louis Untermeyer: "Spratt vs. Spratt" from "—AND OTHER POEMS"; "Prayer" and "Voices" from CHALLENGE. Henry Van Dyke: "The Wind of Sorrow" from COLLECTED POEMS. Harold Vinal: "To One with Hands of Sleep from NOR YOUTH NOR AGE. May Williams Ward: "My House." Carolyn Wells (Mrs. Hadwin Houghton): "A Penitential Week." Grace Hoffman White: "Unvanquished," from WINGS TO DARE. William Butler Yeats: "Into the Twilight," "The Lake Isle of Innisfree," "An Old Song Resung" and "When You are Old" from LATER POEMS; "To a Friend Whose Work Has Come to Nothing" and "To His Heart, Bidding It Have No Fear" from COLLECTED POEMS.

For suggestion and criticism the editor is especially grateful to his friends: Mr. Stephen Vincent Benét, Mr. Hermann Hagedorn, Mr. DuBose Heyward, Miss Winifred Heath, Dr. Everett Dean Martin, Miss Mary Sandall, Dr. Edwin Arlington Robinson and Mrs. Ernst Filsinger (Sara Teasdale); to his friend Mr. Louis Untermeyer for a creative criticism of the manuscript, and for radically rewriting his poem, "Spratt vs. Spratt," with a view to its use here as a "Mental Cocktail"; to Mrs. Sybil Hastings for her devoted labors with the proofs and in preparing the indices; to the New York Society Library, the New York Public Library, and its Library School for many forms of generous assistance; to the audiences who have responded to the editor's lectures on this subject, with information about poems which have proved of therapeutic value; and more than all to the late Dr. S. Weir Mitchell, to whose generous advice and encouragement in 1910 this book is deeply indebted.

DIRECTIONS

(Read Well Before Using!)

To forestall any misapprehension let it be said at once that The Poetry Cure does not mean a cure for poetry, any more than "the rest cure" means a cure for rest, or than "the Keeley cure" means a cure for Keeley.

An essay of mine called "The Musical Pharmacy" appeared fourteen years ago.[1] Its suggestions on the use of certain sorts of music for certain sorts of prevention and cure, were fortunate enough to play an influential part in the movement which soon installed music in hospitals, asylums, homes and sanatoriums as an accepted therapeutic agent.

The success of this movement encouraged me to take up another long cherished plan. For it seemed that one thing was still more needed than musical therapeutics. This was The Poetry Cure.

I had dreamed of a cheap and convenient pocket anthology of remedies for such troubles as fear, fatigue, swollen ego, ingrowing ugliness, the blues, pettiness, impatience, insomnia, torpid imagination, sorrow, hardening of the heart, sluggish blood, myopic vision of the inner eye, and other common ailments.

[1] In *The Outlook* and in *The Musical Amateur*. (Houghton, Mifflin Co., 1911.)

The compilation and testing of this book brought out unforeseen difficulties. The fact soon became evident that few poems affect everybody in exactly the same way. Where half-a-dozen people react similarly to a dose of aconite, they may react in three or four different ways to Henley's "Invictus." What is salvation for the average Jones may be poison for the exceptional Smith. What would lift me out of the blues might conceivably plunge you deeper within them. (Only I should think you abnormal.) And a lyric which filled me with eager vitality might possibly lull you to sleep—if you were outside the common run of people.

But even in spite of such wide variations as these, poetry was found to be still more dependably uniform in its healing effect than the dependable but vaguer art of music. Perhaps this is because the subject matter of a poem is much the same for everyone; while, within certain wide limits, a Chopin nocturne or a Beethoven minuet can mean all things to all men.

For a long period I studied, collected, and tried the effects of various sorts of verse on patients in my poetic clinic. Finally, a year ago, it grew evident that enough poems might be counted on to affect enough people with enough power and uniformity, to make possible a science of poetic therapeutics, and justify the present book.

Any poem that has genuine healing in its wings, usually commences its medical career the moment it

READ WELL BEFORE USING!   xix

is conceived. It begins by promptly curing its creator.

Charles Kingsley once went, on friendly invitation, to preach in a London church. After the sermon, his reverend host rushed to the pulpit, coarsely repudiated everything that Kingsley had said, and branded him with various impolite epithets ranging from Judas Iscariot downwards. A riot was narrowly averted.

Naturally the poet was furious. But, as he went home, a line of verse began to take form in his mind; then another and another. Before he knew it, his most famous poem, "The Three Fishers," was born. And Kingsley was surprised to find that his fury had vanished. The act of creation had absorbed the poisonous secretions of anger like so much blotting paper. It had richly compensated him for a bad quarter of an hour.

Such experiences are common among poets. Goethe once remarked: "I habitually convert whatever rejoices or worries or otherwise concerns me into a poem, and so get rid of it, and at once correct my conception of outward things and set my mind at rest."

William Blake was in the secret too:

> "I was angry with my friend:
> I told my wrath, my wrath did end.
> I was angry with my foe:
> I told it not, my wrath did grow."

And William H. Davies, the tramp and beggar poet, confesses:

> "My mind has thunderstorms,
> That brood for heavy hours;
> Until they rain me words."

But, once the relieving rain has begun to fall, the poet admits—

> "My thoughts are dancing flowers
> And joyful singing birds."

According to Ribot, the French psychologist, "all invention presupposes a want, a craving . . . an unsatisfied impulse. . . . The origin of all imaginative creation is a need, a desire." The poet can usually find quicker and easier relief from his troubles than other artists can, because the apparatus he requires for self-expression is so simple and portable. He is not encumbered with the problem of how to get at a lump of clay or a yard of canvas or a grand piano. If anything mental or spiritual ails him he can alleviate it instantly by scribbling on his cuff just the poem for the complaint. As Shakespeare puts it, he can "turn diseases to commodity."

When the new psychology discovers the poet at work on his cuff, it will pull a long face and declare that he is starting up a thing called a psychic mechanism. There are three principal kinds: mechanisms of escape, of self-defence and of compensation.

A word about this trio. As I understand it, escape is simply taking refuge from the actual. Obeying a strong, primordial instinct of self-preservation, we flee

READ WELL BEFORE USING! xxi

from a reality that is unpleasant or even dangerous, into a delightful region suffused with "the light that never was on sea or land." Philosophy, religion, music and poetry all conspire to lure us into this never-never world of topsy-turvy, where loss is gain, torture—bliss, failure—success, loneliness—fellowship, and death—life. The escape mechanism shatters experience to bits, and then remoulds it "nearer to the heart's desire." It affords us a respite in which we may gather renewed strength for the old struggle to adapt ourselves to reality.

The defence mechanism consists in the sort of thinking through which the ego protects itself against harmful obsessions and actions, and preserves its self-respect. Purposeful forgetting, neurotic symptoms and religious or patriotic or ascetic fanaticism may all be defences which protect one from more destructive unconscious impulses.

Lastly, compensation is a way of recovering one's psychic balance. *It is closely akin to defence.* A person whose unconscious mind is corroded by an inferiority complex, will often consciously, but without realizing why he does it,—cultivate a feeling of competence and solid self-esteem. War heroism, like charity, may cover a multitude of sins. The loss of a limb may be compensated by a sense of gain in character. Grief may be offset by a heightened capacity for esthetic appreciation. In the words of A. E's "Hope in Failure,"[1]

[1] see p. 13.

"The beauty that breathes in thy spirit shall shape of thy sorrow a flower."

Ugliness may be compensated by virtue; old age by knowing better than the young; a bad stutter by literary fluency; tuberculosis by optimism.

These three mechanisms, then, build up within us the spiritual factors which, in their turn, construct the ideal that makes our actual existence. Through escape, defence and compensation our unconsciousness legitimately preserves those vital and indispensable fictions about ourselves which are the most valuable things in life for us. They are so valuable because, as Everett Dean Martin explains,[1] they help men to keep their "personality pictures" unbroken, "to save their self-valuations—their souls."

Now, when we find the poet at work on his cuff, curing himself by starting up some mechanism or other, let us not be disgusted or disconcerted by all this technical jargon. Let us simply realize that folks were unconsciously using poetry as a means of escape, defence and compensation some thousands of years before Freud, Adler and Jung discovered the polysyllable and popularized psycho-analysis.

Without the aid of these gentlemen, Homer, David, Sophocles and Dante made their own lives more bearable. In our century, William H. Davies defended himself against the agitations of his budding fame

[1] In his brilliant book "The Mystery of Religion," Harper's, 1924.

READ WELL BEFORE USING! xxiii

and the lion-hunters of the metropolis, by writing "Leisure,"[1] which begins:

> "What is this life if, full of care,
> We have no time to stand and stare?"

Without knowing anything about psycho-analysis, Coleridge once escaped on the wings of song from the dreariness of a petty, drab life of duns and domestic worry. One afternoon while he slept, his unconscious mind masterfully took charge. In a trice it built him, for immediate occupancy, the glamorous dream palace of Kubla Khan.[2] It was unfortunate that before the estate was quite complete, with dancing pavilion, shrine of love and beauty, bowling green, marble pool and hanging gardens of the moon, that miserable butcher's man arrived with an overdue account, so that the sprite-builder vanished in alarm and never came back to finish the job. But all the same, the adventure helped Coleridge over a very difficult time.

Now this sort of fairy intervention in the life of the bard is all very well. But what interests me most about The Poetry Cure is its effect, not on the few hundreds of poets, but on their many millions of readers.

For the best thing about this sort of therapeutics is: that the very poem which a poet has created for

[1] see p. 305.
[2] see p. 167.

himself as a means of escape or defence or compensation, *can very often provide these same luxuries for uncreative folk,* who are not so lucky as to be able to cure themselves with a few strokes of a pencil.

All they need is a little imagination and a pocket medicine chest of verse. Anatole France somewhere says: "It is the imagination with its lies—that sows all the virtue and beauty in life,"—also most of the mental and spiritual health,—he might well have added.

When Mrs. Quicksilver was shown the eminent sculptor's portrait medallion of her son, she wrinkled up her nose at the beautiful greenish-brown bronze, and cried: "But my Billy ain't as dark-complected as that!" Any reader with no more imagination than the good Mrs. Quicksilver had better lay this volume down. Unless he can allow for that slight element of illusion without which all art becomes poor photography, he will find nothing for him in The Poetry Cure.

I do not know if "The Three Fishers" ever compensated any reader for the loss of his cherished anger. Charles Kingsley never bore malice long. And it may be that the distraction of writing almost any sort of poem would have cooled him off.

But his case is exceptional. There are few sufferers from the strenuous life of cities who can not get from reading "Leisure" the same sort of comforting defence that Davies found in writing it. And, after escaping into the enchanted kingdom of Kubla Khan, the stimulated imagination of almost any reader can distinctly hear the milk of paradise purling deliciously down the cobbled ways of Xanadu,—or even of Jersey City!

This apparent miracle is easy to explain. The unconscious mind of the poet rises to the emergency of the moment, and invents a poem whose argument provides a dream-solution of his—and your—mental or spiritual ailment. It puts the reader, as Goethe says, 'into the same mood the poet is in during the poem's creation.'

If the poet is of the first rank, he does more. He clothes the argument in hypnotic word-music that doubles the therapeutic effect. Few people realize what a powerful combination we have in such a union of argument and melody. Everyone now admits the healing value of the music of Schubert, Beethoven, Brahms, Wagner and Franck. But the healing value of the music of Shakespeare, Milton, Browning, Masefield and Guiney has hardly begun to win recognition.

Doubtless, as old George Herbert pointed out,

"Music helps not the toothache."

I would not claim that Keats can set a smashed collarbone, or that Edna St. Vincent Millay is sovereign for lumbago. But in the less material sphere of the mental and the spiritual, poetry can help far worse ills than these, although its action may prove somewhat more indirect, subtle and deferred than the patient expects.

The ancient Greeks apparently knew more about

The Poetry Cure than any other folk before or since. They believed with Aristotle that poetic tragedy purged the mind "through pity and terror." Certainly the pity acted efficaciously when the Greek prisoners in the quarries of Syracuse gained their liberty by reciting Euripides to their cruel captors.

But all this was long ago. Between that day and ours I know of only one advocate of the therapeutic value of verse. It is significant that Ernst von Feuchtersleben, one of the leading pioneers of psychotherapy, should also have been the well-known poet who wrote *"Ess ist bestimmt in Gottes Rat."* He insisted that poetry was one of the chief sources of mental and spiritual well-being.

Four current writers touch briefly on this subject.

Stekel, a German scientist, has recently described [1] how one can cure himself with poetry through an unconscious psychological analysis of his own hidden emotions, by which the latter are cleared up.

Prof. F. C. Prescott explains [2] why poetry is a safeguard for the individual and the race against mental disturbances and disease.

Poul Bjerre, M.D., the eminent Swedish psychotherapist, declares: [3] "The specific qualities of the poet are more essential for the development of health than are those of the logician. . . . Psychotherapy must be considered a form of poetry."

[1] In "Dichtung und Neurose."
[2] In "The Poetic Mind" (The Macmillan Co., 1922).
[3] In "The History and Practice of Psychanalysis," 1920

READ WELL BEFORE USING! xxvii

David Seabury shows [1] how the genius of the poet "is able to release for us our own inmost urgings. . . . It reaches back into us and stirs primal impulses in our own depths that we have longed to express." When unexpressed, these impulses may turn against us in the form of various neurotic disturbances. When expressed through poetry or other arts, they bring release and health. This is "as essential to the cure of neurosis as hygienic procedure in the handling of contagious disease. . . . Not until mankind learns the importance of creative expression to his health, shall we have a better moral world."

Let us pay no attention to any faddy psychologists who would persuade us that it is harmful to use our psychic mechanisms for escape, defence and compensation. To stimulate such a use has always been one of the chief functions of the fine arts. It has always been legitimate, and always will be.

A large, ordinary anthology of verse is like a drug store. It contains just the thing for your complaint, —that is, if you know where to look for it. But an indiscriminate sampling of the stock may have serious consequences. Be careful to pass by the skull and cross-bones bottles! Mental or spiritual troubles may be aggravated as well as helped by verse. Avoid a bitter or cruel poem as you would a maniac or a leper. St. Augustine called poetry "devil's wine." This sort is.

Evade the blasé or grouchy bard who infests the foot-

[1] In "Unmasking Our Minds," Boni & Liveright, 1924.

hills of Parnassus, as though he had developed a new kind of contagious paralysis. Hasten from the empested frivolity of the Pollyanna optimist as though he had the laughing sickness. How often do I tremble for the unwary when I see him turned loose in such a vast metrical pharmacy as "The Home Book of Verse"!

I am not so Pollyannesque as to feel that the medicated music of poetry can work any sudden, radical change in character. But it undoubtedly exercises a subtly powerful effect on mood. And is not the persistent correction of adverse moods, bound in time to have a permanent effect on character?

Why should not poetry coöperate with those sensible Chinese doctors who charge only for their success in keeping the patients from falling ill? Some day our physicians may come to agree with Robert Graves that verse is good "for prevention as well as cure."

In one respect, at least, I resemble the leaders of the medical profession. I do not promise to refund your money in case I fail. I merely prescribe the best preventatives or remedies yet discovered for your particular case,—and relapse into watchful waiting.

Possibly all the poems in this medicine chest are not for you. Some of them may make you bristle like the traditional Frenchman of fiction at the sight of drinking water. For, in almost every compartment of the chest you will find poems both of escape, defence and compensation. One of these kinds may meet the need of the moment. The others may irritate you, or leave you cold.

READ WELL BEFORE USING! xxix

For instance, if you are sorrowful, and I come at you suddenly and exuberantly with:

> "God's in His heaven—
> All's right with the world!" [1]

your bloodshot eye may possibly peer about for the first lethal weapon handy. You are so constituted that, when in the depths, you do not want a poem of escape.[2] But tastes differ. I know an exceedingly intellectual woman who, when at her lowest, can be cured by a rendition of "There'll be a hot time in the old town tonight!" It takes all sorts to make a clinic.

On the other hand, if, instead of "God's in His heaven," I begin reciting you a poem of self-defence like

> "Out of the night that covers me,
> Black as the pit from pole to pole,
> I thank whatever gods may be
> For my unconquerable soul [3] . . ."—

you may be simply bored.

In that case you are probably of the compensation type. You need the sort of poem that chimes with your emotional mood by asserting that things are pretty bad. You can compensate your painful feelings by sympathetically sharing the relief which the poet feels

[1] see p. 371.
[2] see Advice to Worriers, p. 83.
[3] see p. 367.

xxx   DIRECTIONS

when he spreads his sorrow on paper. Perhaps he goes a step further, and modulates around to the position that things are really not so wretched after all. And seeing the bad offset by the good under your eyes, may help you still more. So William Vaughn Moody might possibly perform a service in bringing you "Pandora's Song:"[1]

> "Of wounds and sore defeat
> I made my battle stay;
> Winged sandals for my feet
> I wove of my delay;
> Of weariness and fear
> I made my shouting spear;
> Of loss and doubt and dread,
> And swift oncoming doom
> I made a helmet for my head
> And a floating plume." . . .

It is advisable, therefore, not to decide about the efficacy of The Poetry Cure without giving it a fair trial. Time, patience, ingenuity and an open mind may possibly be needed before you can discover your own psychological type and find out just which of the poems between these covers will do the most for you in various hours of emergency.

A word as to quality. The drugs in this chest are warranted pure, and of the highest grade to be obtained in the market. It is hoped that nobody will be

[1] From "The Fire Bringer." See p. 376.

READ WELL BEFORE USING! xxxi

offended if he does not find his favorite poem, or even his favorite poet. Why add one more to the myriad existing anthologies of the world's best poetry?

The aim here has been merely to include those of the best poems written in English which have also proved to be the best medicine for fourteen particular complaints. It would have been easy to include thousands of poems for scores of other troubles, and to rival an unabridged dictionary in bulk.

But ease of instant use seemed more important than compendiousness. To whisk from one's pocket the appropriate poetic remedy the instant the first premonitory symptoms of a trouble are noticed, will probably help the patient more than hours of reading after prolonged "enjoyment" of bad mental health. A poem in time saves nine.

We of to-day have fallen heir to the agreeable privilege of being the first to exploit the therapeutic values of verse, with any degree of intelligent deliberateness. Every time we use the stored genius of the poets to construct and maintain for us the only sort of life that really satisfies, we are performing one of those rare acts, like the burning of carbonized, prehistoric trees, by which a small effort yields a disproportionately large return. We are practically getting something for nothing.

On the day when India paper editions of this work begin to dispute front window space in our drug stores, with beauty clays, heating pads and gland preparations, the market value of the poet will rise. He will shoot forward in popular esteem from the dubiously ornamental to the solidly useful class. We now believe in bards if they are far enough away. The spread of the Poetry Cure will shorten the range. And the discovery of a new vein of high-grade verse will then receive almost as warm a welcome as the discovery of a new seam of high-grade coal.

When that day arrives, and poetry makes its destined appeal to our pockets as a reducer of doctors' bills and an uplifter of salaries, then we shall come into full agreement with an eminent person named Ludwig van Beethoven, who exclaimed: "How can we ever sufficiently thank that most precious treasure of a nation,—a great poet?"

R. H. S.

New York City
Aug. 30, 1925

TEN MINUTE CURES

Compounded for the hurried reader who has no more than ten minutes a day in which to test out the healing value of verse. In each Cure he is advised to look for that poem which best answers to his own particular psychological type,[1] and focus on that. When he has, in this summary way, satisfied himself that The Poetry Cure really cures, it might be well to go through the whole book and mark those poems which seem likely to be of the most help to him in an emergency.

MENTAL COCKTAILS AND SPIRITUAL PICK-ME-UPS

(Poems of Laughter)

Suppose you are fatigued. Or suppose you have temporarily become one of those stuffily earnest souls who—even if all conceivable objects of earnestness were to be annihilated—would go right on being earnest about nothing in particular,—intransitively, as it were. Apply uplift to your vitality, and to the corners of your mouth, with one of the following prescriptions.

I

Herford	*The Chimpanzee, p. 54*
Guiterman	*Strictly Germ-Proof, p. 60*

[1] For an explanation of the three types, see p. xx

TEN MINUTE CURES

Tabb	*The Difference*, p. 61
Carroll	*Father William*, p. 85

II

Gilbert	*Ferdinando and Elvira*, p. 55

III

Marquis	*Spring Ode*, p. 53
Carroll	*Poeta Fit, Non Nascitur*, p. 70

SEDATIVES FOR IMPATIENCE

(Poems of Reassurance)

Are your nerves raw and jumpy with impatience and unsatisfied ambition? This may help them.

Burroughs	*Waiting*, p. 275
Patmore	*Magna Est Veritas*, p. 281
Myers	*From Saint Paul*, p. 280
Milton	*On His Blindness*, p. 276

FOR HARDENING OF THE HEART

(Poems of Sympathy)

Hardening of the heart is worse for a man than hardening of the arteries. Do sympathy, fellowship, compassion and the call of brotherhood begin to sound like "the horns of elfland faintly blowing"? Why not take something for this dangerous condition?

I

Hodgson	*The Bells of Heaven*, p. 205
Patmore	*The Toys*, p. 214
Markham	*Outwitted*, p. 242
Helton	*The Song of Dark Waters*, p. 232

TEN MINUTE CURES xxxv

II

Cleghorn	*To Safeguard the Heart from Hardness, p. 213*
Burns	*Auld Lang Syne, p. 241*
Frost	*The Tuft of Flowers, p. 242*

III

Crosby	*From Town Pictures, p. 225*

HASHEESH FOR A TORPID IMAGINATION

(Magic Carpet Poems)

For a lame, sluggish imagination and a stiff, rusty, creaking fancy.

I

Coleridge	*Kubla Khan, p. 167*
Dickinson	*Morning, p. 169*
Flecker	*The Old Ships, p. 171*

II

Blake	*The Tiger, p. 183*
R. Browning	*My Star, p. 180*
De la Mare	*Tartary, p. 188*

STIMULANTS FOR A FAINT HEART

(Poems of Courage)

To redden pale blood-corpuscles, counteract "quitting" and induce a brave glow.

I

Guiney	*The Kings, p. 4*
R. Browning	*Prospice, p. 9*
W. R. Benét	*His Ally, p. 36*

xxxvi   TEN MINUTE CURES

II

Tennyson	*From Ulysses, p. 17*
Anon.	*Psalm XCI, p. 49*

The old ballad of Jonnë Armstrong, p. 7

III

Hovey	*At the End of the Day, p. 3*
Guiney	*Doves, p. 16*
Speyer	*From Of Mountains, p. 19*
Garrison	*One Fight More, p. 47*

POPPY JUICE FOR INSOMNIA

(Soothers and Soporifics)

There are many useful antidotes for insomnia. (I trust this whole book may not prove one of them!) Get yourself into a comfortable position. Relax all your muscles. Whisper rapidly to yourself a score of times: "I'm getting sleepy." Then softly mull over such poems as:

I

Wordsworth	*To Sleep, p. 133*
Tennyson	*From The Lotus Eaters, p. 122*
Gates	*Sleep Sweet, p. 133*

II

Keats	*To Sleep, p. 117*
Sidney	*To Sleep, p. 121*
Old Rhyme	*The White Paternoster, p. 120*
Belloc	*The Night, p. 120*

ACCELERATORS FOR SLUGGISH BLOOD

(Poems of High Voltage)

Suppose your blood has the sparkle and dash of a Nebraska river in the dry season. Give it electric treatment.

TEN MINUTE CURES   xxxvii

I

Guiney	*The Wild Ride, p. 270*
Tennyson	*The Charge of the Light Brigade, p. 258*
R. Browning	*The Wild Joys of Living, p. 263*

II

Chesterton	*Lepanto, p. 249*

CONTENTS

STIMULANTS FOR A FAINT HEART

(Poems of Courage)

	PAGE
At the End of the Day	3
The Kings	4
O Altitudo!	6
To His Heart, Bidding It Have No Fear	6
Jonnë Armstrong	7
Prospice	9
Last Lines	10
Epilogue to Asolando	12
Hope in Failure	13
The Helmsman	14
Lessons	14
Be Strong!	15
From Psalm XLVI	15
Doves	16
From Ulysses	17
Death, Life, Fear	18
From "Of Mountains"	19
Do You Fear the Wind?	21
From The Poem of Joys	21
Grief	22
Prayer	22
From Apparent Failure	24
Prayer	24
All Night the Lone Cicada	25
Enamored Architect of Airy Rhyme	26
Don Quixote	26
Epitaph for a Poet	27
Courage	28

xl CONTENTS

	PAGE
Say Not the Struggle Naught Availeth	28
From Captain Craig	29
Psalm CXXI	31
Before Action	32
A Prayer for the Old Courage	33
The Pillar of Cloud	34
Suicide's Stone	35
The Soldier	35
From to Homer	36
His Ally	36
Courage	37
Unvanquished	38
For Those Who Fail	38
The Old Stoic	39
Psalm XXIII	39
Immortality	40
Let Me Live Out My Years	41
To Althea, from Prison	41
Protest in Passing	42
The Riderless Horse	42
Horseman Springing from the Dark: A Dream	43
If This Were Faith	44
From Character of the Happy Warrior	45
Heroism	46
From Columbus	46
One Fight More	47
From Ode to the West Wind	48
Closing Lines of Prometheus Unbound	49
Psalm XCI	49

MENTAL COCKTAILS AND SPIRITUAL PICK-ME-UPS

(Poems of Laughter)

Spring Ode	53
The Chimpanzee	54

CONTENTS xli

	PAGE
FERDINANDO AND ELVIRA OR THE GENTLE PIEMAN	55
STRICTLY GERM-PROOF	60
THE DIFFERENCE	61
EPITAPH FOR ANY NEW YORKER	61
THE JUMBLIES	62
THE BALLADE OF ADAPTATION	64
A PENITENTIAL WEEK	65
ODE TO DISCORD	66
A FINE NEW BALLAD OF CAWSAND BAY OR THE SPIRITED LASS AND THE BRAVE YOUNG SAILOR	68
POETA FIT, NON NASCITUR	70
THE AMATEUR BARD ON WOMAN	74
THE RICH MAN	76
THE KISS	76
BALLAD	77
"SUCH STUFF AS DREAMS"	78
A SONNET	79
ON A MAGAZINE SONNET	80
SPRATT VS. SPRATT	80
A CREW POEM	82
THE HEAVY DRAGOON	82
ADVICE TO WORRIERS	83
FROM DUCKS	84
FATHER WILLIAM	85

MASSAGE FOR A MUSCLE-BOUND SPIRIT

(Poems of Emancipation)

FIRST FIG	89
VAGABONDIA	89
TO MR. LAWRENCE	93
TO CYRIACK SKINNER	94
INTO THE TWILIGHT	94
MORE LIFE . . . MORE!	95
ECSTASY	95

xlii CONTENTS

	PAGE
THE IDLE LAKE	96
THE BELL	96
ODE IN MAY	98
A ROAD SONG	100
A SELECTION FROM SONG OF THE OPEN ROAD	101
ALE	104
LIFE-DRUNK	105
WE	106
COURAGE, MON AMI!	107
FROM TAMAR	107
THE CELESTIAL SURGEON	108
FROM THE COLLAR	109
AN OLD SONG RESUNG	110
A SELECTION FROM THE POEM OF JOYS	110
FROM PASSAGE TO INDIA	112

POPPY JUICE FOR INSOMNIA

(Soothers and Soporifics)

TO SLEEP	117
KIND SLEEP	117
FOR SLEEP WHEN OVERTIRED OR WORRIED	118
SLEEP	119
COME, BLESSÈD SLEEP	119
THE NIGHT	120
THE WHITE PATERNOSTER	120
TO SLEEP	121
FROM SLEEP	121
FROM THE LOTOS-EATERS	122
FROM THE FAERIE QUEENE	122
FROM IL PENSEROSO	123
CARE-CHARMING SLEEP	123
TO SLEEP (EXTRACT)	124
MIDSUMMER NIGHT	125
SWEET AND LOW	126
WYNKEN, BLYNKEN AND NOD	127

CONTENTS xliii

	PAGE
My Soul Is An Enchanted Boat	128
Bells in the Rain	129
From The Faerie Queene	130
To One With Hands of Sleep	130
Sleep	131
A Translation from Michael Angelo	131
Let Me Sleep	131
The Pool of Sleep	132
Sleep	132
Sleep Sweet	133
To Sleep	133

TO DEFLATE THE EGO

(Ingredients for a Humble Pie)

I'm Nobody	137
Ozymandias of Egypt	137
To the Stone Cutters	138
My House	138
The Beasts	139
One In the Infinite	139
From The House of a Hundred Lights	140
From Psalm XIX	140
My Wage	141
Days	142
After Blenheim	143
To A Staring Baby in a Perambulator	145
From The Rubáyát of Omar Khayyám	146
On One Ignorant and Arrogant	147
An August Mood	147
The Mountain and the Squirrel	148

TONICS FOR AN ANÆMIC SOUL

(Tissue Builders and Vision Strengtheners)

Creeds	153
Measure Me, Sky!	153

CONTENTS

	PAGE
"An Air of Coolness Plays Upon His Face"	154
From A Summer Night	154
From A Vision	155
Ladders Through the Blue	155
Each and All	156
Flower in the Crannied Wall	158
Not Our Good Luck	158
At the Heart	160
Fool and Wise	160
Sonnet	161
Finis	161
Joy	161
Compensation	162
The Anodyne	163

HASHEESH FOR A TORPID IMAGINATION

(Magic Carpet Poems)

Kubla Khan	167
Morning	169
A Child's Song Overheard	169
Buttercups	170
Queen Mab	171
The Old Ships	171
Portrait of a Boy	173
The Falconer of God	174
A Street Car Symphony	175
Dead Men Tell No Tales	179
My Star	180
What is the Grass?	181
His Pilgrimage	182
The Tiger	183
From Il Penseroso	184
Going up to London	185

CONTENTS

	PAGE
Tartary	188
The Blessèd Damozel	190
The Madman	196
From Herod	196
The Poet's Dream	197
Where is Fancy Bred?	198
Fancy	198
Verification	201

FOR HARDENING OF THE HEART

(Poems of Sympathy)

The Bells of Heaven	205
A Lyrical Epigram	205
From Lines on a Lap Dog	205
Concerning Brownie	206
The Spark	207
So I May Feel the Hands of God	208
Salmon Fishing	209
On the Death of a Favourite Canary	210
From The Rime of the Ancient Mariner	212
To Safeguard the Heart from Hardness	213
Little Boy Blue	213
The Toys	214
To My Godchild	216
The Flower Factory	217
The Factories	218
They Will Say	219
A Pitcher of Mignonette	220
Rufus Prays	220
The Bridge of Sighs	221
From Town Pictures	225
Abou Ben Adhem	228
Harvest	229

CONTENTS

	PAGE
A Woman	229
God's Pity	230
Portrait of an Old Woman	231
The Door	232
The Song of Dark Waters	232
"Scum o' the Earth"	233
From Passage to India	237
The Man with the Hoe	237
The Second Coming	239
Mercy	240
Dedication	240
Auld Lang Syne	241
Outwitted	242
The Tuft of Flowers	242
Byron	245
For Mercy, Courage, Kindness, Mirth	245
The World's Need	245

ACCELERATORS FOR SLUGGISH BLOOD

(Poems of High Voltage)

Lepanto	249
Comrades	256
Give a Rouse	257
The Charge of the Light Brigade	258
"How They Brought the Good News from Ghent to Aix"	261
The Wild Joys of Living	263
The Odyssey	264
King Henry Before Harfleur	265
Unrest	266
Exultation	267
From Sursum Corda	268
The Wild Ride	270

CONTENTS

SEDATIVES FOR IMPATIENCE

(*Poems of Reassurance*)

Waiting	275
Envoy	276
On His Blindness	276
Work	277
A Treasure House	277
Found on an English Sun Dial	278
The Arrow and the Song	278
From The Word at St. Kavin's	279
The Recompense	279
From Saint Paul	280
To a Friend	280
"With Whom is No Variableness, Neither Shadow of Turning"	280
Magna Est Veritas	281

BEAUTY'S WINE

(*A Specific for Ugliness*)

Ode to a Nightingale	285
Sonnet	288
To Helen	288
To ——	289
Song	290
From Il Penseroso	291
From Lycidas	291
From the Paraphrase of The Rubáiyát of Omar Khayyám	292
Tears, Idle Tears	296
From The Eve of Saint Agnes	297
Moonlight Music	298
Such Stuff as Dreams	298
Mutability	299
Ode to a Grecian Urn	299

FOR TIMES WHEN "THE WORLD IS TOO MUCH WITH US"

(Antidotes for the Strenuous Life)

THE WORLD	305
LEISURE	305
SIMPLICITY	306
NATURE CURE	307
BALLADE TO THEOCRITUS, IN WINTER	308
CLEAR AND COOL	309
WHERE NONE INTRUDES	310
THE MARSHES OF GLYNN	310
A CALIFORNIA VIGNETTE	316
IN THE WOOD	317
ENGLAND AND SWITZERLAND, 1802	317
THE INVITATION	318
ON A SUBWAY EXPRESS	320
SONG OF THE OPEN COUNTRY	322
DISCOVERY	322
WALLS	323
SOLITUDE	324
THE ESCAPE	324
UP! UP! MY FRIEND	325
THERE IS STRENGTH IN THE SOIL	326
A BALLAD OF TREES AND THE MASTER	327
BEFORE DAWN IN THE WOOD	328
ESCAPE	328
FLOOD TIDE	330
MY NOSEGAYS ARE FOR CAPTIVES	330
THE CREED OF THE WOOD	331
"WITH PIPE AND FLUTE"	332
HOMESICK IN ENGLAND	332
THE HILL-BORN	334
THE BROOK	335
FROM THE DEEP	337

CONTENTS

	PAGE
MY GARDEN	337
COUPLET	338
VOICES	338
IN ROMNEY MARSH	339
THE DAFFODILS	340
FROM LINES COMPOSED A FEW MILES ABOVE TINTERN ABBEY	341
SONNET	342
THE LAKE ISLE OF INNISFREE	343

"PILLS TO PURGE MELANCHOLY"

(Poems of Cheer)

LAUGH AND BE MERRY	347
SADNESS AND JOY	348
TO A FRIEND WHOSE WORK HAS COME TO NOTHING	349
GLADNESS	349
OVER THE SHOULDERS AND SLOPES OF THE DUNE	350
GOLDEN HANDS	351
FROM PSALM XCV	351
THE PLACE OF REST	352
A BLACKBIRD SUDDENLY	353
ANGLER	353
THE SECRET	354
JOY	354
FROM L'ALLEGRO	355
JENNY KISSED ME	358
VILLANELLE, WITH STEVENSON'S ASSISTANCE	358
COMMUNION	359
WHEN YOU ARE OLD	360
FROM THE DEATH SONG	360
THE OPTIMIST	361
A LITTLE SONG OF LIFE	362
FROM PSALM CIII	363

CONTENTS

ANODYNES FOR SORROW

(To be Taken in the Hour of Great Need)

	PAGE
INVICTUS	367
IF SO TOMORROW SAVES	367
THE BALANCE	368
ILLUSION	369
THE WIND OF SORROW	369
VICTORY IN DEFEAT	370
SONGS OF JOY	370
PIPPA'S SONG	371
IDLE TO GRIEVE	372
DUET	372
COMFORT	373
THE MINISTERING SPIRITS	374
I LOVE THE FRIENDLY FACES OF OLD SORROWS	374
TEARS	375
TEARS	375
PANDORA'S SONG	376

PREFACE TO THE SIXTH EDITION

*Have you hastened and aspired
Till your very bones are tired?—
Poetry can give you rest
With its laughter and its zest,
Or can conjure you to sleep
By the flocks of misty sheep
Where the lotos flowers weep.*

*Has dumb terror grazed your heart
With his dusky-feathered dart?—
Poetry may do for you
More than Galen's tribe can do,—
More than winds of sea or mountain,
More than old De Leon's fountain.
It can suck the poison out,
Dry the wound with moly, rout
Every imp of care and doubt,
Give you armor fit to break
Any missile fear can make.*

*Windy pride has puffed you double?—
Poetry can prick your bubble.
It can rouse your stagnant blood
To an effervescent flood.*

*Have the city claims and clamors
Mauled you with their reddened hammers?—
Run to Romney Marsh or Glynn,
To the peace of God within
The Theocritean sea
Or the isle of Innisfree.*

*Children cause your heart to harden?
Pups and beggars in the garden?—
You require poetic doses
Versus cardiac sclerosis.
See if Patmore on The Toys
Softens you toward little boys,
And The Tuft of Flowers evokes
Fellowship for other folks.*

*Does your lame, rheumatic fancy
Long to feel youth's necromancy?
Does your stiff imagination
Need a little lubrication?—
With Grace Conkling be beguiled
By the visions of a child.
Touch at Tyre with Elroy Flecker
In his rose-leaved single-decker;
Steer the glamorous galley on
To the realm of Kubla Khan;
On to Samarkand and Niger;
Quizz with Blake the burning tiger;
Loose your falcon-soul to slay
Silver herons with Benét.*

PREFACE

Frolic's dearth and labor's glut
Clamp your mind into a rut?
Does your spirit cease to burgeon?—
Summon the Celestial Surgeon;
Bid R. Hovey make you play;
Pluck the figs of E. Millay,
(Serve them with a pinch of salt!);
Take the open road with Walt.

Is the world drab, gross, malign?—
Flush your brow with beauty's wine.
Through its dream stuff be new born;
Stand with Ruth amid the corn;
Heed "the studious cloister's" hymn
And "the young-eyed cherubim."

Are you cold with melancholy?—
Certain psalms are passing jolly.
Never let a sigh disgrace you
When Bliss Carman's tune can brace you!
Rout the imps with Yeats's guile,
Masefield's chuckle, Milton's smile.

Or is life so blurred with sorrow
That you shudder at tomorrow?—
Feel the Stygian world new born
As you sound Pandora's horn!
See the murky sky relume
As you touch her helm and plume!

                                              R. H. S.

℞ I

STIMULANTS FOR A FAINT HEART

(Poems of Courage)

AT THE END OF THE DAY

By Richard Hovey

There is no escape by the river,
There is no flight left by the fen;
We are compassed about by the shiver
Of the night of their marching men.
Give a cheer!
For our hearts shall not give way.
Here's to a dark to-morrow,
And here's to a brave to-day!

The tale of their hosts is countless,
And the tale of ours a score;
But the palm is naught to the dauntless,
And the cause is more and more.
Give a cheer!
We may die, but not give way.
Here's to a silent morrow,
And here's to a stout to-day!

God has said: "Ye shall fail and perish;
But the thrill ye have felt to-night
I shall keep in my heart and cherish
When the worlds have passed in night."
Give a cheer!
For the soul shall not give way.

Here's to the greater to-morrow
That is born of a great to-day!

Now shame on the craven truckler
And the puling things that mope!
We've a rapture for our buckler
That outwears the wings of hope.
Give a cheer!
For our joy shall not give way.
Here's in the teeth of to-morrow
To the glory to to-day!

THE KINGS

By Louise Imogen Guiney

A man said unto his angel:
"My spirits are fallen thro',
And I cannot carry this battle;
O brother! what shall I do?

"The terrible Kings are on me,
With spears that are deadly bright,
Against me so from the cradle
Do fate and my fathers fight."

Then said to the man his angel:
"Thou wavering, foolish soul,
Back to the ranks! What matter
To win or to lose the whole,

"As judged by the little judges
Who hearken not well, nor see?
Not thus, by the outer issue,
The Wise shall interpret thee.

"Thy will is the very, the only,
The solemn event of things;
The weakest of hearts defying
Is stronger than all these Kings.

"Tho' out of the past they gather,
Mind's Doubt and Bodily Pain,
And pallid Thirst of the Spirit
That is kin to the other twain,

"And Grief, in a cloud of banners,
And ringleted Vain Desires,
And Vice, with the spoils upon him
Of thee and thy beaten sires,

"While Kings of eternal evil
Yet darken the hills about,
Thy part is with broken sabre
To rise on the last redoubt,

"To fear not sensible failure,
Nor covet the game at all,
But fighting, fighting, fighting,
Die, driven against the wall!"

STIMULANTS FOR A FAINT HEART

O ALTITUDO!

By Sarah N. Cleghorn

Into the loud surf,
Down over the sands of safety,
I come running and shouting.
Against me the breakers
Crouch and spring, hurtle and roar.
I make myself an arrow;
Dizzily I dive through them,
Blinded, with singing ears,
And pounding heart.
Suddenly I am in the clear water,
The deep-sea water,
The buoyant and calm water
Beyond the breasted danger,
On the far side of courage.

TO HIS HEART, BIDDING IT HAVE NO FEAR

By William Butler Yeats

Be you still, be you still, trembling heart;
Remember the wisdom out of the old days:
Him who trembles before the flame and the flood,
And the winds that blow through the starry ways,
Let the starry winds and the flame and the flood
Cover over and hide, for he has no part
With the lonely, majestical multitude.

JONNË ARMSTRONG

(OLD BALLAD)

There dwelt a man in faire Westmerland,
   Jonnë Armstrong men did him call,
He had nither lands nor rents coming in,
   Yet he kept eight score men in his hall.

He had horse and harness for them all,
   Goodly steeds were all milke-white;
O the golden bands an about their necks,
   And their weapons, they were all alike.

Newes then was brought unto the king
   That there was sicke a won as hee,
That livëd lyke a bold out-law,
   And robbed all the north country.

The king he writt a letter then,
   A letter which was large and long;
He signëd it with his owne hand,
   And he promised to doe him no wrong.

When this letter came Jonnë untill,
   His heart was as blyth as birds on the tree:
"Never was I sent for before any king,
   My father, my grandfather, nor none but mee.

"And if wee goe the king before,
   I would wee went most orderly;

Every man of you shall have his scarlet cloak,
  Laced with silver laces three.

"Every won of you shall have his velvett coat,
  Laced with silver lace so white;
O the golden bands an about your necks,
  Black hatts, white feathers, all alyke."

By the morrow morninge at ten of the clock,
  Towards Edenburough gon was hee,
And with him all his eight score men;
  Good lord, it was a goodly sight for to see!

When Jonnë came befower the king,
  He fell downe on his knee;
"O pardon, my soveraine leige," he said,
  "O pardon my eight score men and mee."

"Thou shalt have no pardon, thou traytor strong,
  For thy eight score men nor thee;
For to-morrow morning by ten of the clock,
  Both thou and them shall hang on the gallow-tree."

But Jonnë looked over his left shoulder,
  Good Lord, what a grevious look looked hee!
Saying, "Asking grace of a graceles face—
  Why there is none for you nor mee."

But Jonnë had a bright sword by his side,
  And it was made of the mettle so free,
That had not the king stept his foot aside,
  He had smitten his head from his faire boddee.

Saying, "Fight on, my merry men all,
   And see that none of you be taine;
For rather than men shall say we were hangd,
   Let them report how we were slaine."

Then, God wott, faire Edenburough rose,
   And so besett poore Jonnë rounde,
That fower score and tenn of Jonnës best men
   Lay gasping all upon the ground.

Then like a mad man Jonnë laid about,
   And like a mad man then fought hee,
Untill a falce Scot came Jonnë behinde,
   And runn him through the faire boddee.

Saying, "Fight on my merry men all,
   I am a little hurt, but I am not slain;
I will lay me down for to bleed a while,
   Then I'le rise and fight with you again."

PROSPICE

By Robert Browning

Fear death?—to feel the fog in my throat,
   The mist in my face,
When the snows begin, and the blasts denote
   I am nearing the place,
The power of the night, the press of the storm,
   The post of the foe;

Where he stands, the Arch Fear in a visible form,
  Yet the strong man must go:
For the journey is done and the summit attain'd,
  And the barriers fall,
Though a battle's to fight ere the guerdon be gain'd,
  The reward of it all.
I was ever a fighter, so—one fight more,
  The best and the last!
I would hate that death bandaged my eyes, and forbore,
  And bade me creep past.
No! let me taste the whole of it, fare like my peers
  The heroes of old,
Bear the brunt, in a minute pay glad life's arrears
  Of pain, darkness and cold.
For sudden the worst turns the best to the brave,
  The black minute's at end,
And the elements' rage, the fiend-voices that rave,
  Shall dwindle, shall blend,
Shall change, shall become first a peace out of pain,
  Then a light, then thy breast,
O thou soul of my soul! I shall clasp thee again,
  And with God be the rest!

LAST LINES

By Emily Brontë

No coward soul is mine,
No trembler in the world's storm-troubled sphere:

I see Heaven's glories shine,
And faith shines equal, arming me from fear.

O God within my breast,
Almighty, ever-present Deity!
Life—that in me hast rest,
As I—undying Life—have power in thee!

Vain are the thousand creeds
That move men's hearts: unutterably vain;
Worthless as wither'd weeds,
Or idlest froth amid the boundless main,

To waken doubt in one
Holding so fast by thine infinity;
So surely anchor'd on
The steadfast rock of immortality.

With wide-embracing love
Thy spirit animates eternal years,
Pervades and broods above,
Changes, sustains, dissolves, creates, and rears.

Though earth and man were gone,
And suns and universes ceas'd to be,
And Thou wert left alone,
Every existence would exist in Thee.

There is not room for Death,
Nor atom that his might could render void:
Thou—Thou art Being and Breath,
And what Thou art may never be destroy'd.

EPILOGUE TO ASOLANDO

By Robert Browning

At the midnight in the silence of the sleep-time,
  When you set your fancies free,
Will they pass to where—by death, fools think, imprison'd—
Low he lies who once so lov'd you, whom you lov'd so,
            —Pity me?

Oh to love so, be so lov'd, yet so mistaken!
  What had I on earth to do
With the slothful, with the mawkish, the unmanly?
Like the aimless, helpless, hopeless did I drivel
            —Being—who?

One who never turn'd his back but march'd breast forward,
  Never doubted clouds would break,
Never dream'd, though right were worsted, wrong would triumph,
Held we fall to rise, are baffled to fight better,
            Sleep to wake.

No, at noonday in the bustle of man's work-time
  Greet the unseen with a cheer!
Bid him forward, breast and back as either should be,
"Strive and thrive!" cry "Speed,—fight on, fare ever
            There as here!"

HOPE IN FAILURE

By A. E.

Though now thou hast failed and art fallen, despair not because of defeat,
Though lost for a while be thy heaven and weary of earth be thy feet,
For all will be beauty about thee hereafter through sorrowful years,
And lovely the dews for thy chilling and ruby thy heart-drip of tears.

The eyes that had gazed from afar on a beauty that blinded the eyes
Shall call forth its image for ever, its shadow in alien skies.
The heart that had striven to beat in the heart of the Mighty too soon
Shall still of that beating remember some errant and faltering tune.

For thou hast but fallen to gather the last of the secrets of power;
The beauty that breathes in thy spirit shall shape of thy sorrow a flower,
The pale bud of pity shall open the bloom of its tenderest rays,
The heart of whose shining is bright with the light of the Ancient of Days.

THE HELMSMAN

By M. A. DeWolfe Howe

What shall I ask for the voyage I must sail to the end alone?
Summer and calms and rest from never a labor done?
Nay, blow, ye life-winds all; curb not for me your blast,
Strain ye my quivering ropes, bend ye my trembling mast.
Then there can be no drifting, thank God! for boat or me,—
Eager and swift our course over a living sea.
Mine is a man's right arm to steer through fog and foam;
Beacons are shining still to guide each farer home.
Give me your worst, O winds! others have braved your stress;
E'en if it be to sink, give me no less, no less.

LESSONS

By Sara Teasdale

Unless I learn to ask no help
　From any other soul but mine,
To seek no strength in waving reeds
　Nor shade beneath a straggling pine;
Unless I learn to look at Grief

Unshrinking from her tear-blind eyes,
And take from Pleasure fearlessly
　　Whatever gifts will make me wise—
Unless I learn these things on earth,
Why was I ever given birth?

BE STRONG!

By Duncan Campbell Scott

Be strong O warring soul! For very sooth
　　Kings are but wraiths, republics fade like rain,
　　Peoples are reaped and garnered as the grain,
And that alone prevails which is the truth;
Be strong when all the days of life bear ruth
　　And fury, and are hot with toil and strain:
　　Hold thy large faith and quell thy mighty pain:
Dream the great dream that buoys thine age with youth.

Thou art an eagle mewed in a sea-stopped cave:
　　He, poised in darkness with victorious wings,
　　　　Keeps night between the granite and the sea,
Until the tide has drawn the warder-wave:
　　Then, from the portal where the ripple rings,
　　　　He bursts into the boundless morning—free!

From PSALM XLVI

God is our refuge and strength,
A very present help in trouble.

Therefore will not we fear, though the earth be removed,
And though the mountains be carried into the midst of the sea;

Though the waters thereof roar and be troubled,
Though the mountains shake with the swelling thereof. Selah.

There is a river,
The streams whereof shall make glad the city of God,
The holy place of the tabernacles of the Most High.

God is in the midst of her; she shall not be moved:
God shall help her, and that right early. . . .

Be still, and know that I am God:
I will be exalted among the heathen,
I will be exalted in the earth.
The LORD of hosts is with us;
The God of Jacob is our refuge.　　Selah.

DOVES

BY LOUISE IMOGEN GUINEY

Ah, if man's boast, and man's advance be vain,
And yonder bells of Bow, loud-echoing home,
And the lone Tree foreknow it, and the Dome,
The monstrous island of the middle main;

If each inheritor must sink again
Under his sires, as falleth where it clomb
Back on the gone wave the disheartened foam—
I crossed Cheapside, and this was in my brain.

What folly lies in forecasts and in fears!
Like a wide laughter sweet and opportune,
Wet from the fount, three hundred doves of Paul's
Shook their warm wings, drizzling the golden noon,
And in their rain-cloud vanished up the walls.
"God keeps," I said, "our little flock of years."

From ULYSSES

By Alfred Tennyson

There lies the port; the vessel puffs her sail:
There gloom the dark broad seas. My mariners,
Souls that have toil'd, and wrought, and thought with
    me—
That ever with a frolic welcome took
The thunder and the sunshine, and opposed
Free hearts, free foreheads—you and I are old;
Old age hath yet his honour and his toil;
Death closes all: but something ere the end,
Some work of noble note, may yet be done,
Not unbecoming men that strove with Gods.
The lights begin to twinkle from the rocks:
The long day wanes: the slow moon climbs: the deep
Moans round with many voices. Come, my friends,

'Tis not too late to seek a newer world.
Push off, and sitting well in order smite
The sounding furrows; for my purpose holds
To sail beyond the sunset, and the baths
Of all the western stars, until I die.
It may be that the gulfs will wash us down:
It may be we shall touch the Happy Isles,
And see the great Achilles, whom we knew.
Tho' much is taken, much abides; and tho'
We are not now that strength which in old days
Moved earth and heaven; that which we are, we are;
One equal temper of heroic hearts,
Made weak by time and fate, but strong in will
To strive, to seek, to find, and not to yield.

DEATH, LIFE, FEAR

By Lilla Cabot Perry

I will confront Death smiling, and no tremor
Shall shake my eager heart at his approach;
Why should I fear him, since his hand brings freedom?
Does the plant turn in shrinking from the light?
The bud refuse to feel the blossom growing
Within its heart that soon must open wide?
Brief is the pang of that divine compelling
Which frees its petals to the blessed sun.
No! Death I fear not! Even Life I challenge,
With all its cruelties and possible wrongs!
Love, joy and torture, sin and aspiration,

All would I know and clasp them to my breast,
From many-colored threads weave to completion
The garment of my soul, as is Thy will.
But, Lord, one pang alone I pray Thee, spare me,
Lord, never let me meet the eyes of Fear,
Or meet them but as conqueror to destroy them,
And never let me bow an abject head!
Set firm my feet upon Life's narrow pathway!
Cold, writhing hands from the dread chasm below
Snatch at my ankles! Let me walk unwavering,
And conquer Fear as the sun does the mist.

Lord, I beseech Thee, keep my soul unshaken;
Thou, the unfearing, conquering Source of all things,
Thou would'st not that Thy child should be afraid.

From "OF MOUNTAINS"

By Leonora Speyer

Who is the pioneer?
He is the follower here,
Perhaps the last
Of all who passed.

He does not fear nor scorn
To tread
The ventured path, the worn,
Of those ahead;
Nor shall he fail

To blaze his own brave trail
Along the beaten track,
Make of the old a newer way
Of stouter clay,
For others at his back.

He is the pioneer who climbs,
Who dares to climb,
His own high heart,
Although he fall
A thousand times;
Who dares to crawl
On bloody hands and knees
Along its stony ecstasies
Up to the utmost snows;
Nor knows
He stands on these . . .

Or knowing, does not care,
Save to climb on from there!

Who is the pioneer?
He is the follower here,
Dogged and undeterred,
Perhaps the last
Of all who passed.

He passes too,
The heavy bird,
Limping along . . .

Ah but his song,
His song!

DO YOU FEAR THE WIND?

By Hamlin Garland

Do you fear the force of the wind,
The slash of the rain?
Go face them and fight them,
Be savage again.
Go hungry and cold like the wolf,
Go wade like the crane:
The palms of your hands will thicken,
The skin of your cheek will tan,
You'll grow ragged and weary and swarthy,
But you'll walk like a man!

From THE POEM OF JOYS

By Walt Whitman

O joy of suffering!
To struggle against great odds! to meet enemies undaunted!
To be entirely alone with them! to find how much one can stand!
To look strife, torture, prison, popular odium, death, face to face!

To mount the scaffold! to advance to the muzzles of
   guns with perfect nonchalance!
To be indeed a God!

GRIEF

By Angela Morgan

Upon this trouble shall I whet my life
As 'twere a dulling knife;
Bade I my friend be brave?
I shall still braver be.
No man shall say of me,
"Others he saved, himself he cannot save."
But, swift and fair
As the primeval Word that smote the night—
"Let there be light!"
Courage shall leap from me, a gallant sword
To rout the enemy and all his horde,
Cleaving a kingly pathway through despair.

PRAYER

(From The Image in the Sand; Arranged by permission of the author.)

By E. F. Benson

The dawn of the everlasting day
And of the full knowledge of the One Spirit
Which moves the world.

POEMS OF COURAGE

Infinite Lord of life,
Shine on me;
Make me to know that there is but one all-encompassing
    power,
That everything that might seem to me an exception,
    an evil,
Is but the effect of my own blindness.

Pour, then, thy light upon my eyes;
Remove the shadows from me and the doubtings.
Let thy cloud of witnesses be close about me,
And, though not visible, make it known to me
That they watch,
That they wait,
That my soul, too, even now is one of them,—
Is as close to them
As is my body to those who live with me on this
    earth.

Fill me with the knowledge of their presence,
Of their nearness to me
And of their dearness.

And even as I fill my whole being
With the air I breathe,
Let this knowledge of my communion with them
Flood and overflow my soul.

From APPARENT FAILURE

By Robert Browning

My own hope is, a sun will pierce
The thickest cloud earth ever stretched;
That, after Last, returns the First,
Though a wide compass round be fetched;
That what began best, can't end worst,
Nor what God blessed once, prove accurst.

PRAYER [1]

By Louis Untermeyer

God, though this life is but a wraith,
 Although we know not what we use,
Although we grope with little faith,
 Give me the heart to fight—and lose.

Ever insurgent let me be,
 Make me more daring than devout;
From sleek contentment keep me free,
 And fill me with a buoyant doubt.

Open my eyes to visions girt
 With beauty, and with wonder lit—
But let me always see the dirt,
 And all that spawn and die in it.

[1] From "Challenge" by Louis Untermeyer, by permission of Harcourt, Brace and Company, Inc., holders of the copyright.

Open my ears to music; let
　Me thrill with Spring's first flutes and drums—
But never let me dare forget
　The bitter ballads of the slums.

From compromise and things half-done,
　Keep me, with stern and stubborn pride;
And when, at last, the fight is won
　God, keep me still unsatisfied.

ALL NIGHT THE LONE CICADA

By Charles G. D. Roberts

All night the lone cicada
　Kept shrilling through the rain,
A voice of joy undaunted
　By unforgotten pain.

Down from the tossing branches
　Rang out the high refrain,
By tumult undisheartened,
　By storm assailed in vain.

To looming vasts of mountain,
　To shadowy deeps of plain
The ephemeral, brave defiance
　Adventured not in vain,—

Till to my faltering spirit,
  And to my weary brain,
From loss and fear and failure
  My joy returned again.

ENAMORED ARCHITECT OF AIRY RHYME

By Thomas Bailey Aldrich

Enamored architect of airy rhyme
Build as thou wilt; heed not what each man says:
Good souls, but innocent of dreamers' ways,
Will come, and marvel why thou wastest time;
Others, beholding how thy turrets climb
'Twixt theirs and heaven, will hate thee all thy days;
But most beware of those who come to praise.
O Wondersmith, O worker in sublime
And heaven-sent dreams, let art be all in all;
Build as thou wilt, unspoiled by praise or blame,
Build as thou wilt, and as thy light is given:
Then, if at last the airy structure fall,
Dissolve, and vanish—take thyself no shame.
They fail, and they alone, who have not striven.

DON QUIXOTE

By Austin Dobson

Behind thy pasteboard, on thy battered hack,
  Thy lean cheek striped with plaster to and fro,

Thy long spear levelled at the unseen foe,
And doubtful Sancho trudging at thy back,
Thou wert a figure strange enough, good lack!
  To make wiseacredom, both high and low,
  Rub purblind eyes, and (having watched thee go)
Despatch its Dogberrys upon thy track:
Alas! poor Knight! Alas! poor soul possest!
  Yet would to-day, when Courtesy grows chill,
And life's fine loyalties are turned to jest,
  Some fire of thine might burn within us still!
Ah! would but one might lay his lance in rest,
  And charge in earnest—were it but a mill.

EPITAPH FOR A POET

By DuBose Heyward

Here lies a spendthrift who believed
That only those who spend may keep;
Who scattered seeds, yet never grieved
Because a stranger came to reap;

A failure who might well have risen;
Yet, ragged, sang exultantly
That all success is but a prison,
And only those who fail are free:

Who took what little Earth had given,
And watched it blaze, and watched it die;
Who could not see a distant Heaven
Because of dazzling nearer sky;

Who never flinched till Earth had taken
The most of him back home again,
And the last silences were shaken
With songs too lovely for his pen.

COURAGE

By Virginia Moore

Because I coveted courage
  As keen as candle-flare,
I lit a yellow candle
  And set it staunchly there

Upon my heart's high altar
  Where courage seldom came
(O tall and blue and lovely
  O urgent candle flame!)

And now no wind of weakness,
  No sudden draught of doubt,
For all their sly maneuvres,
  Can puff my candle out!

SAY NOT THE STRUGGLE NAUGHT AVAILETH

By Arthur Hugh Clough

Say not the struggle naught availeth,
  The labour and the wounds are vain,

The enemy faints not, nor faileth,
   And as things have been they remain.

If hopes were dupes, fears may be liars;
   It may be, in yon smoke conceal'd,
Your comrades chase e'en now the fliers,
   And, but for you, possess the field.

For while the tired waves, vainly breaking,
   Seem here no painful inch to gain,
Far back, through creeks and inlets making,
   Comes silent, flooding in, the main.

And not by eastern windows only,
   When daylight comes, comes in the light;
In front the sun climbs slow, how slowly!
   But westward, look, the land is bright!

From CAPTAIN CRAIG [1]

By Edwin Arlington Robinson

          "I had a dream last night:
A dream not like to any other dream
That I remember. I was all alone,
Sitting as I do now beneath a tree,
But looking not, as I am looking now,
Against the sunlight. There was neither sun

[1] From "Captain Craig," By Edwin Arlington Robinson, copyrighted by the Macmillan Company.

Nor moon, nor do I think of any stars;
Yet there was light, and there were cedar trees,
And there were sycamores. I lay at rest,
Or should have seemed at rest, within a trough
Between two giant roots. A weariness
Was on me, and I would have gone to sleep,
But I had not the courage. If I slept,
I feared that I should never wake again;
And if I did not sleep I should go mad,
And with my own dull tools, which I had used
With wretched skill so long, hack out my life.
And while I lay there, tortured out of death,
Faint waves of cold, as if the dead were breathing,
Came over me and through me; and I felt
Quick fearful tears of anguish on my face
And in my throat. But soon, and in the distance,
Concealed, importunate, there was a sound
Of coming steps,—and I was not afraid;
No, I was not afraid then, I was glad;
For I could feel, with every thought, the Man,
The Mystery, the Child, a footfall nearer.
Then, when he stood before me, there was no
Surprise, there was no questioning, I knew him,
As I had known him always; and he smiled.
'Why are you here?' he asked; and reaching down,
He took up my dull blades and rubbed his thumb
Across the edges of them and then smiled
Once more.—'I was a carpenter,' I said,
'But there was nothing in the world to do.'—
'Nothing?' said he.—'No, nothing,' I replied.—

'But are you sure,' he asked, 'that you have skill?
And are you sure that you have learned your trade?
No, you are not.'—He looked at me and laughed
As he said that; but I did not laugh then,
Although I might have laughed.—'They are dull,' said he;
'They were not very sharp if they were ground;
But they are what you have, and they will earn
What you have not. So take them as they are,
Grind them and clean them, put new handles to them,
And then go learn your trade in Nazareth.
Only be sure that you find Nazareth.'—
'But if I starve—what then?' said I.—He smiled."

PSALM CXXI

I will lift up mine eyes unto the hills,
From whence cometh my help.
My help cometh from the Lord, which made heaven and earth.
He will not suffer thy foot to be moved:
He that keepeth thee will not slumber.
Behold, he that keepeth Israel shall neither slumber nor sleep.
The Lord is thy keeper:
The Lord is thy shade upon thy right hand.
The sun shall not smite thee by day, nor the moon by night.
The Lord shall preserve thee from all evil:
He shall preserve thy soul.

The Lord shall preserve thy going out and thy coming in
From this time forth, and even for evermore.

BEFORE ACTION

By William Noel Hodgson

By all the glories of the day
   And the cool evening's benison,
By that last sunset touch that lay
   Upon the hills when day was done,
By beauty lavishly outpoured
   And blessings carelessly received,
   By all the days that I have lived,
Make me a soldier, Lord.

By all of all man's hopes and fears,
   And all the wonders poets sing,
The laughter of unclouded years,
   And every sad and lovely thing;
By the romantic ages stored
   With high endeavour that was his,
   By all his mad catastrophes,
Make me a man, O Lord.

I, that on my familiar hill
   Saw with uncomprehending eyes
A hundred of Thy sunsets spill
   Their fresh and sanguine sacrifice.

Ere the sun swings his noonday sword
  Must say good-bye to all of this;—
  By all delights that I shall miss,
Help me to die, O Lord.

A PRAYER FOR THE OLD COURAGE [1]

By Charles Hanson Towne

Still let us go the way of beauty; go
The way of loveliness; still let us know
Those paths that lead where Pan and Daphne run,
Where roses prosper in the summer sun.

The earth may rock with War. Still is there peace
In many a place to give the heart release
From this too-vibrant pain that drives men mad.
Let us go back to the old loves we had.

Let us go back, to keep alive the gleam,
To cherish the immortal, Godlike dream;
Not as poor cravens flying from the fight,
But as sad children seeking the clean light.

Oh, doubly precious now is solitude;
Thrice dear yon quiet star above the wood,
Since panic and the sundering shock of War
Have laid in ruins all we hungered for.

[1] From A World of Windows by Charles Hanson Towne, copyright 1919, George H. Doran Co., publishers.

Brave soldiers of the spirit, guard ye well
Mountain and fort and massive citadel;
But keep ye white forever—keep ye whole
The battlements of dream within the soul!

THE PILLAR OF CLOUD

By John Henry, Cardinal Newman

Lead, kindly Light, amid the encircling gloom,
    Lead Thou me on!
The night is dark, and I am far from home—
    Lead Thou me on!
Keep Thou my feet; I do not ask to see
The distant scene,—one step enough for me.

I was not ever thus, nor pray'd that Thou
    Shouldst lead me on.
I loved to choose and see my path, but now
    Lead Thou me on!
I loved the garish day, and, spite of fears,
Pride ruled my will: remember not past years.

So long Thy power hath blest me, sure it still
    Will lead me on,
O'er moor and fen, o'er crag and torrent, till
    The night is gone;
And with the morn those angel faces smile
Which I have loved long since, and lost awhile.

SUICIDE'S STONE

By Robinson Jeffers

Peace is the heir of dead desire,
Whether abundance killed the cormorant
In a happy hour, or sleep or death
Drowned him deep in dreamy waters,
Peace is the ashes of that fire,
The heir of that king, the inn of that journey.

This last and best and goal: we dead
Hold it so tight you are envious of us
And fear under sunk lids contempt.
Death-day greetings are the sweetest.
Let trumpets roar when a man dies
And rockets fly up, he has found his fortune.

Yet hungering long and pitiably
That way, you shall not reach a finger
To pluck it unripe and before dark
Creep to cover: life broke ten whipstocks
Over my back, broke faith, stole hope,
Before I denounced the covenant of courage.

THE SOLDIER

By Sophie Jewett

"Non vi si pensa quanto sangue costa."
PARADISO XXIX. 91.

The soldier fought his battle silently.
  Not his the strife that stays for set of sun;

It seemed this warfare never might be done;
  Through glaring day and blinding night fought he.
There came no hand to help, no eye to see;
  No herald's voice proclaimed the fight begun;
  No trumpet, when the bitter field was won,
  Sounded abroad the soldier's victory.
As if the struggle had been light, he went,
  Gladly, life's common road a little space;
  Nor any knew how his heart's blood was spent;
Yet there were some who after testified
  They saw a glory grow upon his face;
  And all men praised the soldier when he died.

From TO HOMER

By John Keats

Aye, on the shores of darkness there is light,
And precipices show untrodden green;
There is a budding morrow in mid-night;
There is a triple sight in blindness keen.

HIS ALLY

By William Rose Benét

He fought for his soul, and the stubborn fighting
    Tried hard his strength.
"One needs seven souls for this long requiting,"
    He said at length.

"Six times I come where my first hope jeered me
    And laughed me to scorn;
But now I fear as I never feared me
    To fall forlorn.

"God! when they fight upright and at me
    I give them back
Even such blows as theirs that combat me;
    But now, alack!

"They fight with the wiles of fiends escaping
    And underhand.
Six times, O God, and my wounds are gaping!
    I—reel to stand.

"Six battles' span! By this gasping breath,
    No pantomime.
'Tis all that I can. I am sick unto death.
    And—a seventh time?

"This is beyond all battles' soreness!"
    Then his wonder cried:
For Laughter, with shield and steely harness,
    Stood up at his side!

COURAGE

By Karle Wilson Baker

    Courage is armor
    A blind man wears;
    The calloused scar

Of outlived despairs:
Courage is Fear
That has said its prayers.

UNVANQUISHED

By Grace Hoffmann White

Ravaged of faith I fled,
Beat life to a blade,
Cut from my stiffened body
Love's enticing coils—
Unvanquished—unafraid . . .

FOR THOSE WHO FAIL

By Joaquin Miller

"All honour to him who shall win the prize,"
  The world has cried for a thousand years;
But to him who tries and who fails and dies,
  I give great honour and glory and tears.

O great is the hero who wins a name,
  But greater many and many a time
Some pale-faced fellow who dies in shame,
  And lets God finish the thought sublime.

And great is the man with a sword undrawn,
  And good is the man who refrains from wine;
But the man who fails and yet fights on,
  Lo he is the twin-born brother of mine!

THE OLD STOIC

By Emily Brontë

Riches I hold in light esteem,
   And Love I laugh to scorn;
And lust of fame was but a dream
   That vanish'd with the morn;

And if I pray, the only prayer
   That moves my lips for me
Is, "Leave the heart that now I bear,
   And give me liberty!"

Yes, as my swift days near their goal,
   'Tis all that I implore:
In life and death a chainless soul,
   With courage to endure.

PSALM XXIII

By David

The LORD is my shepherd;
I shall not want.
He maketh me to lie down in green pastures:
He leadeth me beside the still waters.

He restoreth my soul:
He leadeth me in the paths of righteousness
For his name's sake.

Yea, though I walk through the valley of the shadow
   of death,
I will fear no evil:
For thou art with me;
Thy rod and thy staff they comfort me.

Thou preparest a table before me
In the presence of mine enemies:
Thou anointest my head with oil;
My cup runneth over.

Surely goodness and mercy shall follow me
All the days of my life:
And I will dwell in the house of the Lord for ever.

IMMORTALITY

By Matthew Arnold

Foil'd by our fellowmen, depress'd, outworn,
   We leave the brutal world to take its way,
   And, *Patience! in another life,* we say,
The world shall be thrust down, and we up-borne.
And will not, then, the immortal armies scorn
   The world's poor, routed leavings? or will they
   Who fail'd under the heat of this life's day,
Support the fervours of the heavenly morn?
No, no! the energy of life may be
   Kept on after the grave, but not begun;
      And he who flagg'd not in the earthly strife,

From strength to strength advancing—only he,
  His soul well-knit, and all his battles won,
    Mounts, and that hardly, to eternal life.

LET ME LIVE OUT MY YEARS

By John G. Neihardt

Let me live out my years in heat of blood!
Let me die drunken with the dreamer's wine!
Let me not see this soul-house built of mud
Go toppling to the dust—a vacant shrine.

Let me go quickly, like a candle light
Snuffed out just at the heyday of its glow.
Give me high noon—and let it then be night!
Thus would I go.

And grant that when I face the grisly Thing,
My song may trumpet down the gray Perhaps.
Let me be as a tune-swept fiddlestring
That feels the Master Melody—and snaps!

TO ALTHEA, FROM PRISON

By Richard Lovelace

Stone walls do not a prison make,
  Nor iron bars a cage;
Minds innocent and quiet take
  That for an hermitage;

> If I have freedom in my love
> And in my soul am free,
> Angels alone, that soar above,
> Enjoy such liberty.

PROTEST IN PASSING

By Leonora Speyer

This house of flesh was never loved of me,
Though I have known much love beneath its roof,
Always was I a guest who stood aloof,
Loth to accept such hospitality.
When the house slumbered, how I woke! for then
I knew of half-escapes along the night,
But now there comes a safer, swifter flight:
I go; nor need endure these rooms again.

I have been cowed too long by closed-in walls,
By masonry of muscle, blood and bone;
This quaking house of flesh that was my own,
High roof-tree of the heart, see how it falls!
I go . . . but pause upon the threshold's rust
To shake from off my feet my own dead dust.

THE RIDERLESS HORSE

By Harold Trowbridge Pulsifer

> Close ranks and ride on!
> Though his saddle be bare,

The bullet is sped,
Now the dead
Cannot care.
Close ranks and ride on!
Let the pitiless stride
Of the host that he led,
Though his saddle be red,
Sweep on like the tide.
Close ranks and ride on!
The banner he bore
For God and the right
Never faltered before.
Quick, up with it, then!
For the right! For the light!
Lest legions of men
Be lost in the night!

HORSEMAN SPRINGING FROM THE DARK: A DREAM

By Lilla Cabot Perry

"Horseman, springing from the dark,
   Horseman, flying wild and free,
Tell me what shall be thy road,
   Whither speedest far from me?"

"From the dark into the light,
   From the small unto the great,
From the valleys dark I ride
   Over the hills to conquer fate!"

"Take me with thee, horseman mine!
    Let me madly ride with thee!"
As he turned I met his eyes,
    My own soul looked back at me!

IF THIS WERE FAITH

By Robert Louis Stevenson

God, if this were enough,
That I see things bare to the buff
And up to the buttocks in mire;
That I ask nor hope nor hire,
Nut in the husk,
Nor dawn beyond the dusk,
Nor life beyond death:
God, if this were faith?

Having felt thy wind in my face
Spit sorrow and disgrace,
Having seen thine evil doom
In Golgotha and Khartoum,
And the brutes, the work of thine hands,
Fill with injustice lands
And stain with blood the sea:
If still in my veins the glee
Of the black night and the sun
And the lost battle, run:
If, an adept,
The iniquitous lists I still accept

With joy, and joy to endure and be withstood,
And still to battle and perish for a dream of good:
God, if that were enough?

If to feel, in the ink of the slough,
And the sink of the mire,
Veins of glory and fire
Run through and transpierce and transpire,
And a secret purpose of glory in every part,
And the answering glory of battle fill my heart;
To thrill with the joy of girded men,
To go on forever and fail and go on again,
And be mauled to the earth and arise,
And contend for the shade of a word and a thing not
    seen with the eyes:
With the half of a broken hope for a pillow at night
That somehow the right is the right
And the smooth shall bloom from the rough:
Lord, if that were enough?

From CHARACTER OF THE HAPPY WARRIOR

By William Wordsworth

Whose powers shed round him in the common strife,
Or mild concerns of ordinary life,
A constant influence, a peculiar grace;
But who, if he be called upon to face
Some awful moment to which Heaven has joined
Great issues, good or bad for human kind,

Is happy as a Lover; and attired
With sudden brightness, like a Man inspired . . .

HEROISM

By Lizette Woodworth Reese

Whether we climb, whether we plod,
   Space for one task the scant years lend—
To choose some path that leads to God,
   And keep it to the end.

From COLUMBUS

By Joaquin Miller

Behind him lay the great Azores,
   Behind the Gates of Hercules,
Before him not the ghost of shores,
   Before him only shoreless seas.
The good mate said: "Now must we pray;
   For lo, the very stars are gone.
Brave Admiral, speak, what shall I say?"
   "Why, say, Sail on, sail on, and on."

The men grew mutinous by day,
   The men grew ghastly pale and weak;
The sad mate thought of home, a spray
   Of salt wave washed his swarthy cheek.
"What shall I say, brave Admiral, say
   If we sight naught but seas at dawn?"

"Why you shall say, at break of day,
  Sail on, sail on, sail on, and on."

They sailed, they sailed. Then spoke the mate
  "This mad sea shows its teeth to-night,
He curls his lip, he lies in wait,
  With lifted teeth, as if to bite.
Brave Admiral, say but one good word,
  What shall we do when hope is gone?"
The words leaped as a flaming sword,—
    "Sail on, sail on, sail on, and on."

ONE FIGHT MORE

By Theodosia Garrison

Now, think you, Life, I am defeated quite?
  More than a single battle shall be mine
  Before I yield the sword and give the sign
And turn, a crownless outcast, to the night.
Wounded, and yet unconquered in the fight,
  I wait in silence till the day may shine
  Once more upon my strength, and all the line
Of your defences break before my might.

Mine be that warrior's blood who, stricken sore,
  Lies in his quiet chamber till he hears
    Afar the clash and clang of arms, and knows
The cause he lived for calls for him once more;
  And straightway rises, whole and void of fears,
    And armèd, turns him singing to his foes.

From ODE TO THE WEST WIND

By Percy Bysshe Shelley

O! lift me as a wave, a leaf, a cloud!
I fall upon the thorns of life! I bleed!

A heavy weight of hours has chained and bowed
One too like thee: tameless, and swift, and proud.

Make me thy lyre, even as the forest is:
What if my leaves are falling like its own!
The tumult of thy mighty harmonies

Will take from both a deep, autumnal tone,
Sweet though in sadness. Be thou, spirit fierce,
My spirit! Be thou me, impetuous one!

Drive my dead thoughts over the universe
Like withered leaves to quicken a new birth!
And, by the incantation of this verse,

Scatter, as from an unextinguished hearth
Ashes and sparks, my words among mankind!
Be through my lips to unawakened earth

The trumpet of a prophecy! O wind,
If Winter comes, can Spring be far behind?

CLOSING LINES OF PROMETHEUS UNBOUND

By Percy Bysshe Shelley

Demorgorgon:

  To suffer woes which Hope thinks infinite;
  To forgive wrongs darker than death or night;
    To defy Power, which seems omnipotent;
  To love, and bear; to hope till Hope creates
  From its own wreck the thing it contemplates;
    Neither to change, nor falter, nor repent;
  This, like thy glory, Titan, is to be
  Good, great and joyous, beautiful and free;
  This is alone Life, Joy, Empire, and Victory.

PSALM XCI

He that dwelleth in the secret place of the Most High
Shall abide under the shadow of the Almighty.
I will say of the Lord,
He is my refuge and my fortress:
My God; in him will I trust.
Surely he shall deliver thee from the snare of the fowler,
And from the noisome pestilence.
He shall cover thee with his feathers,
And under his wings shalt thou trust:
His truth shall be thy shield and buckler.
Thou shalt not be afraid for the terror by night;

Nor for the arrow that flieth by day;
Nor for the pestilence that walketh in darkness;
Nor for the destruction that wasteth at noonday.
A thousand shall fall at thy side,
And ten thousand at thy right hand;
But it shall not come nigh thee.
Only with thine eyes shalt thou behold
And see the reward of the wicked.
Because thou hast made the Lord, which is my refuge,
Even the Most High, thy habitation;
There shall no evil befall thee,
Neither shall any plague come nigh thy dwelling.
For he shall give his angels charge over thee,
To keep thee in all thy ways.
They shall bear thee up in their hands,
Lest thou dash thy foot against a stone.
Thou shalt tread upon the lion and adder:
The young lion and the dragon shalt thou trample under feet.
Because he hath set his love upon me,
Therefore will I deliver him:
I will set him on high, because he hath known my name.
He shall call upon me, and I will answer him:
I will be with him in trouble; I will deliver him, and honour him.
With long life will I satisfy him,
And shew him my salvation.

℞ II

MENTAL COCKTAILS AND SPIRITUAL PICK-ME-UPS

(Poems of Laughter)

SPRING ODE

By Don Marquis

I

Fill me with sassafras, nurse,
    And juniper juice!
Let me see if I'm still any use!
For I want to be young and to sing again,
    Sing again, sing again!
    Middle age is a curse!
It is Spring again, Spring again, Spring again!
And the big bull oyster comes out of his cave
    At the flood of the tides
And bellows his love to his mate where she rides
    On the crest of the wave!
The crimson pylorus is singing his song
And the scarlet sciaticas flame in the grass,
The snail is abroad with his periscope prong—
    Fill me with sassafras!
    I want to be one
With the joy of the earth, under the sun,
For the purple convolvulus convolves and volutes
    And the arbutus ups and arbutes—
    Fill me with sassafras,
And cohosh and buchu and juniper juice
    And then turn me loose!

II

Out of the prison of Winter
The earth and its creatures emerge
And the woodlouse sits on a splinter
   And flirts with the cosmic urge;
   Steep me in camomile tea,
   Or give me a shot with a needle,
For I want to be young again—Me!
   And woo with a lyrical wheedle!
   Go page Amaryllis,
And tell her Spring's here with a heluva moon—
        Oh, Chloe, come hither!
Here's a bald-headed Strephon that's willing to spoon!
He brings to the business a lyre and a zither
And a heart that's been chewed by the romance bacillus;
      Nurse, the juniper juice,
And the sassafras, nurse, and then turn me loose,
   Let me see if I'm still any use!

THE CHIMPANZEE

By Oliver Herford

Children, behold the Chimpanzee:
He sits on the ancestral tree
From which we sprang in ages gone.
I'm glad we sprang: had we held on,
We might, for aught that I can say,
Be horrid Chimpanzees to-day.

FERDINANDO AND ELVIRA

or, THE GENTLE PIEMAN

By W. S. Gilbert

PART I

At a pleasant evening party I had taken down to supper
One whom I will call Elvira, and we talked of love and Tupper,

Mr. Tupper and the poets, very lightly with them dealing,
For I've always been distinguished for a strong poetic feeling.

Then we let off paper crackers, each of which contained a motto,
And she listened while I read them, till her mother told her not to.

Then she whispered, "To the ball-room we had better, dear, be walking;
If we stop down here much longer, really people will be talking."

There were noblemen in coronets, and military cousins,
There were captains by the hundred, there were baronets by dozens.

Yet she heeded not their offers, but dismissed them with a blessing;
Then she let down all her back hair which had taken long in dressing.

Then she had convulsive sobbings in her agitated throttle,
Then she wiped her pretty eyes and smelt her pretty smelling-bottle.

So I whispered, "Dear Elvira, say—what can the matter be with you?
Does anything you've eaten, darling Popsy, disagree with you?"

But spite of all I said, her sobs grew more and more distressing,
And she tore her pretty back hair, which had taken long in dressing.

Then she gazed upon the carpet, at the ceiling then above me,
And she whispered, "Ferdinando, do you really, *really* love me?"

"Love you?" said I, then I sighed, and then I gazed upon her sweetly—
For I think I do this sort of thing particularly neatly—

POEMS OF LAUGHTER 57

"Send me to the Arctic regions, or illimitable azure,
On a scientific goose-chase, with my Coxwell or my Glaisher.

"Tell me whither I may hie me, tell me, dear one, that I *may* know—
Is it up the highest Andes? down a horrible volcano?"

But she said, "It isn't polar bears, or hot volcanic grottoes,
Only find out who it is that writes those lovely cracker mottoes!"

PART II

"Tell me, Henry Wadsworth, Alfred, Poet Close, or Mister Tupper,
Do you write the bonbon mottoes my Elvira pulls at supper?"

But Henry Wadsworth smiled, and said he had not had that honour;
And Alfred, too, disclaimed the words that told so much upon her.

"Mister Martin Tupper, Poet Close, I beg of you inform us";
But my question seemed to throw them both into a rage enormous.

Mister Close expressed a wish that he could only get anigh to me.
And Mister Martin Tupper sent the following reply to me:—

"A fool is bent upon a twig, but wise men dread a bandit."
Which I think must have been clever, for I didn't understand it.

Seven weary years I wandered—Patagonia, China, Norway,
Till at last I sank exhausted at a pastrycook his doorway.

There were fuchsias and geraniums, and daffodils and myrtle,
So I entered, and I ordered half a basin of mock turtle.

He was plump and he was chubby, he was smooth and he was rosy,
And his little wife was pretty, and particularly cosy.

And he chirped and sang, and skipped about, and laughed with laughter hearty—
He was wonderfully active for so very stout a party.

And I said, "Oh, gentle pieman, why so very, very merry?

POEMS OF LAUGHTER 59

Is it purity of conscience, or your one-and-seven sherry?"

But he answered, "I'm so happy—no profession could be dearer—
If I am not humming 'Tra! la! la!' I'm singing, 'Tirer, lirer!'

"First I go and make the patties, and the puddings and the jellies,
Then I make a sugar birdcage, which upon a table swell is;

"Then I polish all the silver, which a supper-table lacquers;
Then I write the pretty mottoes which you find inside the crackers"—

"Found at last!" I madly shouted. "Gentle pieman, you astound me!"
Then I waved the turtle soup enthusiastically round me.

And I shouted and I danced until he'd quite a crowd around him—
And I rushed away, exclaiming, "I have found him! I have found him!"

And I heard the gentle pieman in the road behind me trilling,

"'Tira lira!' stop him, stop him! 'Tra! la! la!' the
  soup's a shilling!"

But until I reached Elvira's home, I never, never
  waited,
And Elvira to her Ferdinand's irrevocably mated!

STRICTLY GERM-PROOF

By Arthur Guiterman

The Antiseptic Baby and the Prophylactic Pup
Were playing in the garden when the Bunny gam-
  boled up;
They looked upon the Creature with a loathing un-
  disguised;—
It wasn't Disinfected and it wasn't Sterilized.

They said it was a Microbe and a Hotbed of Disease;
They steamed it in a vapor of a thousand-odd degrees;
They froze it in a freezer that was cold as Banished
  Hope
And washed it in permanganate with carbolated soap.

In sulphureted hydrogen they steeped its wiggly ears;
They trimmed its frisky whiskers with a pair of hard-
  boiled shears;
They donned their rubber mittens and they took it by
  the hand
And 'lected it a member of the Fumigated Band.

There's not a Micrococcus in the garden where they
    play;
They bathe in pure iodoform a dozen times a day;
And each imbibes his rations from a Hygienic Cup—
The Bunny and the Baby and the Prophylactic Pup.

THE DIFFERENCE

By John B. Tabb

Unc' Si, de Holy Bible say,
    In speakin' of de jus',
Dat he do fall seben times a day;
    Now, how's de sinner wuss?

"Well, chile, de slip may come to all,
    But den de diff'ence foller;
For, ef you watch him when he fall,
    De jus' man do not waller."

EPITAPH FOR ANY NEW YORKER

By Christopher Morley

I, who all my life had hurried,
    Came to Peter's crowded gate;
And, as usual, was worried,
    Fearing that I might be late.
So, when I began to jostle
    (I forgot that I was dead)
Patient smiled the old Apostle:
    "Take your Eternity," he said.

THE JUMBLIES

By Edward Lear

They went to sea in a sieve, they did;
  In a sieve they went to sea;
In spite of all their friends could say,
On a winter's morn, on a stormy day,
  In a sieve they went to sea.
And when the sieve turn'd round and round,
And every one cried, "You'll be drown'd!"
  They call'd aloud, "Our sieve ain't big:
But we don't care a button; we don't care a fig:
  In a sieve we'll go to sea!"
    Far and few, far and few,
      Are the lands where the Jumblies live:
      Their heads are green, and their hands are blue;
      And they went to sea in a sieve.

They sail'd away in a sieve, they did,
  In a sieve they sail'd so fast,
With only a beautiful pea-green veil
Tied with a ribbon, by way of a sail,
  To a small tobacco-pipe mast.
And every one said who saw them go,
"Oh! won't they be soon upset, you know:
For the sky is dark, and the voyage is long;
And, happen what may, it's extremely wrong
  In a sieve to sail so fast."

POEMS OF LAUGHTER

The water it soon came in, it did;
   The water it soon came in:
So, to keep them dry, they wrapp'd their feet
In a pinky paper all folded neat:
   And they fasten'd it down with a pin.
And they pass'd the night in a crockery-jar;
And each of them said, "How wise we are!
Though the sky be dark, and the voyage be long,
Yet we never can think we were rash or wrong,
   While round in our sieve we spin."

And all night long they sail'd away;
   And, when the sun went down,
They whistled and warbled a moony song
To the echoing sound of a coppery gong,
   In the shade of the mountains brown,
"O Timballoo! how happy we are
When we live in a sieve and a crockery-jar!
And all night long, in the moonlight pale,
We sail away with a pea-green sail
   In the shade of the mountains brown."

They sail'd to the Western Sea, they did,—
   To a land all cover'd with trees:
And they bought an owl, and a useful cart,
And a pound of rice, and a cranberry-tart,
   And a hive of silvery bees;
And they bought a pig, and some green jackdaws,
And a lovely monkey with lollipop paws,

And forty bottles of ring-bo-ree,
  And no end of Stilton cheese:

And in twenty years they all came back,—
  In twenty years or more;
And every one said, "How tall they've grown!
For they've been to the Lakes, and the Torrible Zone,
  And the hills of the Chankly Bore."
And they drank their health, and gave them a feast
Of dumplings made of beautiful yeast;
And every one said, "If we only live.
We, too, will go to sea in a sieve,
  To the hills of the Chankly Bore."
    Far and few, far and few,
      Are the lands where the Jumblies live:
    Their heads are green, and their hands are blue;
      And they went to sea in a sieve.

THE BALLADE OF ADAPTATION

By Brander Matthews

The native drama's sick and dying,
  So say the cynic critic crew:
The native dramatist is crying—
  "Bring me the paste! Bring me the glue!
  Bring me the pen, and scissors, too!
Bring me the works of E. Augier!
  Bring me the works of V. Sardou!
I am the man to write a play!"

For want of plays the stage is sighing,
  Such is the song the wide world through:
The native dramatist is crying—
  "Behold the comedies I brew!
  Behold my dramas not a few!
On German farces I can prey,
  And English novels I can hew:
I am the man to write a play!"

There is, indeed, no use denying
  That fashion's turned from old to new:
The native dramatist is crying—
  "Molière, good-bye! Shakespeare, adieu!
  I do not think so much of you.
Although not bad, you've had your day,
  And for the present you won't do.
I am the man to write a play!"

ENVOI

Prince of the stage, don't miss the cue,
  A native dramatist, I say
To every cynic critic, "Pooh!
  I am the man to write a play!"

A PENITENTIAL WEEK

By Carolyn Wells

The week had gloomily begun
For Willie Weeks, a poor man's
                    SUN.

He was beset with bill and dun,
And he had very little
                        MON.

"This cash," said he, "won't pay my dues,
I've nothing here but ones and
                        TUES."

A bright thought struck him, and he said:
"The rich Miss Goldrocks I will
                        WED."

But when he paid his court to her,
She lisped, but firmly said: "No,
                        THUR."

"Alas," said he, "then I must die!
Although hereafter I may
                        FRI."

They found his gloves, and coat, and hat;
The Coroner upon them
                        SAT.

ODE TO DISCORD

(*Inspired by a Strauss Symphony.*)

From the *London Spectator*

Hence loathèd Melody, whose name recalls
The mellow fluting of the nightingale

>   In some sequestered vale,
>   The murmur of the stream
>   Heard in a dream,
> Or drowsy plash of distant waterfalls!
> But thou, divine Cacophony, assume
> The rightful overlordship in her room,
> And with Percussion's stimulating aid
> Expel the heavenly but no longer youthful maid!
>
> Bestir ye, minions of the goddess new,
>   And pay her homage due.
> First let the gong's reverberating clang
>   With clash of shivering metal
> Inaugurate the reign of Sturm and Drang!
>   Let drums (bass, side, and kettle)
> Add to the general welter, and conspire
> To set our senses furiously on fire.
> Noise, yet more noise, I say. Ye trumpets, blare
> In unrelated keys and rend the affrighted air,
> Nor let the shrieking piccolo refrain
> To pierce the midmost marrow of the brain.
> Bleat, cornets, bleat, and let the loud bassoon
> Bay like a bloodhound at an azure moon!
>   Last, with stentorian roar,
> To consummate our musical Majuba,
>   Let the profound bass tuba
> Emit one long and Brobdingnagian snore.

A FINE NEW BALLAD OF CAWSAND BAY

or THE SPIRITED LASS AND THE BRAVE YOUNG SAILOR

By Hamilton Moore

In Cawsand Bay lying,
The *Blue Peter* flying,
The hands all turned up for the anchor to weigh,
There came off a lady,
As fresh as a May day,
Who, looking up modestly, these words did say:
"I wants a young man there,
So do what you can there
To hoist me aboard or send him to me.
His name's Harry Grady,
And I am a lady,
Come off for to save him from going to sea."

The Captain his honour,
When he lookéd upon her,
Ran down the ship's side to assist her on board;
And he said with emotion
"What son of the ocean
Can thus be looked arter by Elinor Ford?"
When thus she gave answer,
"This here is my man, sir,
I'll make him as rich and as fine as a lord."
"That ere," said the Captain,
"Can't very well happen,
We've got sailing orders—you sir, go on board!"

"Avast" says the lady,
"Don't mind him, HAL GRADY,
He once was your captain, but now you're at large,
You sha'nt go aboard her
In spite that chap's order;"
Then out from her bosom she lugg'd his discharge.
Says the CAPTAIN, says he now,
"I'm damned, but he's free now!"
HAL sings out, "Let Weatherface have all my clothes."
For the shore then he steered her,
And all the hands cheered her,
But the CAPTAIN was jealous and looked down his nose

Then she got a shore tailor
To rig her young sailor
In fine nankeen trowsers and blue long-tail coat;
And he looked like a squire
For her to admire
With a dimity handkercher tied round his throat.
"And now," says she, "HARRY,
The next thing, we'll marry,"
And she looked like a dove in his fine manly face.
"That's the thing," says HAL GRADY,
"A parson get ready,
And arter a 'long-splice' we'll 'splice the main brace.'"

Their house it was greater
Nor e'er a first-rater,
With servants in uniform handing the drink;
With a garden to go in

Where flowers was blowin'
Sun-flower, jessamine, lily, and pink.
Then he got eddication
Just fit for his station:
For we know we arn't never too old for to larn.
And his shipmates soon found him
With young uns around him,
All "chips of the old block" from stem to the starn.

POETA FIT, NON NASCITUR

By Lewis Carroll

"How shall I be a poet?
  How shall I write in rhyme?
You told me once 'the very wish
  Partook of the sublime.'
Then tell me how! Don't put me off
  With your 'another time'!"

The old man smiled to see him,
  To hear his sudden sally;
He liked the lad to speak his mind
  Enthusiastically;
And thought "There's no hum-drum in him,
  Nor any shilly-shally.

"And would you be a poet
  Before you've been to school?

Ah, well! I hardly thought you
  So absolute a fool.
First learn to be spasmodic—
  A very simple rule.

"For first you write a sentence,
  And then you chop it small;
Then mix the bits, and sort them out
  Just as they chance to fall:
The order of the phrases makes
  No difference at all.

"Then, if you'd be impressive,
  Remember what I say,
That abstract qualities begin
  With capitals alway:
The True, the Good, the Beautiful—
  Those are the things that pay!

"Next, when you are describing
  A shape, or sound, or tint;
Don't state the matter plainly,
  But put it in a hint;
And learn to look at all things
  With a sort of mental squint."

"For instance, if I wished, Sir,
  Of mutton-pies to tell,
Should I say 'dreams of fleecy flocks
  Pent in a wheaten cell'?"

"Why, yes," the old man said: "that phrase
  Would answer very well.

"Then fourthly, there are epithets
    That suit with any word—
As well as Harvey's Reading Sauce
    With fish, or flesh, or bird—
Of these, 'wild,' 'lonely,' 'weary,' 'strange,'
    Are much to be preferred."

"And will it do, O will it do
    To take them in a lump—
As 'the wild man went his weary way
    To a strange and lonely pump'?"
"Nay, nay! You must not hastily
    To such conclusions jump.

"Such epithets, like pepper,
    Give zest to what you write;
And, if you strew them sparely,
    They whet the appetite:
But if you lay them on too thick,
    You spoil the matter quite!

"Last, as to the arrangement:
    Your reader, you should show him,
Must take what information he
    Can get, and look for no im-
mature disclosure of the drift
    And purpose of your poem.

POEMS OF LAUGHTER 73

"Therefore, to test his patience—
 How much he can endure—
Mention no places, names, or dates,
 And evermore be sure
Throughout the poem to be found
 Consistently obscure.

"First fix upon the limit
 To which it shall extend:
Then fill it up with 'Padding'
 (Beg some of any friend):
Your great SENSATION-STANZA
 You place towards the end."

"And what is a Sensation,
 Grandfather, tell me, pray?
I think I never heard the word
 So used before to-day:
Be kind enough to mention one
 'Exempli gratia.' "

And the old man, looking sadly
 Across the garden-lawn,
Where here and there a dew-drop
 Yet glittered in the dawn,
Said "Go to the Adelphi,
 And see the 'Colleen Bawn.'

"The word is due to Boucicault—
 The theory is his,

Where Life becomes a Spasm,
  And History a Whiz:
If that is not Sensation,
  I don't know what it is.

"Now try your hand, ere Fancy
  Have lost its present glow—"
"And then," his grandson added,
  "We'll publish it, you know:
Green cloth—gold-lettered at the back—
  In duodecimo!"

Then proudly smiled that old man
  To see the eager lad
Rush madly for his pen and ink
  And for his blotting-pad—
But, when he thought of *publishing*,
  His face grew stern and sad.

THE AMATEUR BARD ON WOMAN [1]

Author Unknown

In this imperfect, gloomy scene
  Of complicated ill,
How rarely is a day serene,
  The throbbing bosom still!

[1] This composition secured honorable mention, 1923, in a symposium on the world's worst poems.

Will not a beauteous landscape bright
  Or music's soothing sound,
Console the heart, afford delight,
  And throw sweet peace around?
They may; but never comfort lend
Like an accomplished female friend!

With such a friend the social hour
  In sweetest pleasure glides;
There is, in female charms, a power
  Which lastingly abides;
The fragrance of the blushing rose,
  Its tints and splendid hue,
Will, with the seasons, decompose,
  And pass as flitting dew;
On firmer ties his joys depend
Who has a faithful female friend!

As orbs revolve, and years recede,
  And seasons onward roll,
The fancy may on beauties feed
  With discontented soul;
A thousand objects bright and fair
  May for a moment shine,
Yet many a sigh and many a tear
  But mark their swift decline;
While lasting joys the man attend
Who has a polished female friend!

THE RICH MAN

By Franklin P. Adams

The rich man has his motor-car,
   His country and his town estate.
He smokes a fifty-cent cigar
   And jeers at Fate.

He frivols through the livelong day,
   He knows not Poverty, her pinch,
His lot seems light, his heart seems gay;
   He has a cinch.

Yet though my lamp burns low and dim,
   Though I must slave for livelihood—
Think you that I would change with him?
   You bet I would!

THE KISS

By Coventry Patmore

"I saw you take his kiss!" "'Tis true."
   "O modesty!" "'Twas strictly kept:
He thought me asleep—at least, I knew
   He thought I thought he thought I slept."

BALLAD

By Charles Stuart Calverley

PART I

The auld wife sat at her ivied door,
  (*Butter and eggs and a pound of cheese*)
A thing she had frequently done before;
  And her spectacles lay on her apron'd knees.

The piper he pip'd on the hill-top high,
  (*Butter and eggs and a pound of cheese*)
Till the cow said, "I die," and the goose asked "Why?"
  And the dog said nothing, but search'd for fleas.

The farmer he strode through the square farmyard;
  (*Butter and eggs and a pound of cheese*)
His last brew of ale was a trifle hard,
  The connection of which with the plot one sees.

The farmer's daughter hath frank blue eyes;
  (*Butter and eggs and a pound of cheese*)
She hears the rooks caw in the windy skies,
  As she sits at her lattice and shells her peas.

The farmer's daughter hath ripe red lips;
  (*Butter and eggs and a pound of cheese*)
If you try to approach her away she skips
  Over tables and chairs with apparent ease.

The farmer's daughter hath soft brown hair;
  (*Butter and eggs and a pound of cheese*)
And I met with a ballad, I can't say where,
  Which wholly consisted of lines like these.

PART II

She sat with her hands 'neath her dimpled cheeks,
  (*Butter and eggs and a pound of cheese*)
And spake not a word. While a lady speaks
  There is hope, but she didn't even sneeze.

She sat with her hands 'neath her crimson cheeks;
  (*Butter and eggs and a pound of cheese*)
She gave up mending her father's breeks,
  And let the cat roll in her best chemise.

She sat with her hands 'neath her burning cheeks,
  (*Butter and eggs and a pound of cheese*)
And gaz'd at the piper for thirteen weeks;
  Then she follow'd him out o'er the misty leas.

Her sheep follow'd her, as their tails did them,
  (*Butter and eggs and a pound of cheese*)
And this song is consider'd a perfect gem;
  And as to the meaning, it's what you please.

"SUCH STUFF AS DREAMS"

By Franklin P. Adams

Jenny kiss'd me in a dream;
  So did Elsie, Lucy, Cora,

Bessie, Gwendolyn, Eupheme,
  Alice, Adelaide, and Dora.
Say of honor I'm devoid,
  Say monogamy has missed me,
But don't say to Dr. Freud
  Jenny kiss'd me.[1]

A SONNET [2]

By James Kenneth Stephen

Two voices are there: one is of the deep;
It learns the storm-cloud's thunderous melody,
Now roars, now murmurs with the changing sea,
Now bird-like pipes, now closes soft in sleep:
And one is of an old half-witted sheep
Which bleats articulate monotony,
And indicates that two and one are three,
That grass is green, lakes damp, and mountains steep:
And, Wordsworth, both are thine: at certain times,
Forth from the heart of thy melodious rhymes
The form and pressure of high thoughts will burst:
At other times—good Lord! I'd rather be
Quite unacquainted with the A. B. C.
Than write such hopeless rubbish as thy worst.

[1] This is a parody of Leigh Hunt's poem on p. 358.
[2] A parody of Wordsworth's sonnet, England and Switzerland, 1802. See p. 317.

ON A MAGAZINE SONNET

By Russel Hillard Loines

"Scorn not the sonnet," though its strength be sapped,
   Nor say malignant its inventor blundered;
The corpse that here in fourteen lines is wrapped
   Had otherwise been covered with a hundred.

SPRATT VS. SPRATT

(With genuflections to Owen Seaman and the Ghost of Guy Wetmore Carryl)

By Louis Untermeyer

Of all of the gruesome attempts at a twosome
   The worst of the lot were the Spratts;
Their life was a series of quibbles and queries,
   And quarrels and squabbles and spats.
They argued at breakfast, they argued at tea,
And they argued from midnight till quarter past three.[1]

The paterfamilias was rather a silly ass
   With an appetite passing belief;
A garrulous glutton, he ate up the mutton,
   The chicken, the chops and the beef.
His dining-room manner was almost obscene:
He threw his wife fat while *he* gobbled the lean!

[1] A. M.

He railed at her reading, her brain and her breeding,
  Her goodness, her glands and her girth;
He mentioned with loathing the state of her clothing
  And also the State of her birth.[1]
But his malice exceeded all bounds of control
When he scoffed at her Art and the state of her Soul.

To show her what home meant he gave her no moment
  Of leisure, not even at night.
He bellowed, "I'll teach ye to read Shaw and Nietszche,"
  And quoted from Harold Bell Wright.
"The place for a woman—" he'd start, very glib . . .
And so on for two or three hours *ad lib*.[2]

So very malignant became his indignant
  Remarks about "culture" and "cranks,"
That at last she revolted; she upped and she bolted
  And died in the radical ranks.
Her will left him silent in pique up in Darien [3]
When he found she had founded The New Vegetarian.[4]

And *The Moral* is this (though a bit abstruse):
What's sauce for a more or less proper goose,
When it rouses the violent feminine dander,
Is apt to be sauce for the propaganda!

[1] Oklahoma.
[2] also *ad nauseam*.
[3] Connecticut.
[4] A Journal for Devout Dieticians.

A CREW POEM

By Edward Augustus Blount, Jr.

So happy were Columbia's eight,
  As near the goal they drew,
Each struggling hero all elate,
  The cock-swain almost crew.

THE HEAVY DRAGOON

By W. S. Gilbert

If you want a receipt for that popular mystery,
  Known to the world as a Heavy Dragoon,
Take all the remarkable people in history,
  Rattle them off to a popular tune!
The pluck of Lord Nelson on board of the *Victory*—
  Genius of Bismarck devising a plan;
The humour of Fielding (which sounds contradictory)—
  Coolness of Paget about to trepan—
The grace of Mozart, that unparalleled musico—
  Wit of Macaulay, who wrote of Queen Anne—
The pathos of Paddy, as rendered by Boucicault—
  Style of the Bishop of Sodor and Man—
The dash of a D'Orsay, divested of quackery—
Narrative powers of Dickens and Thackeray—
Victor Emanuel—peak-haunting Peveril—
Thomas Aquinas, and Doctor Sacheverell—
  Tupper and Tennyson—Daniel Defoe—
  Anthony Trollope and Mister Guizot!—

> Take of these elements all that is fusible,
> Melt 'em all down in a pipkin or crucible,
> Set 'em to simmer and take off the scum,
> And a Heavy Dragoon is the residuum!

If you want a receipt for this soldierlike paragon,
  Get at the wealth of the Czar (if you can)—
The family pride of a Spaniard from Arragon—
  Force of Mephisto pronouncing a ban—
A smack of Lord Waterford, reckless and rollicky—
  Swagger of Roderick, heading his clan—
The keen penetration of Paddington Pollaky—
  Grace of an Odalisque on a divan—
The genius strategic of Cæsar or Hannibal—
Skill of Lord Wolseley in thrashing a cannibal—
Flavour of Hamlet—the Stranger, a touch of him—
Little of Manfred (but not very much of him)—
  Beadle of Burlington—Richardson's show—
  Mr. Micawber and Madame Tussaud!
> Take of these elements all that is fusible—
> Melt 'em all down in a pipkin or crucible—
> Set 'em to simmer and take off the scum,
> And a Heavy Dragoon is the residuum!

ADVICE TO WORRIERS

By George Kaupman

Pray list to me a modest while;
I fain would spill an earful:

Don't worry—cultivate a smile—
　　Be always bright and cheerful.

When things are looking dour and black,
　　Then *you* be blithe and hearty;
Just slap me gaily on the back—
　　The life of every party.

Let naught your cheery nature spoil;
　　Be always gay and chipper . . .
And I'll supply the boiling oil,
　　If someone has a dipper.

From DUCKS

By F. W. Harvey

When God had finished the stars and whirl of coloured suns
He turned His mind from big things to fashion little ones,
Beautiful tiny things (like daisies) He made, and then
He made the comical ones in case the minds of men
　　Should stiffen and become
　　Dull, humourless and glum:
And so forgetful of their Maker be
As to take even themselves—*quite seriously.*
Caterpillars and cats are lively and excellent puns:
All God's jokes are good—even the practical ones!

And as for the duck, I think God must have smiled a bit
Seeing those bright eyes blink on the day He fashioned it.
And He's probably laughing still at the sound that came out of its bill!

FATHER WILLIAM

By Lewis Carroll

"You are old, Father William," the young man said,
  "And your hair has become very white;
And yet you incessantly stand on your head—
  Do you think, at your age, it is right?"

"In my youth," Father William replied to his son,
  "I feared it might injure the brain;
But now that I'm perfectly sure I have none,
  Why, I do it again and again."

"You are old," said the youth, "as I mentioned before,
  And have grown most uncommonly fat;
Yet you turned a back-somersault in at the door—
  Pray, what is the reason of that?"

"In my youth," said the sage, as he shook his grey locks,
  "I kept all my limbs very supple

By the use of this ointment—one shilling the box—
  Allow me to sell you a couple."

"You are old," said the youth, "and your jaws are too weak
  For anything tougher than suet;
Yet you finished the goose, with the bones and the beak—
  Pray, how did you manage to do it?"

"In my youth," said his father, "I took to the law,
  And argued each case with my wife;
And the muscular strength which it gave to my jaw,
  Has lasted the rest of my life."

"You are old," said the youth; "one would hardly suppose
  That your eye was as steady as ever;
Yet you balanced an eel on the end of your nose—
  What made you so awfully clever?"

"I have answered three questions, and that is enough,"
  Said his father. "Don't give yourself airs!
Do you think I can listen all day to such stuff?
  Be off, or I'll kick you down stairs!"

℞ III

MASSAGE FOR A MUSCLE-BOUND SPIRIT

(Poems of Emancipation)

FIRST FIG [1]

By Edna St. Vincent Millay

My candle burns at both ends;
 It will not last the night;
But ah, my foes, and oh, my friends—
 It gives a lovely light!

VAGABONDIA

By Richard Hovey

Off with the fetters
That chafe and restrain!
Off with the chain!
Here Art and Letters,
Music and Wine,
And Myrtle and Wanda,
The winsome witches,
Blithely combine.
Here are true riches,
Here is Golconda,
Here are the Indies,
Here we are free—
Free as the wind is,
Free as the sea,
Free!

[1] From a Few Figs from Thistles, published by Harper & Brothers, copyright, 1922, by Edna St. Vincent Millay.

Houp-la!

What have we
To do with the way
Of the Pharisee?
We go or we stay
At our own sweet will;
We think as we say,
And we say or keep still
At our own sweet will,
At our own sweet will.

Here we are free
To be good or bad,
Sane or mad,
Merry or grim
As the mood may be,—
Free as the whim
Of a spook on a spree,—
Free to be oddities,
Not mere commodities,
Stupid and salable,
Wholly available,
Ranged upon shelves;
Each with his puny form
In the same uniform,
Cramped and disabled;
We are not labelled,
We are ourselves.

POEMS OF EMANCIPATION 91

Here is the real,
Here the ideal;
Laughable hardship
Met and forgot,
Glory of bardship—
World's bloom and world's blot;
The shock and the jostle,
The mock and the push,
But hearts like the throstle
A-joy in the bush;
Wits that would merrily
Laugh away wrong,
Throats that would verily
Melt Hell in Song.

. . . . . .

    With the comrade heart
    For a moment's play,
    And the comrade heart
    For a heavier day,
    And the comrade heart
    Forever and aye.

    For the joy of wine
    Is not for long;
    And the joy of song
    Is a dream of shine;

But the comrade heart
Shall outlast art
And a woman's love
The fame thereof.

But wine for a sign
Of the love we bring!
And song for an oath
That Love is king!
And both, and both
For his worshipping!

Then up and away
Till the break of day,
With a heart that's merry,
And a Tom-and-Jerry,
And a derry-down-derry—
What's that you say,
You highly respectable
Buyers and sellers?
We should be decenter?
Not as we please inter
Custom, frugality,
Use and morality
In the delectable
Depths of wine-cellars?

Midnights of revel,
And noondays of song!
Is it so wrong?
Go to the Devil!

I tell you that we,
While you are smirking
And lying and shirking
Life's duty of duties,
Honest sincerity
We are in verity
Free!
Free to rejoice
In blisses and beauties!
Free as the voice
Of the wind as it passes!
Free as the bird
In the weft of the grasses!
Free as the word
Of the sun to the sea—
Free!

TO MR. LAWRENCE

By John Milton

Lawrence of vertuous Father vertuous Son,
   Now that the Fields are dank, and ways are mire,
   Where shall we sometimes meet, and by the fire
   Help waste a sullen day; what may be won
From the hard Season gaining: time will run
   On smoother, till Favonius re-inspire
   The frozen earth; and cloth in fresh attire
   The Lillie and Rose, that neither sow'd nor spun.

What neat repast shall feast us, light and choice,
  Of Attick tast, with Wine, whence we may rise
  To hear the Lute well toucht, or artfull voice
Warble immortal Notes and Tuskan Ayre?
  He who of those delights can judge, and spare
  To interpose them oft, is not unwise.

TO CYRIACK SKINNER

By John Milton

Cyriack, whose Grandsire on the Royal Bench
  Of Brittish Themis, with no mean applause
  Pronounc't and in his volumes taught our Lawes,
  Which others at their Barr so often wrench:
To day deep thoughts resolve with me to drench
  In mirth, that after no repenting drawes;
  Let Euclid rest and Archimedes pause,
  And what the Swede intend, and what the French.
To measure life, learn thou betimes, and know
  Toward solid good what leads the nearest way;
  For other things mild Heav'n a time ordains,
And disapproves that care, though wise in show,
  That with superfluous burden loads the day,
  And when God sends a cheerful hour, refrains.

INTO THE TWILIGHT

By William Butler Yeats

Out-worn Heart, in a time out-worn,
  Come clear of the nets of wrong and right;

Laugh, heart, again in the grey twilight,
Sigh, heart, again in the dew of morn . . .

MORE LIFE . . . MORE!

By Lee Wilson Dodd

Set me over the main again,
   Loose me for China, loose me for France,
Give me to rolic through Spain again
   Or ever the years advance!
Or ever the sordid clutch of the years
   Tear the leaping heart from my side,
Grant me a gust of laughter and tears,
   And the breathing earth for bride!

God of Wanderers! send me the seas,
   Blustering blue-throats shagged at the nape;
Shoulder me forth from my prison of ease,
   Spurn me from Cape to Cape!
   Lash me onward from Land to Land,
   Star-bronzed, stained with the brine;
With the roofless reach of the iris-spanned
   Soul's lust, that is . . . life! be mine.

ECSTASY

By Harold Trowbridge Pulsifer

I heard the wind among the trees,
The surf along the sea:

MASSAGE FOR A MUSCLE-BOUND SPIRIT

    Star-deep, soul-wide,
    The sudden tide
    Swept on and over me.

    My hidden dreams, a rushing sea,—
    All glorious they came,—
    A blazing light
    That made the night
    A living thing of flame!

THE IDLE LAKE

By Edmund Spenser

In this wide Inland sea, that hight by name
The Idle lake, my wandring ship I row,
That knowes her port, and thither sayles by ayme,
Ne care, ne feare I how the wind do blow,
Or whether swift I wend, or whether slow . . .

THE BELL

By James Rorty

On the day when I stopped begging at the heels of life,
On that day, as I sat on a high hill, looking at the sun,
I heard a bell strike far up in the sky, and my heart swelled,
And into my heart with laughter came trooping the lovely young-wise children of the wisdom of the earth.

POEMS OF EMANCIPATION 97

Years had passed before that day; each year the circling seasons found me sad and mournful in the same place.
The fifes of spring played to me, the green grass cried to me, but I would not dance;
The winds of autumn tugged at me, but I would not sail;
Love found me frightened, questioning, and swept on.

In terror I fled to the schools, and pulling at the philosopher's beard, asked why, and why?
I listened respectfully to the wheeze and clatter of the editor's office;
I slept through the professor's lecture and humbly knew that I must be respectful, even while I slept.
There was not a drum beaten or a tambourine clashed anywhere, but I was there, beating time, beating time.

Until one day I heard a sweet bell pealing, far in the blue sky pealing, pealing,
And into my heart with laughter came trooping the lovely young-wise children of the wisdom of the earth.

It is long since I have seen the philosopher, but my laughing heart tells me he is still drawing triangles in the sky;
Having business elsewhere, I left the editor pleasuring in the midst of his favorite indignations;

Sitting at the foot of a stone, listening to the blue jays squalling wisdom in the trees, I could find a pension in my heart for every professor in the world.

On the day when I stopped begging at the heels of life, lo,
The brown-robed mother of the western hills taught me quietness;
The blue-eyed mother of waters taught me peace.
Love shall have his toll of me; I have honey for every bee and seeds for every winging bird.

ODE IN MAY

By William Watson

Let me go forth, and share
  The overflowing Sun
  With one wise friend, or one
Better than wise, being fair,
Where the pewit wheels and dips
  On heights of bracken and ling,
And Earth, unto her leaflet tips,
  Tingles with the Spring.

What is so sweet and dear
  As a prosperous morn in May,
  The confident prime of the day,
And the dauntless youth of the year,
When nothing that asks for bliss,
  Asking aright, is denied,

And half of the world a bridegroom is,
   And half of the world a bride?

The Song of Mingling flows,
   Grave, ceremonial, pure,
   As once, from lips that endure,
The cosmic descant rose,
When the temporal lord of life,
   Going his golden way,
Had taken a wondrous maid to wife
   That long had said him nay.

For of old the Sun, our sire,
   Came wooing the mother of men,
   Earth, that was virginal then,
Vestal fire to his fire.
Silent her bosom and coy,
   But the strong god sued and press'd;
And born of their starry nuptial joy
   Are all that drink of her breast.

And the triumph of him that begot,
   And the travail of her that bore,
   Behold they are evermore
As warp and weft in our lot.
We are children of splendour and flame,
   Of shuddering, also, and tears.
Magnificent out of the dust we came,
   And abject from the Spheres.

O bright irresistible lord!
    We are fruit of Earth's womb, each one,
    And fruit of thy loins, O Sun,
Whence first was the seed outpour'd.
To thee as our Father we bow,
    Forbidden thy Father to see,
Who is older and greater than thou, as thou
    Art greater and older than we.

Thou art but as a word of his speech;
    Thou art but as a wave of his hand;
    Thou art brief as a glitter of sand
'Twixt tide and tide on his beach;
Thou art less than a spark of his fire,
    Or a moment's mood of his soul:
Thou art lost in the notes on the lips of his choir
    That chant the chant of the Whole.

A ROAD SONG

By Duncan Campbell Scott

Up heart, away heart,
Never heed the weather.
Leave the lowland reaches
Where the grain's in seed.
Take the powerful wind in face,
All in highest feather,
Lift your burden with a shout,
Fit for every need.

Front the mountains, cross the passes,
Pioneer the sheer crevasses,
Where the glaciers breed,
Where the imminent avalanches,
Tremble with their air-held motions,
Where below the balsam branches
Start the rills in the erosions,
Follow where they lead;
Where the sunlight ebbs in oceans,
Cast away your load!
Life is not the goal,
It is the road.

A Selection from SONG OF THE OPEN ROAD

By Walt Whitman

Afoot and light-hearted, I take to the open road,
Healthy, free, the world before me,
The long brown path before me, leading wherever I choose.

Henceforth I ask not good-fortune—I myself am good fortune;
Henceforth I whimper no more, postpone no more, need nothing,
Strong and content, I travel the open road. . . .

I think heroic deeds were all conceiv'd in the open air, and all great poems also;

MASSAGE FOR A MUSCLE-BOUND SPIRIT

I think I could stop here myself, and do miracles;
I think whatever I shall meet on the road I shall like,
    and whoever beholds me shall like me;
I think whoever I see must be happy. . . .

I am larger, better than I thought;
I did not know I held so much goodness.
All seems beautiful to me;
I can repeat over to men and women, You have done
    such good to me, I would do the same to you.

I will recruit for myself and you as I go;
I will scatter myself among men and women as I go;
I will toss the new gladness and roughness among them;
Whoever denies me, it shall not trouble me;
Whoever accepts me, he or she shall be blessed, and
    shall bless me. . . .

Allons! whoever you are, come travel with me!
Traveling with me, you find what never tires. . . .

Allons! with power, liberty, the earth, the elements!
Health, defiance, gayety, self-esteem, curiosity;
Allons! from all formules! . . .

Allons! yet take warning!
He traveling with me needs the best blood, thews,
    endurance;
None may come to the trial, till he or she bring cour-
    age and health. . . .

POEMS OF EMANCIPATION 103

Allons! after the GREAT COMPANIONS! and to belong to them!
They too are on the road! they are the swift and majestic men! they are the greatest women. . . .

Allons! to that which is endless, as it was beginningless. . . .
To see nothing anywhere but what you may reach it and pass it,
To conceive no time, however distant, but what you may reach it and pass it,
To look up and down no road but it stretches and waits for you—however long but it stretches and waits for you . . .
To see no possession but you may possess it—enjoying all without labor or purchase—abstracting the feast, yet not abstracting one particle of it. . . .

Allons! whoever you are! come forth!
You must not stay sleeping and dallying there in the house, though you built it, or though it has been built for you.
Allons! out of the dark confinement! . . .

Allons! through struggles and wars!
The goal that was named can not be countermanded. . . .

Allons! the road is before us!
It is safe—I have tried it—my own feet have tried it well.

Allons! be not detain'd!
Let the paper remain on the desk unwritten, and the book on the shelf unopen'd!
Let the tools remain in the workshop! let the money remain unearn'd! . . .

Mon enfant! I give you my hand!
I give you my love, more precious than money,
I give you myself, before preaching or law;
Will you give me yourself? will you come travel with me?
Shall we stick by each other as long as we live?

ALE

By William H. Davies

Now do I hear thee weep and groan,
   Who hast a comrade sunk at sea?
Then quaff thee of my good old ale,
   And it will raise him up for thee;
Thou'lt think as little of him then
As when he moved with living men.

If thou hast hopes to move the world,
   And every effort it doth fail,
Then to thy side call Jack and Jim,
   And bid them drink with thee good ale;
So may the world, that would not hear,
Perish in hell with all your care.

One quart of good old ale, and I
    Feel then what life immortal is:
The brain is empty of all thought,
    The heart is brimming o'er with bliss;
Time's first child, Life, doth live; but Death,
The second, hath not yet his breath.

LIFE-DRUNK

By Arthur Stringer

On opal Aprilian mornings like this
I seem dizzy and drunk with life.
I waken and wander and laugh in the sun;
With some mystical knowledge enormous
I lift up my face to the light.
Drunk with a gladness stupendous I seem;
With some wine of Immensity god-like I reel;
And my arm could fling Time from his Throne;
I could pelt the awed taciturn arch
Of Morning with music and mirth;
And I feel, should I find but a voice for my thought,
That the infinite orbits of all God's loneliest stars
That are weaving vast traceries out on the fringes of Night
Could never stand more than a hem on the robe of my Song!

WE

By Hervey Allen

We who have come back from the war,
And stand upright and draw full breath,
Seek boldly what life holds in store
And eat its whole fruit rind and core,
Before we enter through the door
To keep our rendezvous with death.

We who have walked with death in France,
When all the world with death was rife,
Who came through all that devils' dance,
When life was but a circumstance,
A sniper's whim, a bullet's glance,
We have a rendezvous with life!

With life that hurtles like a spark
From stricken steel where anvils chime,
That leaps the space from dark to dark,
A blinding, blazing, flaming arc,
As clean as fire, and frank and stark—
White life that lives while there is time.

We will not live by musty creeds,
Who learned the truth through love and war,
Who tipped the scales for right by deeds,
When old men's lies were broken reeds,
We follow where the cold fact leads
And bow our heads no more.

We have come back who broke the line
The hard Hun held by bomb and knife!
All but the blind can read the sign;
The time is ours by right divine,
Who drank with Death in blood red wine,
We have a rendezvous with life!

COURAGE, MON AMI!

By Willard Wattles

Oh, it is good to camp with the spirit,
  Oh, it is jaunty to walk with the mind,
When the soul sees all the future to share it
  Knowing the road that stretches behind.

Courage, my comrade, the devil is dying!
  Here's the bright sun and a cloud scudding free;
The touch of your hand is too near for denying,
  And laughter's a tavern sufficient for me.

Hang your old hat on the smoke-mellowed rafter,
  Strike an old song on your crazy guitar;
Hey, hustle, old lady, it's heaven we're after—
  God, but I'm glad we can be what we are!

From TAMAR

By Robinson Jeffers

She answered, standing dark against the west in the
    window, the death of the winter rose of evening

Behind her little high-poised head, and threading the
    brown twilight of the room with the silver
Exultance of her voice, "My brother can you feel how
    happy I am, but how far off too?
If I have done wrong it has turned good to me, I could
    almost be sorry that I have to die now
Out of such freedom; if I were standing back of the
    evening crimson on a mountain in Asia
All the fool shames you can whip up into a filth of
    words would not be farther off me,
Nor any fear of anything, if I stood in the evening star
    and saw this dusty dime's worth
A dot of light, dropped up the star-gleam."

THE CELESTIAL SURGEON

By Robert Louis Stevenson

If I have faltered more or less
In my great task of happiness;
If I have moved among my race
And shown no glorious morning face;
If beams from happy human eyes
Have moved me not; if morning skies,
Books, and my food, and summer rain
Knocked on my sullen heart in vain:—
Lord, thy most pointed pleasure take
And stab my spirit broad awake;
Or, Lord, if too obdurate I,
Choose thou, before that spirit die,

A piercing pain, a killing sin,
And to my dead heart run them in!

From **THE COLLAR**

By George Herbert

I struck the board and cry'd, "No more;
    I will abroad."
What, shall I ever sigh and pine?
My lines and life are free; free as the road,
    Loose as the winde, as large as store . . .
    Is the yeare onely lost to me?
    Have I no bayes to crown it,
No flowers, no garlands gay? all blasted,
    All wasted?
    Not so, my heart; but there is fruit,
    And thou hast hands.
    Recover all thy sigh-blown age
On double pleasures; leave thy cold dispute
Of what is fit and not; forsake thy cage,
    Thy rope of sands
Which pettie thoughts have made; and made to thee
    Good cable, to enforce and draw,
    And be thy law,
    While thou didst wink and wouldst not see.
    Away! take heed;
    I will abroad.
Call in thy death's-head there, tie up thy fears;
    He that forbears

110 MASSAGE FOR A MUSCLE-BOUND SPIRIT

> To suit and serve his need
> Deserves his load.

AN OLD SONG RESUNG

By William Butler Yeats

Down by the salley gardens my love and I did meet;
She passed the salley gardens with little snow-white feet.
She bid me take love easy, as the leaves grow on the tree;
But I, being young and foolish, with her would not agree.

In a field by the river my love and I did stand,
And on my leaning shoulder she laid her snow-white hand.
She bid me take life easy, as the grass grows on the weirs;
But I was young and foolish, and now am full of tears.

A Selection from THE POEM OF JOYS

By Walt Whitman

. . . O the joy of my spirit! it is uncaged! it darts like lightning!
It is not enough to have this globe, or a certain time—
I will have thousands of globes, and all time . . .

O something pernicious and dread!
Something far away from a puny and pious life!
Something unproved! Something in a trance!
Something escaped from the anchorage, and driving free . . .

O to realize space!
The plenteousness of all—that there are no bounds;
To emerge, and be of the sky—of the sun and moon, and the flying clouds, as one with them.

O the joy of a manly self-hood!
Personality—to be servile to none—to defer to none—not to any tyrant, known or unknown,
To walk with erect carriage, a step springy and elastic,
To look with calm gaze, or with a flashing eye,
To speak with a full and sonorous voice, out of a broad chest,
To confront with your personality all the other personalities of the earth . . .

O, while I live, to be the ruler of life—not a slave,
To meet life as a powerful conqueror,
No fumes—no ennui—no more complaints, or scornful criticisms . . .

O, to sail to sea in a ship!
To leave this steady and unendurable land!
To leave the tiresome sameness of the streets, the sidewalks and the houses;

To leave you, O solid and motionless land, and entering a ship,
To sail, and sail, and sail.

O to have my life henceforth a poem of new joys!
To dance, clap hands, exult, shout, skip, leap, roll on, float on,
To be a sailor of the world, bound for all ports,
A ship itself, (see indeed these sails I spread to the sun and air,)
A swift and swelling ship, full of rich words—full of joys.

From PASSAGE TO INDIA

By Walt Whitman

Passage to more than India!
O secret of the earth and sky!
Of you, O waters of the sea! O winding creeks and rivers!
Of you, O woods and fields! Of you, strong mountains of my land!
Of you, O prairies, Of you, gray rocks,
O morning red! O clouds! O rains and snows!
O day and night, passage to you!

O sun and moon, and all you stars! Sirius and Jupiter!
Passage to you!

Passage—immediate passage! the blood burns in my veins!
Away, O soul! hoist instantly the anchor!
Cut the hawsers—haul out—shake out every sail!
Have we not stood here like trees in the ground long enough?
Have we not grovell'd here long enough, eating and drinking like mere brutes?
Have we not darken'd and dazed ourselves with books long enough?

Sail forth! steer for the deep waters only!
Reckless, O soul, exploring, I with thee, and thou with me;
For we are bound where mariner has not yet dared to go,
And we will risk the ship, ourselves and all.

O my brave soul!
O farther, farther sail!
O daring joy, but safe! Are they not all the seas of God?
O farther, farther, farther sail!

℞ IV

POPPY JUICE FOR INSOMNIA

(Soothers and Soporifics)

TO SLEEP

By John Keats

O soft embalmer of the still midnight!
  Shutting with careful fingers and benign
Our gloom-pleased eyes, embower'd from the light,
  Enshaded in forgetfulness divine;
O soothest Sleep! if so it please thee, close,
  In midst of this thine hymn, my willing eyes,
Or wait the amen, ere thy poppy throws
  Around my bed its lulling charities;
  Then save me, or the passèd day will shine
Upon my pillow, breeding many woes;
Save me from curious conscience, that still lords
  Its strength for darkness, burrowing like a mole;
Turn the key deftly in the oilèd wards,
  And seal the hushèd casket of my soul.

KIND SLEEP

By Isabel Fiske Conant

Slip into sleep as easy as a gown
The soft and clinging draperies of dream
The under-sea-green trail that down and down,
Sinks rhythmically with a sunless gleam,—
Then wake as gradually as lilies rise
Spreading wet, yielding petals, new to suns,

To waterless, light element of skies,
Unoceanic, and yet native ones.
Slip into death as birds drop down the side
Of rugged canyons that they never fear,
As wings upon the blue that, rising, ride,
Then waken to a better time of year.
 Tossing away a far too long November,
 Returning to the April you remember.

FOR SLEEP WHEN OVERTIRED OR WORRIED

By Sarah N. Cleghorn

Cares and anxieties,
I roll you all up in a bundle together;
I carry you across the meadow to the river.
River, I am throwing in a bundle of cares and anxieties.
Float it away to the sea!

Now I come slowly back across the meadow,
Slowly into the house,
Slowly up to my room.
The night is quiet and cool;
The lights are few and dim;
The sounds are drowsy and far away and melting
 into each other;
Melting into the night.
Sleep comes creeping nearer, creeping nearer;
It goes over my head like a wave.
I sleep . . . I rest . . . I sleep.

SLEEP

By Sophie Jewett

Dear gray-eyed Angel, wilt thou come to-night?
  Spread the soft shadow of thy sheltering wings,
And banish every hint of thought and light,
  And all the clamoring crowd of waking things?
Wilt thou bend low above wide weary eyes,
As o'er the worn world bend the tireless skies?

COME, BLESSÈD SLEEP

By Christina Rossetti

Come, blessèd Sleep, most full, most perfect, come.
  Come, sleep, if so I may forget the whole;
  Forget my body and forget my soul,
Forget how long life is and troublesome.
Come, happy sleep, to soothe my heart or numb,
  Arrest my weary spirit or control:
  Till light be dark to me from pole to pole,
And winds and echoes and low songs be dumb.
Come, sleep, and lap me into perfect calm,
  Lap me from all the world and weariness.
Come, secret sleep, with thine unuttered psalm,
Come, heavy dreamless sleep, and close and press
  Upon mine eyes thy fingers dropping balm.

THE NIGHT

By Hilaire Belloc

Most Holy Night, that still dost keep
The keys of all the doors of sleep,
To me when my tired eyelids close
　　Give thou repose.

And let the far lament of them
That chaunt the dead day's requiem
Make in my ears, who wakeful lie,
　　Soft lullaby.

Let them that guard the hornèd Moon
By my bedside their memories croon.
So shall I have new dreams and blest
　　In my brief rest.

Fold thy great wings about my face,
Hide day-dawn from my resting-place,
And cheat me with thy false delight,
　　Most Holy Night.

THE WHITE PATERNOSTER

(*Old Rhyme*)

Matthew, Mark, Luke and John,
Bless the bed that I lie on!
Four corners to my bed,
Five angels there lie spread;

Two at my head,
Two at my feet,
One at my heart, my soul to keep.

TO SLEEP

By Sir Philip Sidney

Come, Sleep, O Sleep, the certain knot of peace,
The baiting-place of wit, the balm of woe,
The poor man's wealth, the prisoner's release,
The indifferent judge between the high and low.
With shield of proof shield me from out the prease
Of those fierce darts, Despair at me doth throw;
O make in me those civil wars to cease!
I will good tribute pay, if thou do so.
Take thou of me smooth pillows, sweetest bed;
A chamber deaf to noise and blind to light;
A rosy garland, and a weary head.
And if these things, as being thine by right,
Move not thy heavy grace, thou shalt in me
Livelier than elsewhere Stella's image see.

From SLEEP [1]

By Christopher Morley

Yet, in the end, you take us all, dear Sleep—
And not as now, when, even while we drowse
The mind, still rocking like an ocean bird,
Knows itself poised upon the unknowing gulf;

[1] From Parson's Pleasure by Christopher Morley, copyright 1923, George H. Doran Co., publishers.

But when, all grateful and without wild words
The dark sea-rim enfolds us, circle-round.
A clear unrippled sea of endless calm
And on the wave, not even a lonely gull.

From THE LOTOS-EATERS

By Alfred Tennyson

There is sweet music here that softer falls
Than petals from blown roses on the grass,
Or night-dews on still waters between walls
Of shadowy granite, in a gleaming pass;
Music that gentlier on the spirit lies,
Than tir'd eyelids upon tir'd eyes;
Music that brings sweet sleep down from the blissful skies.
Here are cool mosses deep,
And thro' the moss the ivies creep,
And in the stream the long-leaved flowers weep,
And from the craggy ledge the poppy hangs in sleep.

From THE FAERIE QUEENE

By Edmund Spenser

And more to lulle him in his slumber soft,
A trickling streame from high rock tumbling downe,
And ever-drizling raine upon the loft,
Mixt with a murmuring winde, much like the sowne
Of swarming Bees, did cast him in a swowne.

SOOTHERS AND SOPORIFICS

No other noyse, nor peoples troublous cryes,
As still are wont t'annoy the wallèd towne,
Might there be heard; but carelesse Quiet lyes
Wrapt in eternall silence farre from enimyes.

From IL PENSEROSO

By John Milton

There in close covert by some brook
Where no profaner eye may look,
Hide me from Day's garish eye,
While the bee with honey'd thigh,
That at her flowery work doth sing,
And the waters murmuring,
With such concert as they keep,
Entice the dewy-feathered sleep.
And let some strange mysterious dream
Wave at his wings in airy stream
Of lively portraiture display'd,
Softly on my eyelids laid,
And, as I wake, sweet music breathe
Above, about, or underneath,
Sent by some spirit to mortals good,
Or the unseen genius of the wood.

CARE-CHARMING SLEEP

By John Fletcher

Care-charming Sleep, thou easer of all woes,
Brother to Death, sweetly thyself dispose

On this afflicted prince; fall like a cloud,
In gentle showers; give nothing that is loud,
Or painful to his slumbers; easy, sweet,
And as a purling stream, thou son of Night,
Pass by his troubled senses; sing his pain,
Little hollow murmuring wind or silver rain;
Into this prince gently, oh, gently slide,
And kiss him into slumber like a bride.

TO SLEEP (Extract)

By Norman Gale

But thou, O Sleep, bend down and give
My fevered frame apparent death;
Receive my hands, caress my brow,
And send the incense of thy breath
About my temples while I weep,
Sleep, lest thou shouldst not hear me, Sleep.

On aching balls that roam the room
Thus set thy seals as one who stirs
About the bedside of the dead
And weighs down rebel lids of eyes
That look beyond for Paradise
With silver circles from a purse:
And when thy spell is on me cast,
And thou from out my chamber passed,
If haply Wakefulness be near
Say not that I am sleeping, dear,

For oftentimes, methinks, her mood
Is wry, and not to do me good.
O God, 'twould better be if she
To wake me should delay too long,
And find with face all still and cold
Me unresponsive to her song!

The blind grows pale with dawn, and hark!
It is the matin of the lark.
Though there be virtue in thy touch
I will not pray thee overmuch,
Lest I should weary thee, and be
Cast out of all thy love by thee;
And, Sleep, I will not moan or weep
If thou wilt come to-morrow, Sleep.

MIDSUMMER NIGHT

By Archibald Lampman

Mother of balms and soothings manifold,
  Quiet-breathed Night, whose brooding hours are seven,
  To whom the voices of all rest are given,
And those few stars whose scattered names are told.
Far off, beyond the westward hills outrolled,
  Darker than thou, more still, more dreamy even,
  The golden moon leans in the dusky heaven,
And under her, one star, a point of gold.

And all go slowly lingering toward the west,
As we go down forgetfully to our rest,
  Weary of daytime, tired of noise and light.
Ah, it was time that thou shouldst come, for we
Were sore athirst, and had great need of thee,
  Thou sweet physician, balmy-bosomed Night.

SWEET AND LOW

By Alfred Tennyson

Sweet and low, sweet and low
  Wind of the western sea;
Low, low, breathe and blow,
  Wind of the western sea!
Over the rolling waters go,
Come from the dying moon, and blow,
  Blow him again to me;
While my little one, while my pretty one, sleeps.

Sleep and rest, sleep and rest,
  Father will come to thee soon;
Rest, rest, on mother's breast,
  Father will come to thee soon;
Father will come to his babe in the nest,
Silver sails all out of the west
  Under the silver moon:
Sleep, my little one, sleep, my pretty one, sleep.

WYNKEN, BLYNKEN AND NOD

By Eugene Field

Wynken, Blynken, and Nod one night
  Sailed off in a wooden shoe,—
Sailed on a river of crystal light
  Into a sea of dew.
"Where are you going, and what do you wish?"
  The old moon asked the three:
"We have come to fish for the herring-fish
  That live in this beautiful sea:
  Nets of silver and gold have we,"
     Said Wynken,
     Blynken,
     And Nod.

The old moon laughed and sang a song,
  As they rocked in the wooden shoe;
And the wind that sped them all night long
  Ruffled the waves of dew;
The little stars were the herring-fish
  That lived in the beautiful sea.
"Now cast your nets wherever you wish,—
  Never afeard are we!"
  So cried the stars to the fishermen three,
     Wynken,
     Blynken,
     And Nod.

All night long their nets they threw
  To the stars in the twinkling foam,—
Then down from the skies came the wooden shoe,
  Bringing the fishermen home:
'Twas all so pretty a sail, it seemed
  As if it could not be;
And some folk thought 'twas a dream they'd dreamed
  Of sailing that beautiful sea;
  But I shall name you the fishermen three:
    Wynken,
    Blynken,
    And Nod.

Wynken and Blynken are two little eyes,
  And Nod is a little head,
And the wooden shoe that sailed the skies
  Is a wee one's trundle-bed;
So shut your eyes while Mother sings
  Of wonderful sights that be,
And you shall see the beautiful things
  As you rock on the misty sea
  Where the old shoe rocked the fishermen three,—
    Wynken,
    Blynken,
    And Nod.

MY SOUL IS AN ENCHANTED BOAT

By Percy Bysshe Shelley

My soul is an enchanted boat,
Which, like a sleeping swan doth float

Upon the silver waves of thy sweet singing;
　And thine does like an angel sit
　Beside the helm conducting it,
Whilst all the winds with melody are ringing.
　It seems to float ever, for ever,
　Upon that many-winding river,
　Between mountains, woods, abysses,
　A paradise of wildernesses!
Till, like one in slumber bound,
Borne to the ocean, I float down, around,
Into a sea profound, of ever spreading sound.

BELLS IN THE RAIN [1]

By Elinor Wylie

Sleep falls, with limpid drops of rain,
Upon the steep cliffs of the town.
Sleep falls; men are at peace again
While the small drops fall softly down.

The bright drops ring like bells of glass
Thinned by the wind, and lightly blown;
Sleep cannot fall on peaceful grass
So softly as it falls on stone.

Peace falls unheeded on the dead
Asleep; they have had deep peace to drink;
Upon a live man's bloody head
It falls most tenderly, I think.

[1] From "Nets to Catch the Wind" by Elinor Wylie, copyright, 1921, by Harcourt, Brace and Company, Inc.

From THE FAERIE QUEENE

By Edmund Spenser

And fast beside there trickled softly downe
A gentle streame, whose murmuring wave did play
Emongst the pumy stones, and made a sowne,
To lull him soft asleepe that by it lay:
The wearie Traveiler, wandring that way,
Therein did often quench his thirsty heat,
And then by it his wearie limbes display,
Whiles creeping slomber made him to forget
His former payne, and wypt away his toilsom sweat.

TO ONE WITH HANDS OF SLEEP

By Harold Vinal

She moves as other women move
Across the arc of day and night,
And every utterance is love,
And every look a holy light.

She speaks as other women speak,
But the faint echo of a word,
Is quietness against the cheek
And balm and myrrh administered.

She is as water to the mind,
A reservoir, where shadows are.
I take her beauty, being blind,
But give her gall and vinegar.

SOOTHERS AND SOPORIFICS

SLEEP

By John Fletcher

Come, Sleep, and with thy sweet deceiving
  Lock me in delight awhile;
  Let some pleasing dreams beguile
  All my fancies; that from thence
  I may feel an influence
All my powers of care bereaving!

Though but a shadow, but a sliding,
  Let me know some little joy!
  We that suffer long annoy
  Are contented with a thought
  Through an idle fancy wrought:
O let my joys have some abiding!

A TRANSLATION FROM MICHAEL ANGELO

By William Wordsworth

Come, gentle Sleep, Death's image tho' thou art,
Come share my couch, nor speedily depart;
How sweet thus living without life to lie,
Thus without death how sweet it is to die.

LET ME SLEEP

By Christina Rossetti

Sleep, let me sleep, for I am sick of care;
  Sleep, let me sleep, for my pain wearies me.

Shut out the light, thicken the heavy air
With drowsy incense; let a distant stream
Of music lull me, languid as a Dream,
   Soft as the whisper of a summer sea.

THE POOL OF SLEEP

By Arlo Bates

I dragged my body to the pool of sleep,
  Longing to drink; but ere my throbbing lip
  From the cool flood one Dives-drop might sip,
The wave sank fluctuant to some unknown deep.
With aching eyes that could not even weep,
  I saw the dark, deluding water slip,
  Slow eddying, down; the weeds and mosses drip
With maddening waste. I watched the sweet tide creep
A little higher, but to fall more fast.
  Fevered and wounded in the strife of men
I burned with anguish, till, endurance past,
  The fount crept upward; sank, and rose again,—
Swelled slowly, slowly, slowly,—till at last
  My seared lips met the soothing wave, and then—

SLEEP

By John B. Tabb

What art thou, balmy sleep?
"Foam from the fragrant deep
Of silence, hither blown
From the hushed waves of tone."

SLEEP SWEET

By Ellen M. Huntington Gates

Sleep sweet within this quiet room,
  O thou, whoe'er thou art,
And let no mournful yesterdays
  Disturb thy quiet heart.

Nor let to-morrow scare thy rest
  With dreams of coming ill;
Thy Maker is thy changeless friend,
  His love surrounds thee still.

Forget thyself and all the world;
  Put out each feverish light;
The stars are watching overhead,
  Sleep sweet, goodnight! good night!

TO SLEEP

By William Wordsworth

A flock of sheep that leisurely pass by,
One after one; the sound of rain, and bees
Murmuring; the fall of rivers, winds and seas,
Smooth fields, white sheets of water, and pure sky;
I have thought of all by turns, and yet do lie
Sleepless! and soon the small birds' melodies
Must hear, first uttered from my orchard trees;
And the first cuckoo's melancholy cry.

Even thus last night, and two nights more, I lay,
And could not win thee, Sleep! by any stealth;
So do not let me wear to-night away:
Without Thee what is all the morning's wealth?
Come, blessed barrier between day and day,
Dear mother of fresh thoughts and joyous health!

ṚV

TO DEFLATE THE EGO

(Ingredients for a Humble Pie)

I'M NOBODY!

By Emily Dickinson

I'm nobody! Who are you?
Are you nobody, too?
Then there's a pair of us—don't tell!
They'd banish us, you know.

How dreary to be somebody!
How public, like a frog
To tell your name the livelong day
To an admiring bog!

OZYMANDIAS OF EGYPT

By Percy Bysshe Shelley

I met a traveller from an antique land
Who said: Two vast and trunkless legs of stone
Stand in the desert. Near them on the sand,
Half sunk, a shattered visage lies, whose frown
And wrinkled lip and sneer of cold command
Tell that its sculptor well those passions read
Which yet survive, stamped on those lifeless things,
The hand that mocked them and the heart that fed;
And on the pedestal these words appear:
"My name is Ozymandias, king of kings;

Look on my works, ye mighty, and despair!"
Nothing besides remains. Round the decay
Of that colossal wreck, boundless and bare,
The lone and level sands stretch far away.

TO THE STONE CUTTERS

By Robinson Jeffers

Stone-cutters fighting time with marble, you foredefeated
Challengers of oblivion,
Eat cynical earnings, knowing rock splits, records fall down,
The square-limbed Roman letters
Scale in the thaws, wear in the rain. The poet as well
Builds his monument mockingly;
For man will be blotted out, the blithe earth die, the brave sun
Die blind, his heart blackening:
Yet stones have stood for a thousand years, and pained thoughts found
The honey peace in old poems.

MY HOUSE

By May Williams Ward

My house is small,
An irrelevant cube;
Absurdity

>   Sucked by gravity
>   Against immensity,
>   Walled by diversity,
>   Roofed by infinity.

THE BEASTS

By Walt Whitman

I think I could turn and live with animals, they are so placid and self-contain'd;
I stand and look at them long and long.
They do not sweat and whine about their condition;
They do not lie awake in the dark and weep for their sins;
They do not make me sick discussing their duty to God;
Not one is dissatisfied—not one is demented with the mania of owning things;
Not one kneels to another, nor to his kind that lived thousands of years ago;
Not one is respectable or industrious over the whole earth.

ONE IN THE INFINITE

By George Francis Savage-Armstrong

Roll on, and with thy rolling crust
  That round thy poles thou twirlest,

Roll with thee, Earth, this grain of dust,
    As through the Vast thou whirlest;
On, on through zones of dark and light
    Still waft me, blind and reeling,
Around the sun, and with his flight
    In wilder orbits wheeling.

Speed on through deeps without a shore,
    This Atom with thee bearing,
Thyself a grain of dust—no more—
    'Mid fume of systems flaring.
Ah, what am I to thirst for power,
    Or pore on Nature's pages,—
Whirl'd onward, living for an hour,
    And dead through endless ages?

From THE HOUSE OF A HUNDRED LIGHTS

By Ridgely Torrence

What! doubt the Master Workman's hand
    because my fleshly ills increase?
No; for there still remains one chance
    that I am not His Masterpiece.

From PSALM XIX

By David

The heavens declare the glory of God;
And the firmament sheweth his handywork.

Day unto day uttereth speech,
And night unto night sheweth knowledge.
There is no speech nor language
Where their voice is not heard.
Their line is gone out through all the earth,
And their words to the end of the world.
In them hath he set a tabernacle for the sun,
Which is as a bridegroom coming out of his chamber,
And rejoiceth
As a strong man to run a race.
His going forth is from the end of the heaven,
And his circuit unto the ends of it:
And there is nothing hid from the heat thereof. . . .

Who can understand his errors?
Cleanse thou me from secret faults.
Keep back thy servant also from presumptuous sins;
Let them not have dominion over me:
Then shall I be upright, and I shall be innocent
From the great transgression.
Let the words of my mouth,
And the meditations of my heart,
Be acceptable in thy sight,
O Lord, my strength, and my redeemer.

MY WAGE

By Jessie B. Rittenhouse

I bargained with Life for a penny,
And Life would pay no more,

However I begged at evening
   When I counted my scanty store;

For Life is a just employer,
   He gives you what you ask,
But once you have set the wages,
   Why, you must bear the task.

I worked for a menial's hire,
   Only to learn, dismayed,
That any wage I had asked of Life,
   Life would have paid.

DAYS

By Ralph Waldo Emerson

Daughters of Time, the hypocritic Days,
Muffled and dumb like barefoot dervishes,
And marching single in an endless file,
Bring diadems and fagots in their hands.
To each they offer gifts after his will,
Bread, kingdoms, stars, and sky that holds them all.
I, in my pleachèd garden, watched the pomp,
Forgot my morning wishes, hastily
Took a few herbs and apples, and the Day
Turned and departed silent. I, too late,
Under her solemn fillet saw the scorn.

AFTER BLENHEIM

By Robert Southey

It was a summer evening,
   Old Kaspar's work was done,
And he before his cottage door
   Was sitting in the sun;
And by him sported on the green
His little grandchild Wilhelmine.

She saw her brother Peterkin
   Roll something large and round
Which he beside the rivulet
   In playing there had found;
He came to ask what he had found
That was so large and smooth and round.

Old Kaspar took it from the boy
   Who stood expectant by;
And then the old man shook his head,
   And with a natural sigh
" 'Tis some poor fellow's skull," said he,
"Who fell in the great victory.

"I find them in the garden,
   For there's many here about,
And often when I go to plow
   The ploughshare turns them out.

For many thousand men," said he,
"Were slain in that great victory."

"Now tell us what 'twas all about,"
　　Young Peterkin he cries;
And little Wilhelmine looks up
　　With wonder-waiting eyes;
"Now tell us all about the war,
And what they fought each other for."

"It was the English," Kaspar cried,
　　"Who put the French to rout;
But what they fought each other for
　　I could not well make out.
But every body said," quoth he,
"That 'twas a famous victory.

"My father lived at Blenheim then,
　　Yon little stream hard by;
They burnt his dwelling to the ground,
　　And he was forced to fly:
So with his wife and child he fled,
Nor had he where to rest his head.

"With fire and sword the country round
　　Was wasted far and wide,
And many a childing mother then
　　And newborn baby died:
But things like that, you know, must be
At every famous victory.

"They say it was a shocking sight
  After the field was won;
For many thousand bodies here
  Lay rotting in the sun:
But things like that, you know, must be
After a famous victory.

"Great praise the Duke of Marlbro' won
  And our good Prince Eugene";
"Why 'twas a very wicked thing!"
  Said little Wilhelmine;
"Nay . . . nay . . . my little girl," quoth he,
"It was a famous victory.

"And every body praised the Duke
  Who this great fight did win."
"But what good came of it at last?"
  Quoth little Peterkin:—
"Why that I cannot tell," said he,
"But 'twas a famous victory."

TO A STARING BABY IN A PERAMBULATOR

By Nancy Byrd Turner

Child, I surrender—and hereby declare
Whatever you may think I've done, I've done it:
Theft, arson, murder. You have laid bone-bare
My innermost being, weighed and passed upon it.
I had some prideful secrets, and a pair
Of fond delusions, and a scheme or two,

But all have perished in that long, light blue
Appraisal,—in that bland, unblenching stare.

They call you "blessed innocent" and "lamb";—
I'd rather meet the Sphinx and Sophocles,
The Delphian sybil and Demosthenes
And Einstein, all together in one pram,
If so I might evade in any wise
The inquisition of your awful eyes.

From THE RUBÁIYÁT OF OMAR KHAYYÁM

As Paraphrased

By Edward Fitzgerald

We are no other than a moving row
Of magic shadow-shapes that come and go
   Round with this sun-illumin'd lantern held
In midnight by the Master of the Show;

Impotent pieces of the game He plays
Upon this checker-board of nights and days;
   Hither and thither moves, and checks, and slays,
And one by one back in the closet lays.

The ball no question makes of ayes and noes
But right or left as strikes the Player goes;
   And He that toss'd you down into the field,
He knows about it all—HE knows—HE knows!

The Moving Finger writes; and, having writ,
Moves on: nor all your piety nor wit
  Shall lure it back to cancel half a line,
Nor all your tears wash out a word of it.

And that inverted bowl they call the Sky,
Whereunder crawling coop'd we live and die,
  Lift not your hands to *It* for help—for It
As impotently rolls as you or I.

ON ONE IGNORANT AND ARROGANT

Translated from the Latin of Owen

By William Cowper

Thou mayst of double ignorance boast,
Who knows't not that thou nothing knows't.

AN AUGUST MOOD

By Duncan Campbell Scott

Where the pines have fallen on the hillside
The green needles burning in the sun
Make sweet incense in the vacant spaces
All along the run
Of the rill; and by the rillside
Rushes waver and shine;
In remote and shady places
Wintergreen abounds and interlaces
With the twinflower vine.

The young earth appears aloof and lonely
Swinging in the ether, only
Nature left with all her golden foison;
No ambitions here to wound or poison
With their fears and wishes,
The pure life of birds and beasts and fishes.

All our human passion and endeavour
Idle as a thistle-down
Lightly wheeling, blown about forever;
All our vain renown
Slighter is than flicker of the rushes;
All our prate of evil and of good
Lesser than the comment of two thrushes
Talking in the wood.

THE MOUNTAIN AND THE SQUIRREL

By Ralph Waldo Emerson

The Mountain and the Squirrel
Had a quarrel,
And the former called the latter "Little Prig,"
Bun replied:
"You are doubtless very big;
But all sorts of things and weather
Must be taken in together
To make up a year,
And a sphere;
And I think it no disgrace

To occupy my place.
If I'm not so large as you,
You're not so small as I,
And not half so spry;
I'll not deny you make
A very pretty squirrel track.
Talents differ; all is well and wisely put;
If I cannot carry forests on my back,
Neither can you crack a nut."

℞ VI

TONICS FOR AN ANÆMIC SOUL
(Tissue Builders and Vision Strengtheners)

CREEDS

By Willard Wattles

How pitiful are little folk—
They seem so very small;
They look at stars, and think they are
Denominational.

MEASURE ME, SKY!

By Leonora Speyer

Measure me, sky!
Tell me I reach by a song
Nearer the stars;
I have been little so long!

Weigh me, high wind!
What will your wild scales record?
Profit of pain,
Joy by the weight of a word!

Horizon, reach out!
Catch at my hands, stretch me taut,
Rim of the world;
Widen my eyes by a thought!

Sky, be my depth,
Wind, be my width and my height,
World, my heart's span;
Loneliness, wings for my flight!

"AN AIR OF COOLNESS PLAYS UPON HIS FACE"

By Sarah N. Cleghorn

Out of the four and twenty hours,
To take one sheaf of moments
To open the house and air it
In the May morning of Eternity,
Will not, O my dear Self,
Leave all your cares and duties
Naked to the little foxes,
But guard them with a golden bayonet!
Efficient would we be with the farming,
The baking, the children,—
Swing wide the dormer windows of Now
To the sunlit breezes of Forever!

From A SUMMER NIGHT

By Matthew Arnold

Plainness and clearness without shadow of stain!
Clearness divine!
Ye heavens, whose pure dark regions have no sign
Of languor, though so calm, and though so great,

Are yet untroubled and unpassionate;
Who, though so noble, share in the world's toil,
And, though so task'd, keep free from dust and soil!
I will not say that your mild deeps retain
A tinge, it may be, of their silent pain
Who have long'd deeply once, and long'd in vain—
But I will rather say that you remain
A world above man's head, to let him see
How boundless might his soul's horizons be,
How vast, yet of what clear transparency!
How it were good to live there, and breathe free;
How fair a lot to fill
Is left to each man still!

From A VISION

By Henry Vaughan

I saw Eternity the other night,
Like a great ring of pure and endless light,
   All calm, as it was bright:—
And round beneath it, Time, in hours, days, years,
   Driven by the spheres,
Like a vast shadow moved; in which the World
   And all her train were hurl'd.

LADDERS THROUGH THE BLUE [1]

By Hermann Hagedorn

I have climbèd ladders through the blue!
   For apples some, and some for heaven!

[1] Copyrighted 1925, by Doubleday, Page & Co.

> The rungs of some were six and seven,
> But some no earthly number knew.
>
> Some were of oak and some of dew,
>   Some spider-woven, zephyr-riven.
> I have climbed ladders through the blue!
>   For apples some and some for heaven!
>
> The tallest, firmest, ah, too few!—
>   Were of such substance as at even
>   By Truth to the awed heart is given;
> And, oh, the pure air, oh, the view,
> Climbing the ladders through the blue!

EACH AND ALL

By Ralph Waldo Emerson

Little thinks, in the field, yon red-cloaked clown
Of thee, from the hill-top looking down;
The heifer that lows in the upland farm
Far heard, lows not thine ear to charm;
The sexton, tolling his bell at noon,
Deems not that great Napoleon
Stops his horse, and lists with delight
Whilst his files sweep round yon Alpine height;
Nor knowest thou what argument
Thy life to thy neighbor's creed has lent.
All are needed by each one—
Nothing is fair or good alone.

TISSUE BUILDERS

I thought the sparrow's note from heaven,
Singing at dawn on the alder-bough;
I brought him home; in his nest, at even,
He sings the song, but it pleases not now;
For I did not bring home the river and sky;
He sang to my ear—they sang to my eye.

The delicate shells lay on the shore;
The bubbles of the latest wave
Fresh pearls to their enamel gave,
And the bellowing of the savage sea
Greeted their safe escape to me.
I wiped away the weeds and foam—
I fetched my sea-born treasures home;
But the poor, unsightly, noisome things
Had left their beauty on the shore,
With the sun, and the sand, and the wild uproar.

The lover watched his graceful maid,
As 'mid the virgin train she strayed;
Nor knew her beauty's best attire
Was woven still by the snow-white choir.
At last she came to his hermitage,
Like the bird from the woodlands to the cage;
The gay enchantment was undone—
A gentle wife, but fairy none.

Then I said: "I covet truth;
Beauty is unripe childhood's cheat;
I leave it behind with the games of youth."—
As I spoke, beneath my feet

The ground-pine curled its pretty wreath,
Running over the club-moss burrs;
I inhaled the violet's breath;
Around me stood the oaks and firs;
Pine-cones and acorns lay on the ground;
Over me soared the eternal sky,
Full of light and of deity;
Again I saw, again I heard,
The rolling river, the morning bird;
Beauty through my senses stole—
I yielded myself to the perfect whole.

FLOWER IN THE CRANNIED WALL

By Alfred Tennyson

Flower in the crannied wall,
I pluck you out of the crannies,
I hold you here, root and all, in my hand,
Little flower—but *if* I could understand
What you are, root and all, and all in all,
I should know what God and man is.

NOT OUR GOOD LUCK

By Robinson Jeffers

Not our good luck nor the instant peak and fulfillment
    of time gives us to see
The beauty of things, nothing can bridle it.
God who walks lightning-naked on the Pacific has never
    been hidden from any

Puddle or hillock of the earth behind us.
Between the mean mud tenements and huddle of the
 filth of Babylon, the river Euphrates;
And over the tiled brick temple buttresses
And the folly of a garden on arches, the ancienter
 simple and silent tribe of the stars
Filed, and for all her gods and the priests' mouths
God also moved on the city. . . .

Dark ships drawing in from the sundown and the
 islands of the south, great waves with gray vapor
 in your hollows
And whitening of high heads coming home from the
 west,
From Formosa or the skerries of Siberia and the sight
 of the eyes that have widened for the sky-peaks of
 Asia:
That he touched you is no wonder, that you slid from
 his hand
Is an old known tale to our foreland cypresses, no news
 to the Lobos granite, no marvel
To Point Pinos Light and the beacon at Point Sur,
But here is the marvel, he is nowhere not present, his
 beauty, it is burning in the midland villages
And tortures men's eyes in the alleys of cities.

Far-flown ones, you children of the hawk's dream
 future, when you lean from a crag of the last planet
 on the ocean
Of the far stars, remember we also have known beauty,

AT THE HEART

By M. A. DeWolfe Howe

The heart is but a narrow space
For paltriness to find a place;
But in its precincts there is room
Sufficient unto bliss or doom.
The certainties, so few, are there,
The doubts that feed the soul with care;
The passions battling with the will
To guide their liege to good or ill;
The saving grace of reverence,
The saving hatred of pretence;
The sympathy of common birth
With all the native things of earth:
The love begun with life, the love
That years diminish not, nor move;
And—more in such a narrow space?—
The image of a woman's face.

FOOL AND WISE

By Coventry Patmore

Endow the fool with sun and moon,
   Being his, he holds them mean and low;
But to the wise a little boon
   Is great, because the giver's so.

SONNET

By Snow Longley

I dreamed last night I stood with God on high,
And saw the centuries glide, like falling rain,
Into the still pool of eternity,
Whose calm deeps scarcely rippled with their gain;
And everywhere, in flower and bud and tree,
In savage beast or stirring of the clod,
In the on-marching of humanity,
I seemed to see life reaching up to God;
And little joys that I had counted great,
And loss of love with all its wealth of gain,
Seemed less than that my soul drag not its weight,
Nor stay the age-long welding of life's chain.
O God, when self would seek its own delight,
Renew to me Thy vision of the night.

FINIS

By Walter Savage Landor

I strove with none, for none was worth my strife.
Nature I loved and, next to Nature, Art:
I warm'd both hands before the fire of life;
It sinks, and I am ready to depart.

JOY

By Carl Sandburg

Let a joy keep you.
Reach out your hands

And take it when it runs by,
As the Apache dancer
Clutches his woman.
I have seen them
Live long and laugh loud,
Sent on singing, singing,
Smashed to the heart
Under the ribs
With a terrible love.
Joy always,
Joy everywhere—
Let joy kill you!
Keep away from the little deaths.

COMPENSATION

By Theodosia Garrison

Because I craved a gift too great
  For any prayer of mine to bring,
    To-day with empty hands I go;
    Yet must my heart rejoice to know
  I did not ask a lesser thing.

Because the goal I sought lay far
  In cloud-hid heights, to-day my soul
    Goes unaccompanied of its own;
    Yet this shall comfort me alone,
  I did not seek a nearer goal.

O gift ungained, O goal unwon!
　Still am I glad, remembering this,
　　For all I go unsatisfied,
　　I have kept faith with joy denied,
　Nor cheated life with cheaper bliss.

THE ANODYNE

By Sarah N. Cleghorn

In the late evening, when the house is still,
For an intense instant,
I lift my clean soul out of the soiled garments of mortality.
No sooner is it free to rise than it bends back earthward
And touches mortal life with hands like the hands that troubled the waters of Bethesda.
So this incorruptible touches the corrupt;
This immortal cools with a touch
The beaded forehead of mortality.

℞ VII

HASHEESH FOR A TORPID IMAGINATION
(Magic Carpet Poems)

KUBLA KHAN

By Samuel Taylor Coleridge

In Xanadu did Kubla Khan
  A stately pleasure-dome decree:
Where Alph, the sacred river, ran
Through caverns measureless to man
  Down to a sunless sea.
So twice five miles of fertile ground
With walls and towers were girdled round:
And there were gardens bright with sinuous rills
Where blossom'd many an incense-bearing tree;
And here were forests ancient as the hills,
Enfolding sunny spots of greenery.

But O, that deep romantic chasm which slanted
Down the green hill athwart a cedarn cover!
A savage place! as holy and enchanted
As e'er beneath a waning moon was haunted
By woman wailing for her demon-lover!
And from this chasm, with ceaseless turmoil seething,
As if this earth in fast thick pants were breathing,
A mighty fountain momently was forced;
Amid whose swift half-intermitted burst
Huge fragments vaulted like rebounding hail,
Or chaffy grain beneath the thresher's flail:
And 'mid these dancing rocks at once and ever

It flung up momently the sacred river.
Five miles meandering with a mazy motion
Through wood and dale the sacred river ran,
Then reach'd the caverns measureless to man,
And sank in tumult to a lifeless ocean:
And 'mid this tumult Kubla heard from far
Ancestral voices prophesying war!
    The shadow of the dome of pleasure
        Floated midway on the waves;
    Where was heard the mingled measure
        From the fountain and the caves.
It was a miracle of rare device,
A sunny pleasure-dome with caves of ice!

    A damsel with a dulcimer
        In a vision once I saw:
    It was an Abyssinian maid,
        And on her dulcimer she play'd,
Singing of Mount Abora.
Could I revive within me,
    Her symphony and song,
To such a deep delight 'twould win me,
That with music loud and long,
I would build that dome in air,
That sunny dome! those caves of ice!
And all who heard should see them there,
And all should cry, Beware! Beware!
His flashing eyes, his floating hair!
Weave a circle round him thrice,
    And close your eyes with holy dread,

For he on honey-dew hath fed,
And drunk the milk of Paradise.

MORNING

By Emily Dickinson

Will there really be a morning?
Is there such a thing as day?
Could I see it from the mountains
If I were as tall as they?
Has it feet like water lilies?
Has it feathers like a bird?
Is it brought from famous countries
Of which I've never heard?
Oh some scholar, oh some sailor,
Oh some wise man from the skies,
Please to tell a little pilgrim
Where the place called morning lies.

A CHILD'S SONG OVERHEARD

By Grace Hazard Conkling

I heard you singing, singing alone
Of river-sand and glittering stone,
Of a curved valley like a blade
And one who dwelt there unafraid.

Where was the river? Who the king
Whose deeds you were remembering?

Why did you make his glory high
And spangled like a stretch of sky?

Oh, this must be a land you knew
In dreams all lovely and untrue;
And of the king I heard you say
He lives a million years away

And holds the river in his hand
Between its ribbons of bright sand
Till suddenly he lets it fall
Down like a laughter musical!

BUTTERCUPS

By Wilfrid Thorley

There must be fairy miners
   Just underneath the mould,
Such wondrous quaint designers
   Who live in caves of gold.

They take the shining metals,
   And beat them into shreds;
And mould them into petals,
   To make the flowers' heads.

Sometimes they melt the flowers,
   To tiny seeds like pearls,
And store them up in bowers
   For little boys and girls.

And still a tiny fan turns
  Above a forge of gold;
To keep with fairy lanterns,
  The world from growing old.

QUEEN MAB

(From Romeo and Juliet)

By William Shakespeare

She is the fairies' midwife, and she comes
In shape no bigger than an agate-stone
On the fore-finger of an alderman,
Drawn with a team of little atomies
Athwart men's noses as they lie asleep;
Her waggon-spokes made of long spinners' legs,
The cover of the wings of grasshoppers,
The traces of the smallest spider's web,
The collars of the moonshine's watery beams,
Her whip of cricket's bone, the lash of film,
Her waggoner a small grey-coated gnat,
Not half so big as a round little worm
Prick'd from the lazy finger of a maid;
Her chariot is an empty hazel-nut
Made by the joiner squirrel or old grub,
Time out of mind the fairies' coachmakers.

THE OLD SHIPS

By James Elroy Flecker

I have seen old ships sail like swans asleep
Beyond the village which men still call Tyre,

172 HASHEESH FOR A TORPID IMAGINATION

With leaden age o'ercargoed, dipping deep
For Famagusta and the hidden sun
That rings black Cyprus with a lake of fire;
And all those ships were certainly so old
Who knows how oft with squat and noisy gun,
Questing brown slaves or Syrian oranges,
The pirate Genoese
Hell-raked them till they rolled
Blood, water, fruit, and corpses up the hold.
But now through friendly seas they softly run,
Painted the mid-sea blue or shore-sea green,
Still patterned with the vine and grapes in gold.

But I have seen,
Pointing her shapely shadows from the dawn
And image tumbled on a rose-swept bay,
A drowsy ship of some yet older day;
And, wonder's breath indrawn,
Thought I—who knows—who knows—but that same
(Fished up beyond Æïa, patched up new
—Stern painted brighter blue—)
That talkative, bald-headed seaman came
(Twelve patient comrades sweating at the oar)
From Troy's doom-crimson shore,
And with great lies about his wooden horse
Set the crew laughing, and forgot his course.

It was so old a ship—who knows—who knows?
—And yet so beautiful, I watched in vain
To see the mast burst open with a rose,
And the whole deck put on its leaves again.

PORTRAIT OF A BOY

By Stephen Vincent Benét

After the whipping, he crawled into bed;
Accepting the harsh fact with no great weeping.
How funny uncle's hat had looked striped red!
He chuckled silently. The moon came, sweeping
A black frayed rag of tattered cloud before
In scorning; very pure and pale she seemed,
Flooding his bed with radiance. On the floor
Fat motes danced. He sobbed; closed his eyes and dreamed.

Warm sand flowed round him. Blurts of crimson light
Splashed the white grains like blood. Past the cave's mouth
Shone with a large fierce splendor, wildly bright,
The crooked constellations of the South;
Here the Cross swung; and there, affronting Mars,
The Centaur stormed aside a froth of stars.
Within, great casks like wattled aldermen
Sighed of enormous feasts, and cloth of gold
Glowed on the walls like hot desire. Again,
Beside webbed purples from some galleon's hold,
A black chest bore the skull and bones in white
Above a scrawled "Gunpowder!" By the flames,
Decked out in crimson, gemmed with syenite,
Hailing their fellows by outrageous names

The pirates sat and diced. Their eyes were moons.
"Doubloons!" they said. The words crashed gold.
 "Doubloons!"

THE FALCONER OF GOD

By William Rose Benét

I flung my soul to the air like a falcon flying.
I said, "Wait on, wait on, while I ride below!
 I shall start a heron soon
 In the marsh beneath the moon—
A strange white heron rising with silver on its wings,
  Rising and crying
  Wordless, wondrous things;
 The secret of the stars, of the world's heart-strings
  The answer to their woe.
Then stoop thou upon him, and grip and hold him so!"

My wild soul waited on as falcons hover.
I beat the reedy fens as I trampled past.
 I heard the mournful loon
 In the marsh beneath the moon.
And then, with feathery thunder, the bird of my desire
  Broke from the cover
  Flashing silver fire.
 High up among the stars I saw his pinions spire.
  The pale clouds gazed aghast
As my falcon stooped upon him, and gript and held
  him fast.

My soul dropped through the air—with heavenly
    plunder?—
Gripping the dazzling bird my dreaming knew?
  Nay! but a piteous freight,
  A dark and heavy weight
Despoiled of silver plumage, its voice forever stilled,--
    All of the wonder
  Gone that ever filled
  Its guise with glory. O bird that I have killed,
    How brilliantly you flew
Across my rapturous vision when first I dreamed of
    you!

Yet I fling my soul on high with new endeavor,
And I ride the world below with a joyful mind.
  I shall start a heron soon
  In the marsh beneath the moon—
A wondrous silver heron its inner darkness fledges!
    I beat forever
    The fens and the sedges.
  The pledge is still the same—for all disastrous
    pledges,
    All hopes resigned!
My soul still flies above me for the quarry it shall
    find!

A STREET CAR SYMPHONY

By Roy Helton

Rumble along, over the water
Smooth as glass where the oil spots are;

176 HASHEESH FOR A TORPID IMAGINATION

There by that tug's nose, wide meadows of wonder
Gold like the blood of a splintered star!

Here inside where the straps are swinging
Huddles the freight of a Spruce Street car.

Poke necked spinster, with fumbling eyes,
Flat as a psalm book and ugly and queer;
Blonde in bright taffeta, merry as spring,
With a pearl in each ear;
Young mulatto girl, clean and comely,
All ablaze with a new pink gown,—
White folk's fashions, Gold Coast colors;

Dim red aisles of the broad red town.

Stout bald artist with sandy hair,
Grease marked coat and egg on his mouth;

Oh what a madness of youth in the air
When the wind blows south!

"What are you doing back home, old Kate?
Pretty lonely, I guess, and grey;
Nobody now to meet at the gate
At the end of the day;
You who mothered and smoothed me down,
Buttoned my collars and messed at my tie,—
While the moon rode white on the brow of the wind
And the stars ran high."

Scurry along here! The great folk are frowning.
Frowning? Not they. They are off out of town,
And their solemn old homes, in the broad cloth of twilight,
Like old empty mothers, look hungrily down.

Spoonful of yellow hair
Caught up in a wide red bow,
And the ruddy face of a child
At her noon day glow:
"When father and mother died
I wasn't so pleased at first,
Though I don't know which of the two of them
Was really the worst;
Ma with her weepy smile
Bothering me in my bed,
Or Pa with his drunken snort
And his aching head.
It's good to be all on your own,
Though the lady that works me is slow;
There always are fellows to kid, when a girl
Has a shape and a go;
And Johnnie'll be waiting, I'll bet
On the corner of Seventh and Race,
With a pink in his coat and a shine on his shoes,
And a grin on his face.
He's a looker, and on to the town;
And he knows how I love him all right:
Oh what a strange noise the blood makes in my heart
  When I think of to-night."

178   HASHEESH FOR A TORPID IMAGINATION

Young girl student with calm grave eyes:

Life's aflame on the lamp lit street.

"What will the Lord God make of me
When the true man's eyes and my own eyes meet?
Amo, Amas,—now the wind comes warm;
Over the hills now the daisies roam;
Launcelot! Launcelot! When are you coming
  To carry me home?"

Gay girls in messalines flitting the pavements;
Loom of tall towers that rise through the dusk;
Faint scent of spring where the trees are budding,
  Then garlic and gas and musk.

Drooping pale widow in from the graveyard,
Planning to sell the new tenant their coal;
Figuring how much she'll get for the ice box,
And why God has taken the light from her soul.

Clutter of faded old tenement houses
Warm with the folk of the Ghetto and Rome,
Banked, with sprawled legs, on colonial doorways,
Common and dirty, but making it home.
Women in wigs with the grey hair beneath them,
Wrinkled old grandmas, all shrouded in white,
And a million brown children that dance on the pavements
  And stay up all night.

Pious old man in a choker collar
Conning a speech for the Ladies' Aid
On the dangers of dance, and the open Sabbath,
   And of calling a spade a spade.

Drag along solemnly! Through these dark byways
Washington strolled for a breath of the south,
And Darthea Penniston ventured, or pretty
Peg Shippen with roses of youth on her mouth.

Chicken coops, Swiss chard, sparrow grass, spinach;
Moon over head and a smoke tossed star;

"End of the line! All out, sir, at Dock Street!"

Back into town on the Spruce Street car.

DEAD MEN TELL NO TALES

By Haniel Long

They say that dead men tell no tales!

Except of barges with red sails
And sailors mad for nightingales;

Except of jongleurs stretched at ease
Beside old highways through the trees;

Except of dying moons that break
The hearts of lads who lie awake;

Except of fortresses in shade,
And heroes crumbled and betrayed.

But dead men tell no tales, they say!

Except old tales that burn away
The stifling tapestries of day:

Old tales of life, of love and hate
Of time and space, and will, and fate.

MY STAR

By Robert Browning

All that I know
   Of a certain star
Is, it can throw
   (Like the angled spar)
Now a dart of red,
   Now a dart of blue;
Till my friends have said
   They would fain see, too,
My star that dartles the red and the blue!
Then it stops like a bird; like a flower, hangs furled:
  They must solace themselves with the Saturn above it.
What matter to me if their star is a world?
  Mine has opened its soul to me; therefore I love it.

WHAT IS THE GRASS?

By Walt Whitman

A child said, *What is the grass?* fetching it to me with full hands;
How could I answer the child? I do not know what it is, any more than he.

I guess it must be the flag of my disposition, out of hopeful green stuff woven.

Or I guess it is the handkerchief of the Lord,
A scented gift and remembrancer, designedly dropt,
Bearing the owner's name someway in the corners, that we may see and remark, and say, *Whose?* . . .

And now it seems to me the beautiful uncut hair of graves.

Tenderly will I use you, curling grass;
It may be that you transpire from the breasts of young men;
It may be if I had known them I would have loved them;
It may be you are from old people, and from women, and from offspring taken soon out of their mothers' laps;
And here you are the mothers' laps. . . .

What do you think has become of the young and old men?

And what do you think has become of the women and
    children?

They are alive and well somewhere;
The smallest sprout shows there is really no death;
And if ever there was, it led forward life, and did not
    wait at the end to arrest it,
And ceas'd the moment life appear'd.

All goes onward and outward—nothing collapses;
And to die is different from what any one supposed,
    and luckier.

HIS PILGRIMAGE

By Sir Walter Raleigh

Give me my scallop-shell of quiet,
  My staff of faith to walk upon,
My scrip of joy, immortal diet,
  My bottle of salvation,
My gown of glory, hope's true gage;
And thus I'll take my pilgrimage.

Blood must be my body's balmer;
  No other balm will there be given;
Whilst my soul, like quiet palmer,
  Travelleth towards the land of heaven;
Over the silver mountains,
Where spring the nectar fountains:

There will I kiss
　　　The bowl of bliss;
And drink mine everlasting fill
Upon every milken hill.
My soul will be a-dry before;
But, after, it will thirst no more.

THE TIGER

By William Blake

Tiger, tiger, burning bright
In the forests of the night,
What immortal hand or eye
Could frame thy fearful symmetry?

In what distant deeps or skies
Burnt the fire of thine eyes?
On what wings dare he aspire?
What the hand dare seize the fire?

And what shoulder and what art
Could twist the sinews of thy heart?
And, when thy heart began to beat,
What dread hand and what dread feet?

What the hammer? What the chain?
In what furnace was thy brain?
What the anvil? What dread grasp
Dare its deadly terrors clasp?

When the stars threw down their spears,
And water'd heaven with their tears,
Did He smile His work to see?
Did He who made the lamb make thee?

Tiger, tiger, burning bright
In the forests of the night,
What immortal hand or eye
Dare frame thy fearful symmetry?

From IL PENSEROSO

By John Milton

Oft on a Plat of rising ground,
I hear the far-off Curfeu sound,
Over som wide-water'd shoar,
Swinging slow with sullen roar;
Or if the Ayr will not permit,
Som still removèd place will fit,
Where glowing Embers through the room
Teach light to counterfeit a gloom,
Far from all resort of mirth,
Save the Cricket on the hearth,
Or the Belmans drousie charm,
To bless the dores from nightly harm:
Or let my Lamp at midnight hour,
Be seen in som high lonely Towr,
Where I may oft out-watch the Bear,

With thrice great Hermes, or unsphear
The spirit of Plato to unfold
What Worlds, or what vast Regions hold
The immortal mind that hath forsook
Her mansion in this fleshly nook:
And of those Daemons that are found
In fire, air, flood, or under ground,
Whose power hath a true consent
With Planet or with Element.
Som time let Gorgeous Tragedy
In Scepter'd pall com sweeping by,
Presenting Thebs, or Pelops line,
Or the tale of Troy divine.
Or what (though rare) of later age,
Ennoblèd hath the Buskind stage. . . .
And if ought els, great Bards beside,
In sage and solemn tunes have sung,
Of Turneys and of Trophies hung;
Of Forests, and inchantments drear,
Where more is meant than meets the ear.

GOING UP TO LONDON

By Nancy Byrd Turner

"As I went up to London,"
I heard a stranger say—
Going up to London
In such a casual way!
He turned the magic phrase
That has haunted all my days

As though it were a common thing
For careless lips to say.
As he went up to London!
I'll wager many a crown
He never saw the road that I
Shall take to London town.

When I go up to London
'Twill be in April weather.
I'll have a riband on my rein
And flaunt a scarlet feather;
The broom will toss its brush for me;
Two blackbirds and a thrush will be
Assembled in a bush for me
And sing a song together.
And all the blossomy hedgerows
Will shake their hawthorn down
As I go riding, riding
Up to London town.

Halting on a tall hill
Pied with purple flowers,
Twenty turrets I shall count,
And twice as many towers;
Count them on my finger-tip
As I used to do,
And half a hundred spires
Pricking toward the blue.
There will be a glass dome
And a roof of gold,

And a latticed window high
Tilting toward the western sky,
As I knew of old.
London, London,
They counted me a fool—
I could draw your skyline plain
Before I went to school!

Riding, riding downward
By many a silver ridge
And many a slope of amethyst,
I'll come to London Bridge—
London Bridge flung wide for me,
Horses drawn aside for me,
Thames my amber looking-glass
As I proudly pass;
Lords and flunkies, dukes and dames,
Country folk with comely names
Wondering at my steadfast face,
Beggars curtsying,
Footmen falling back a space;—
I would scarcely stay my pace
If I met the King!
If I met the King himself
He'd smile beneath his frown:
"Who is this comes traveling up
So light to London town?"

Riding, riding eagerly,
Thrusting through the throng,

(Traveling light, Your Majesty,
Because the way was long),
I'll hurry fast to London gate,
(The way was long, and I am late),
I'll come at last to London gate,
Singing me a song—
Some old rhyme of ancient time
When wondrous things befell.
And there the boys and girls at play,
Understanding well,
Quick will hail me, clear and sweet,
Crowding, crowding after;
Every little crooked street
Will echo to their laughter;
Lilting, as they mark my look,
Chanting, two and two,
*Dreamed it, dreamed it in a dream
And waked and found it true!*

Sing, you rhymes, and ring, you chimes,
And swing, you bells of Bow!
When I go up to London
All the world shall know!

TARTARY

By Walter de la Mare

If I were Lord of Tartary,
Myself and me alone,

My bed should be of ivory,
  Of beaten gold my throne;
And in my court should peacocks flaunt,
And in my forests tigers haunt,
And in my pools great fishes slant
  Their fins athwart the sun.

If I were Lord of Tartary,
  Trumpeters every day
To every meal should summon me,
  And in my courtyard bray;
And in the evening lamps would shine,
Yellow as honey, red as wine,
While harp, and flute, and mandoline,
  Made music sweet and gay.

If I were Lord of Tartary,
  I'd wear a robe of beads,
White, and gold, and green they'd be—
  And clustered thick as seeds;
And ere should wane the morning-star,
I'd don my robe and scimitar,
And zebras seven should draw my car
  Through Tartary's dark glades.

Lord of the fruits of Tartary,
  Her rivers silver-pale!
Lord of the hills of Tartary,
  Glen, thicket, wood, and dale!

Her flashing stars, her scented breeze,
Her trembling lakes, like foamless seas,
Her bird-delighting citron-trees
   In every purple vale!

THE BLESSÈD DAMOZEL

By Dante Gabriel Rossetti

The blessèd Damozel lean'd out
   From the gold bar of Heaven:
Her blue grave eyes were deeper much
   Than a deep water, even.
She had three lilies in her hand,
   And the stars in her hair were seven.

Her robe, ungirt from clasp to hem,
   No wrought flowers did adorn,
But a white rose of Mary's gift
   On the neck meetly worn;
And her hair, lying down her back,
   Was yellow like ripe corn.

Herseem'd she scarce had been a day
   One of God's choristers;
The wonder was not yet quite gone
   From that still look of hers;
Albeit, to them she left, her day
   Had counted as ten years.

(To *one* it is ten years of years:
  . . . Yet now, here in this place,
Surely she lean'd o'er me,—her hair
  Fell all about my face. . . .
Nothing: the Autumn-fall of leaves.
  The whole year sets apace.)

It was the terrace of God's house
  That she was standing on,—
By God built over the sheer depth
  In which Space is begun;
So high, that looking downward thence,
  She scarce could see the sun.

It lies from Heaven across the flood
  Of ether, as a bridge.
Beneath, the tides of day and night
  With flame and darkness ridge
The void, as low as where this earth
  Spins like a fretful midge.

But in those tracts, with her, it was
  The peace of utter light
And silence. For no breeze may stir
  Along the steady flight
Of seraphim; no echo there,
  Beyond all depth or height.

Heard hardly, some of her new friends,
  Playing at holy games,

Spake, gentle-mouth'd, among themselves,
   Their virginal chaste names;
And the souls, mounting up to God,
   Went by her like thin flames.

And still she bow'd herself, and stoop'd
   Into the vast waste calm;
Till her bosom's pressure must have made
   The bar she lean'd on warm,
And the lilies lay as if asleep
   Along her bended arm.

From the fixt lull of Heaven, she saw
   Time, like a pulse, shake fierce
Through all the worlds. Her gaze still strove,
   In that steep gulf, to pierce
The swarm; and then she spoke, as when
   The stars sang in their spheres.

"I wish that he were come to me,
   For he will come," she said.
"Have I not pray'd in solemn Heaven?
   On earth, has he not pray'd?
Are not two prayers a perfect strength?
   And shall I feel afraid?

"When round his head the aureole clings,
   And he is clothed in white,
I'll take his hand, and go with him
   To the deep wells of light,

And we will step down as to a stream
   And bathe there in God's sight.

"We two will stand beside that shrine,
   Occult, withheld, untrod,
Whose lamps tremble continually
   With prayer sent up to God;
And where each need, reveal'd, expects
   Its patient period.

"We two will lie i' the shadow of
   That living mystic tree
Within whose secret growth the Dove
   Sometimes is felt to be,
While every leaf that His plumes touch
   Saith His name audibly.

"And I myself will teach to him,—
   I myself, lying so,—
The songs I sing here; which his mouth
   Shall pause in, hush'd and slow,
Finding some knowledge at each pause,
   And some new thing to know."

(Alas! to *her* wise simple mind
   These things were all but known
Before: they trembled on her sense,—
   Her voice had caught their tone.
Alas for lonely Heaven! Alas
   For life wrung out alone!

Alas, and though the end were reach'd? . . .
  Was *thy* part understood
Or borne in trust? And for her sake
  Shall this too be found good?—
May the close lips that knew not prayer
  Praise ever, though they would?)

"We two," she said, "will seek the groves
  Where the lady Mary is,
With her five handmaidens, whose names
  Are five sweet symphonies:—
Cecily, Gertrude, Magdalen,
  Margaret and Rosalys.

"Circle-wise sit they, with bound locks
  And bosoms coverèd;
Into the fine cloth, white like flame,
  Weaving the golden thread,
To fashion the birth-robes for them
  Who are just born, being dead.

"He shall fear, haply, and be dumb.
  Then I will lay my cheek
To his, and tell about our love,
  Not once abash'd or weak:
And the dear Mother will approve
  My pride, and let me speak.

"Herself shall bring us, hand in hand,
  To Him round whom all souls

Kneel—the unnumber'd solemn heads
 Bow'd with their aureoles:
And Angels, meeting us, shall sing
 To their citherns and citoles.

"There will I ask of Christ the Lord
 Thus much for him and me:—
To have more blessing than on earth
 In nowise; but to be
As then we were,—being as then
 At peace. Yea, verily.

"Yea, verily; when he is come
 We will do thus and thus:
Till this my vigil seem quite strange
 And almost fabulous;
We two will live at once, one life;
 And peace shall be with us."

She gazed, and listen'd, and then said,
 Less sad of speech than mild,—
"All this is when he comes." She ceased:
 The light thrill'd past her, fill'd
With Angels, in strong level lapse.
 Her eyes pray'd, and she smiled.

(I saw her smile.) But soon their flight
 Was vague 'mid the poised spheres.
And then she cast her arms along
 The golden barriers,

THE MADMAN

By L. A. G. Strong

I think I'll do a fearful deed
  Of wickedness and cruelty,
And then, if Father Walsh speaks truth,
  Jesus will weep a tear for me:

And I will catch it in my hat
  Just here outside my cabin door,
And put it on my little field
  Where nothing ever grew before.

And it will sprout so fine and brave,
  That lovely birds with yellow bills
Will come to pluck my crowded corn
  From all the Seven Holy Hills.

From HEROD

By Stephen Phillips

Herod speaks:
I dreamed last night of a dome of beaten gold
To be a counter-glory to the Sun.
There shall the eagle blindly dash himself,

There the first beam shall strike, and there the moon
Shall aim all night her argent archery;
And it shall be the tryst of sundered stars,
The haunt of dead and dreaming Solomon;
Shall send a light upon the lost in Hell,
And flashings upon faces without hope.—
And I will think in gold and dream in silver,
Imagine in marble and conceive in bronze,
Till it shall dazzle pilgrim nations
And stammering tribes from undiscovered lands,
Allure the living God out of the bliss,
And all the streaming seraphim from heaven.

THE POET'S DREAM

By Percy Bysshe Shelley

On a Poet's lips I slept
Dreaming like a love-adept
In the sound his breathing kept;
Nor seeks nor finds he mortal blisses,
But feeds on the aërial kisses
Of shapes that haunt Thought's wildernesses.
He will watch from dawn to gloom
The lake-reflected sun illume
The yellow bees in the ivy-bloom,
   Nor heed nor see what things they be—
But from these create he can
Forms more real than living Man,
   Nurselings of Immortality!

WHERE IS FANCY BRED?

By William Shakespeare

Tell me where is Fancy bred,
Or in the heart or in the head?
How begot, how nourishèd?
  Reply, reply.
It is engender'd in the eyes,
With gazing fed; and Fancy dies
In the cradle where it lies.
  Let us all ring Fancy's knell:
  I'll begin it,—Ding, dong, bell.
Ding, dong, bell.

FANCY

By John Keats

Ever let the Fancy roam,
Pleasure never is at home:
At a touch sweet Pleasure melteth,
Like to bubbles when rain pelteth;
Then let wingèd Fancy wander
Through the thought still spread beyond her:
Open wide the mind's cage-door,
She'll dart forth, and cloudward soar.
O sweet Fancy! let her loose;
Summer's joys are spoilt by use,
And the enjoying of the Spring
Fades as does its blossoming:

Autumn's red-lipp'd fruitage too,
Blushing through the mist and dew,
Cloys with tasting: What do then?
Sit thee by the ingle, when
The sear faggot blazes bright,
Spirit of a winter's night;
When the soundless earth is muffled,
And the cakèd snow is shuffled
From the ploughboy's heavy shoon;
When the Night doth meet the Noon
In a dark conspiracy
To banish Even from her sky.
Sit thee there, and send abroad,
With a mind self-overawed,
Fancy, high-commission'd:—send her!
She has vassals to attend her:
She will bring, in spite of frost,
Beauties that the earth hath lost;
She will bring thee, all together,
All delights of summer weather;
All the buds and bells of May,
From dewy sward or thorny spray;
All the heapèd Autumn's wealth,
With a still, mysterious stealth:
She will mix these pleasures up
Like three fit wines in a cup,
And thou shalt quaff it:—thou shalt hear
Distant harvest-carols clear;
Rustle of the reapèd corn;
Sweet birds antheming the morn:

And, in the same moment—hark!
'Tis the early April lark,
Or the rooks, with busy caw,
Foraging for sticks and straw.
Thou shalt, at one glance, behold
The daisy and the marigold;
White-plumed lilies, and the first
Hedge-grown primrose that hath burst;
Shaded hyacinth, alway
Sapphire queen of the mid-May;
And every leaf, and every flower
Pearlèd with the self-same shower.
Thou shalt see the fieldmouse peep
Meagre from its cellèd sleep;
And the snake all winter-thin
Cast on sunny bank its skin;
Freckled nest-eggs thou shalt see
Hatching in the hawthorn-tree,
When the hen-bird's wing doth rest
Quiet on her mossy nest;
Then the hurry and alarm
When the beehive casts its swarm;
Acorns ripe down-pattering
While the autumn breezes sing.

O sweet Fancy! let her loose;
Every thing is spoilt by use:
Where's the cheek that doth not fade,
Too much gazed at? Where's the maid
Whose lip mature is ever new?

Where's the eye, however blue,
Doth not weary? Where's the face
One would meet in every place?
Where's the voice, however soft,
One would hear so very oft?
At a touch sweet Pleasure melteth
Like to bubbles when rain pelteth.
Let, then, wingèd Fancy find
Thee a mistress to thy mind:
Dulcet-eyed as Ceres' daughter,
Ere the God of Torment taught her
How to frown and how to chide;
With a waist and with a side
White as Hebe's, when her zone
Slipt its golden clasp, and down
Fell her kirtle to her feet,
While she held the goblet sweet,
And Jove grew languid.—Break the mesh
Of the Fancy's silken leash;
Quickly break her prison-string,
And such joys as these she'll bring.—
Let the wingèd Fancy roam,
Pleasure never is at home.

VERIFICATION [1]

By Christopher Morley

The half-dream crumbles and falls through:
The dream full-dreamed comes true, comes true!

[1] From Parson's Pleasure by Christopher Morley, copyright 1923, George H. Doran Co., publishers.

℞ VIII

FOR HARDENING OF THE HEART
(Poems of Sympathy)

THE BELLS OF HEAVEN

By Ralph Hodgson

'Twould ring the bells of Heaven
The wildest peal for years,
If Parson lost his senses
And people came to theirs,
And he and they together
Knelt down with angry prayers
For tamed and shabby tigers,
And dancing dogs and bears,
And wretched, blind pit-ponies,
And little hunted hares.

A LYRICAL EPIGRAM

By Edith Wharton

My little old dog:
A heart-beat
At my feet.

From LINES ON A LAP DOG

By John Gay

Here Shock, the pride of all his kind, is laid,
Who fawn'd like man, but ne'er like man betray'd.

CONCERNING BROWNIE

By Nancy Byrd Turner

Let scoffers doubt it if they will—
Too real a little chap he moved,
And ran and romped, and wagged and loved,
Not to be somewhere still.
Granted he did not have a soul,
There's surely some reward of merit
For having such a trustful spirit,
A friendship so heart-whole.

Of course he could not hope for heaven,
—He might not look on seraphim,—
But, somehow, I believe there's given
A place his Maker meant for him;
That if we saw with clearer eyes,
And deeper mysteries had learned,
His small brown form might be discerned
Safe in some humble paradise.

Perched, cheerful, in a cozy niche
(Most like his cherished window-seat,
Cushioned and comforting) from which
He gazes on the pleasant street,
A wise and watchful wrinkle wearing
While all the old-time folk go past;
And pricks a prideful ear, at last
And, all ecstatic, sets abeat

A celebrating tail—keen hearing
The fall of dear familiar feet.

I cannot find it in my creed,
Yet very plain it seems to me
That, off, away at topmost speed,
Afire with hospitality,
He deems himself, and is, indeed,
The little dog he used to be.

THE SPARK

By Helen Gray Cone

Readers of riddles dark,
Solve me the mystery of the Spark!

My good dog died yesternight.
His heart of love through his eyes of light
Had looked out kind his whole life long.
In all his days he had done no wrong.
Like a knight's was his noble face.
What shall I name the inward grace
That leashed and barred him from all things base?
Selfless trust and courage high—
Dust to dust, but are these to die?
(Hate and lust and greed and lies—
Dust to dust, and are these to rise?)

When 'tis kindled, whither it goes,
Whether it fades, or glows and grows—

Readers of riddles dark,
Solve me the mystery of the Spark!

SO I MAY FEEL THE HANDS OF GOD

By Anna Hempstead Branch

How swiftly, once, on silvery feet
I saw thee bound beneath the sun!
Oh, savage innocence! The fleet,
The wild, the sweet, the glistening one!

God made in thee the gentlest sound
To win for thee the dear caress.
Like flowers growing in the ground
We heard that trembling daintiness.

Thou art strange Nature's subtlest child,
The offspring of her alien mood.
Now age has come on thee, the wild,
And stricken thee, the simply good.

Animal sweetness, when it goes,
Leaves emptiness behind.
Dear, thou must wither like the rose
And dimness take thy creature mind.

No more we laugh to see thee run—
The innocent, the fierce, the sweet!
Thy snow-white dancing in the sun!
The rushing of thy happy feet!

The hearthstone and the friendly touch,
Thou art grown needy, now, for these.
How strange that wanting them so much
Thou hast forgot the arts to please.

Oh, creature age! creature distress!
The haunting, old, and dim surprise!
Would I might charm with tenderness
The grief from those bewildered eyes!

Thou hast no more, at love's commands,
The simple sweetness of a purr.
Then let me comfort with my hands
The saddening of thy shining fur.

When cold afflicts thy piteous sod
Then let me warm that need of thine,
So I may feel the hands of God
Laid over thee—more close than mine.

SALMON FISHING

By Robinson Jeffers

The days shorten, the south blows wide for showers now,
The south wind shouts to the rivers,
The rivers open their mouths and the salt salmon
Race up into the freshet.
In Christmas month against the smoulder and menace
Of a long angry sundown,

Red ash of the dark solstice, you see the anglers,
Intent, hieratic, primeval,
Like the priests of the people that built Stonehenge,
Dark silent forms, performing
Remote solemnities in the red shallows
Of the river's mouth at the year's turn,
Drawing landward their live bullion; the bloody mouths
And scales full of the sunset
Twitch on the rocks, no more to wander at will
The wild Pacific pasture nor, wanton and spawning,
Race up into fresh water.

ON THE DEATH OF A FAVOURITE CANARY

By Matthew Arnold

Poor Matthias! Wouldst thou have
More than pity? claim'st a stave?
—Friends more near us than a bird
We dismiss'd without a word.
Rover with the good brown head,
Great Atossa, they are dead;
Dead, and neither prose nor rhyme
Tells the praises of their prime.
Thou didst know them old and gray,
Know them in their sad decay.
Thou hast seen Atossa sage
Sit for hours beside thy cage;

Thou wouldst chirp, thou foolish bird,
Flutter, chirp—she never stirr'd!
What were now these toys to her?
Down she sank amid her fur;
Eyed thee with a soul resign'd—
And thou deemedst cats were kind!
—Cruel, but composed and bland,
Dumb, inscrutable and grand,
So Tiberius might have sat,
Had Tiberius been a cat.

Birds, companions more unknown,
Live beside us, but alone;
Finding not, do all they can,
Passage from their souls to man.
Kindness we bestow, and praise,
Laud their plumage, greet their lays;
Still, beneath their feather'd breast,
Stirs a history unexpress'd.
Wishes there, and feelings strong,
Incommunicably throng;
What they want we cannot guess,
Fail to track their deep distress—
Dull look on when death is nigh,
Note no change, and let them die.

Was it, as the Grecian sings,
Birds were born the first of things,
Before the sun, before the wind,
Before the gods, before mankind,

Airy, ante-mundane throng—
Witness their unworldly song!
Proof they give too, primal powers,
Of a prescience more than ours—
Teach us, while they come and go,
When to sail and when to sow.
Cuckoo calling from the hill,
Swallow skimming by the mill,
Swallows trooping in the sedge,
Starlings swirling from the hedge,
Mark the seasons, map our year,
As they show and disappear.
But, with all this travail sage
Brought from that anterior age,
Goes an unreversed decree
Whereby strange are they and we,
Making want of theirs, and plan,
Indiscernible by man.

From THE RIME OF THE ANCIENT MARINER

By Samuel Taylor Coleridge

O happy living things! no tongue
Their beauty might declare:
A spring of love gush'd from my heart,
And I bless'd them unaware. . . .

He prayeth well who loveth well
Both man and bird and beast.

He prayeth best who loveth best
All things both great and small;
For the dear God who loveth us,
He made and loveth all.

TO SAFEGUARD THE HEART FROM HARDNESS

By Sarah N. Cleghorn

I steadfastly *will*,
I firmly command my heart,
That when next I feel the leaden cooling of friendliness
    and pity within me,
Into my memory shall run
The thought of the child I love best,
Undressed and ready for bed,
Or hiding behind the door,
And cautiously peeping out;
Or stubbing his toe and falling,
And crying a little and climbing up on my lap,
To hear the story of the Three Bears over again.

LITTLE BOY BLUE

By Eugene Field

The little toy dog is covered with dust,
    But sturdy and stanch he stands;
And the little toy soldier is red with rust,
    And his musket moulds in his hands.

Time was when the little toy dog was new,
  And the soldier was passing fair;
And that was the time when our Little Boy Blue
  Kissed them and put them there.

"Now, don't you go till I come," he said,
  "And don't you make any noise!"
So, toddling off to his trundle-bed,
  He dreamt of the pretty toys;
And, as he was dreaming, an angel song
  Awakened our Little Boy Blue—
Oh! the years are many, the years are long,
  But the little toy friends are true!

Ay, faithful to Little Boy Blue they stand,
  Each in the same old place,
Awaiting the touch of a little hand,
  The smile of a little face;
And they wonder, as waiting the long years through
  In the dust of that little chair,
What has become of our Little Boy Blue,
  Since he kissed them and put them there.

THE TOYS

By Coventry Patmore

My little Son, who look'd from thoughtful eyes
And moved and spoke in quiet grown-up wise,

POEMS OF SYMPATHY

Having my law the seventh time disobey'd,
I struck him, and dismiss'd
With hard words and unkiss'd,
—His Mother, who was patient, being dead.
Then, fearing lest his grief should hinder sleep,
I visited his bed,
But found him slumbering deep,
With darken'd eyelids, and their lashes yet
From his late sobbing wet.
And I, with moan,
Kissing away his tears, left others of my own;
For, on a table drawn beside his head,
He had put, within his reach,
A box of counters and a red-vein'd stone,
A piece of glass abraded by the beach,
And six or seven shells,
A bottle with bluebells,
And two French copper coins, ranged there with careful art,
To comfort his sad heart.
So when that night I pray'd
To God, I wept, and said:
Ah, when at last we lie with trancèd breath,
Not vexing Thee in death,
And Thou rememberest of what toys
We made our joys,
How weakly understood
Thy great commanded good,
Then, fatherly not less

Than I whom Thou hast moulded from the clay,
Thou'lt leave Thy wrath, and say,
"I will be sorry for their childishness."

TO MY GODCHILD

Francis M. W. Meynell

(Extract)

BY FRANCIS THOMPSON

And when, immortal mortal, droops your head,
And you, the child of deathless song, are dead;
Then, as you search with unaccustomed glance
The ranks of Paradise for my countenance,
Turn not your tread along the Uranian sod
Among the bearded counsellors of God;
For, if in Eden as on earth are we,
I sure shall keep a younger company:
Pass where beneath their rangèd gonfalons
The starry cohorts shake their shielded suns,
The dreadful mass of their enridgèd spears;
Pass where majestical the eternal peers,
The stately choice of the great Saintdom, meet—
A silvern segregation, globed complete
In sandalled shadow of the Triune feet;
Pass by where wait, young poet-wayfarer,
Your cousined clusters, emulous to share
With you the roseal lightnings burning 'mid their hair;
Pass the crystalline sea, the Lampads seven:—
Look for me in the nurseries of Heaven.

THE FLOWER FACTORY

By Florence Wilkinson Evans

Lisabetta, Marianina, Fiametta, Teresina,
They are winding stems of roses, one by one, one by one,
Little children who have never learned to play;
Teresina softly crying that her fingers ache to-day;
Tiny Fiametta nodding when the twilight slips in, gray.
High above the clattering street, ambulance and fire-gong beat,
They sit, curling crimson petals, one by one, one by one.

Lisabetta, Marianina, Fiametta, Teresina,
They have never seen a rosebush nor a dewdrop in the sun.
They will dream of the vendetta, Teresina, Fiametta,
Of a Black Hand and a face behind a grating;
They will dream of cotton petals, endless, crimson, suffocating,
Never of a wild-rose thicket nor the singing of a cricket,
But the ambulance will bellow through the wanness of their dreams,
And their tired lids will flutter with the street's hysteric screams.

Lisabetta, Marianina, Fiametta, Teresina,
They are winding stems of roses, one by one, one by one.
Let them have a long, long playtime, Lord of Toil, when toil is done,
Fill their baby hands with roses, joyous roses of the sun!

THE FACTORIES

By Margaret Widdemer

I have shut my little sister in from life and light,
   (For a rose, for a ribbon, for a wreath across my hair,)
I have made her restless feet still until the night,
   Locked from sweets of summer and from wild spring air;
I who roamed the meadowlands, free from sun to sun,
   Free to sing and pull the buds and watch the far wings fly,
I have bound my sister till her playing-time is done—
   Oh, my little sister, was it I? Was it I?

I have robbed my sister of her day of maidenhood,
   (For a robe, for a feather, for a trinket's restless spark,)
Shut from Love till dusk shall fall, how shall she know good,
   How shall she go scatheless through the sunlit dark?

I who could be innocent, I who could be gay,
    I who could have love and mirth before the light
        went by,
I have shut my sister in her mating time away—
    Sister, my young sister, was it I? Was it I?

I have robbed my sister of the lips against her breast,
    (For a coin, for the weaving of my children's lace
        and lawn,)
Feet that pace beside the loom, hands that cannot rest,
    How can she know motherhood, whose strength is
        gone?
I, who took no heed of her, starved and labour-worn,
    I, against whose placid heart my sleepy gold-heads
        lie,
Round my path they cry to me, little souls unborn—
    God of Life! Creator! It was I! It was I!

THEY WILL SAY

By Carl Sandburg

Of my city the worst that men will ever say is this:
You took little children away from the sun and the
    dew,
And the glimmers that played in the grass under the
    great sky,
And the reckless rain; you put them between walls
To work, broken and smothered, for bread and wages,
To eat dust in their throats and die empty-hearted
For a little handful of pay on a few Saturday nights.

A PITCHER OF MIGNONETTE

By Henry Cuyler Bunner

A pitcher of mignonette
  In a tenement's highest casement,—
Queer sort of flower-pot—yet
That pitcher of mignonette
Is a garden in heaven set,
  To the little sick child in the basement—
The pitcher of mignonette,
  In a tenement's highest casement.

RUFUS PRAYS

By L. A. G. Strong

In the darkening church
  Where but a few had stayed
At the Litany Desk
  The idiot knelt and prayed.

Rufus, stunted, uncouth,
  The one son of his mother.
"Eh, I'd sooner 'ave Rufie,"
  She said, "than many another:

" 'E's useful about the 'ouse
  And so gentle as 'e can be.
And 'e gets up early o' mornin's,
  And makes me a cup o' tea."

The formal evensong
  Had passed over his head.
He sucked his thumb and squinted
  And dreamed, instead.

Now while the organ boomed
  To the few who still were there,
At the Litany Desk
  The idiot made his prayer:

"Gawd bless Mother,
  'N' make Rufie a good lad;
Take Rufie to Heaven
  'N' forgive him when 'e's bad.

" 'N' early mornin's in Heaven
  'E'll make mother's tea,
'N' a cup for the Lord Jesus
  'N' a cup for Thee."

THE BRIDGE OF SIGHS

By Thomas Hood

One more Unfortunate,
  Weary of breath,
Rashly importunate,
  Gone to her death!

Take her up tenderly,
  Lift her with care;
Fashion'd so slenderly
  Young, and so fair!

Look at her garments
Clinging like cerements;
Whilst the wave constantly
   Drips from her clothing;
Take her up instantly,
   Loving, not loathing.

Touch her not scornfully;
Think of her mournfully,
   Gently and humanly;
Not of the stains of her,
All that remains of her
   Now is pure womanly.

Make no deep scrutiny
Into her mutiny
   Rash and undutiful:
Past all dishonour,
Death has left on her
   Only the beautiful.

Still, for all slips of hers,
   One of Eve's family—
Wipe those poor lips of hers
   Oozing so clammily.

Loop up her tresses
   Escaped from the comb,
Her fair auburn tresses;
Whilst wonderment guesses
   Where was her home?

Who was her father?
  Who was her mother?
Had she a sister?
  Had she a brother?
Or was there a dearer one
Still, and a nearer one
  Yet, than all other?

Alas! for the rarity
Of Christian charity
  Under the sun!
O, it was pitiful!
Near a whole city full,
  Home she had none.

Sisterly, brotherly,
Fatherly, motherly
  Feelings had changed:
Love, by harsh evidence,
Thrown from its eminence;
Even God's providence
  Seeming estranged.

Where the lamps quiver
So far in the river,
  With many a light
From window and casement,
From garret to basement,
She stood, with amazement,
  Houseless by night.

FOR HARDENING OF THE HEART

The bleak wind of March
  Made her tremble and shiver;
But not the dark arch,
Or the black flowing river:
Mad from life's history,
Glad to death's mystery,
  Swift to be hurl'd—
Anywhere, anywhere
  Out of the world!

In she plunged boldly—
No matter how coldly
  The rough river ran—
Over the brink of it,
Picture it—think of it,
  Dissolute Man!
Lave in it, drink of it,
  Then, if you can!

Take her up tenderly,
  Lift her with care;
Fashion'd so slenderly,
  Young, and so fair!

Ere her limbs frigidly
Stiffen too rigidly,
  Decently, kindly,
Smooth and compose them;
And her eyes, close them,
  Staring so blindly!

Dreadfully staring
  Thro' muddy impurity,
As when with the daring
Last look of despairing
  Fix'd on futurity.

Perishing gloomily,
Spurr'd by contumely,
Cold inhumanity,
Burning insanity,
  Into her rest.—
Cross her hands humbly
As if praying dumbly,
  Over her breast!

Owning her weakness,
  Her evil behaviour,
And leaving, with meekness,
  Her sins to her Saviour!

From TOWN PICTURES [1]

By Ernest Crosby

It is an August evening in a free roof-garden built for the people on a pier over the river.
I am in a bad humour to-night, and I come here to cure myself.
Crowds are sitting in rows on benches on each side of the stand where the brass band is playing, and

[1] From Broad-Cast by Ernest Crosby. Published by Funk and Wagnalls Company, New York and London.

round them and up and down the long deck from one end to the other passes a continuous stream of promenaders under the electric lights.

I join the shabby procession, but the vulgar flirting of those shrill shop-girls with the rough young men behind them is quite indecent, and offends me sadly.

I stop at the end of the pier, and look out at the dark river with its lights, white, red and green.

It would be altogether beautiful, if it were not for the shriek of the ferry whistles in the next slip, and the suggestion of sewage in the south breeze.

But this will not do; I have not come here to complain, but to take my regular cure.

I sit down on the corner of a bench, not too near the musicians.

And now I begin to love.

At first it is an effort, and I undertake only the children, for they are the easiest.

There is a baby yonder, jumping on its mother's arm in time with the trumpets, and another tiny tot dancing across the floor holding her pink skirts out with her hands.

Now I am loving them hard, like a new-kindled coal fire with the blower on, and I can almost hear my heart roar.

I have soon reached the point of loving all the children (and how many there are), even the most perverse, and gradually the mothers too move into my focus.

The old people come next. How I love that respectable old Irishwoman there with her cap and red shawl, watching her grandchild (or is it her great-grandchild?)—and the sturdy German grandsire asleep bolt upright in his carefully brushed black coat! I could hug them both, and I do not find it easy to keep my hands off them.

But now my love is boiling over, and becoming indiscriminate.

I can put it to any test and try it on any one; it is a conflagration that would outstrip any fire-extinguisher.

I turn my heart loose on the shabby procession, and now I pronounce it worthy of a place on the frieze of the Parthenon.

I love the pale tailor in his dirty shirt-sleeves, with his sickly boy in his arms.

I love the black hands of the machinist, and I am glad that he has not washed them too thoroughly.

I love the thin, grey-haired old maid with spectacles (how surprised she would be if she knew it!) and the young rowdies who are waltzing together.

Here come the same vulgar youths and maidens who shocked me an hour ago, quite as vulgar as ever, and yet now I love them till I see nothing that is not divine in them.

Love covers a multitude of sins—indeed it does!

But the band is playing "Home, Sweet Home," and the multitude has already half disappeared.

It is time for me to close the draughts and let the fire go down.
My love-cure has worked its wonted miracle, and blues and ill humour have gone.
As a patent-medicine I should like to sing its praises and advertise its virtues, until whole cities should take it for their municipal ailments, and statesmen prescribe it to their several nations.
Who says there is no panacea?
Love is the great panacea!

ABOU BEN ADHEM

By Leigh Hunt

Abou Ben Adhem (may his tribe increase!)
Awoke one night from a deep dream of peace,
And saw within the moonlight of his room,
Making it rich, and like a lily in bloom,
An angel writing in a book of gold.
Exceeding peace had made Ben Adhem bold,
And, to the presence in the room, he said,
"What writest thou?" The vision raised its head,
And, with a look made of all sweet accord,
Answered, "The names of those who love the Lord!"
"And is mine one?" asked Abou.—"Nay, not so,"
Replied the angel. Abou spake more low,
But cheerly still; and said—"I pray thee, then,
Write me as one that loves his fellow-men."

The angel wrote and vanished. The next night
It came again, with a great wakening light,
And showed the names whom love of God had blest;
And lo! Ben Adhem's name led all the rest!

HARVEST

By Robert Haven Schauffler

They heard that she was dying, and they came,
  The reticent New England village folk,
  And wrestled with their tongues and, stammering, spoke
Their very hearts, torn betwixt love and shame.
The wheelwright brought a crock of flowering flame
  And, with moist eyes, said: "Madam, ef a stroke
  O' the axe could save ye—(and this ain't no joke)—
I'd cut my right hand off to do that same!"
When her white soul had sped, the fisherman rowed
  A fare of fish—his parting gift—ashore,
And choked upon the words: "I never knowed
  No one I liked so well as her afore."
And the charwoman sobbed: " 'Twas me she showed
  How not to get downhearted any more."

A WOMAN

By Scudder Middleton

She had an understanding with the years;
For always in her eyes there was a light

As though she kept a secret none might guess—
Some confidence that Time had made her heart.
So calmly did she bear the weight of pain,
With such serenity accept the joy,
It seemed she had a mother-love for life,
And all the days were children at her breast.

GOD'S PITY

By Louise Driscoll

God pity all the brave who go
    The common way and wear
No ribboned medals on their breasts,
    No laurels on their hair.

God pity all the lonely folk
    With griefs they do not tell,
Women waking in the night,
    And men dissembling well.

In common courage of the street
    The crushed grape is the wine,
Wheat in the mill is daily bread
    And given for a sign.

And who but God shall pity them
    Who go so quietly,
And smile upon us when we meet
    And greet us pleasantly?

PORTRAIT OF AN OLD WOMAN

By Arthur Davison Ficke

She limps with halting painful pace,
  Stops, wavers and creeps on again;
Peers up with dim and questioning face,
  Void of desire or doubt or pain.

Her cheeks hang gray in waxen folds
  Wherein there stirs no blood at all.
A hand, like bundled cornstalks, holds
  The tatters of a faded shawl.

Where was a breast, sunk bones she clasps;
  A knot jerks where were woman-hips;
A ropy throat sends writhing gasps
  Up to the tight line of her lips.

Here strong the city's pomp is poured . . .
  She stands, unhuman, bleak, aghast:
An empty temple of the Lord
  From which the jocund Lord has passed.

He has builded him another house,
  Whenceforth his flame, renewed and bright,
Shines stark upon these weathered brows
  Abandoned to the final night.

THE DOOR

By Mary Carolyn Davies

The littlest door, the inner door,
  I swing it wide.
Now in my heart there is no more
  To hide.

The farthest door—the latch at last
  Is lifted; see.
I kept the little fortress fast.
  —Be good to me.

THE SONG OF DARK WATERS

By Roy Helton

I'se de niggah, I'se de niggah;
  I'se de niggah makes de works go round;
I'se a-pullin', I'se a-haulin'
  Wherever dere's a shovel in de ground.
You couldn' lif' de garbage in de old slop cart
  Withouten men lak me;
You couldn' run a vessel on de lakes or ribbahs;
  You couldn' put a steamer on de sea.
I'se a dirt and a black and a filth and a grime;
I'se a-sweatin' and a-laughin' and a-gruntin' all de time
  And dat's my way to be.

I'se de niggah, I'se de niggah;
  I'se de niggah in de woodpile of de worl'.

Up dere in Heaven where de Lord am livin'
  Who laid dem streets of pearl?
De angels all ben ladies. De postles all ben gents;
Jes set and sing and twiddle dere wing
  And live at de Lord's expense.
Who raise dem walls of Shiloh?
Who pave dem streets of pearl?

Some old niggah. Some pore old niggah.
Some old niggah from de woodpile of de worl'.

"SCUM O' THE EARTH"

By Robert Haven Schauffler

I

At the gate of the West I stand,
On the isle where the nations throng.
We call them "scum o' the earth";

Stay, are we doing you wrong,
Young fellow from Socrates' land?—
You, like a Hermes so lissome and strong
Fresh from the master Praxiteles' hand?
So you're of Spartan birth?
Descended, perhaps, from one of the band—
Deathless in story and song—
Who combed their long hair at Thermopylæ's
  pass? . . .

234 FOR HARDENING OF THE HEART

Ah, I forget what straits (alas!),
More tragic than theirs, more compassion-worth,
Have doomed you to march in our "immigrant class"
Where you're nothing but "scum o' the earth."

II

You Pole with the child on your knee,
What dower bring you to the land of the free?
Hark! does she croon
The sad little tune
That Chopin once found on his Polish lea
And mounted in gold for you and for me?
Now a ragged young fiddler answers
In wild Czech melody
That Dvořak took whole from the dancers.
And the heavy faces bloom
In the wonderful Slavic way;
The little, dull eyes, the brows a-gloom,
Suddenly dawn like the day.
While, watching these folk and their mystery,
I forget that we,
In our scornful mirth,
Brand them as "polacks"—and "scum o' the earth."

III

Genoese boy of the level brow,
Lad of the lustrous, dreamy eyes
Agaze at Manhattan's pinnacles now
In the first, sweet shock of a hushed surprise;

Within your far-rapt seer's eyes
I catch the glow of the wild surmise
That played on the Santa Maria's prow
In that still gray dawn,
Four centuries gone,
When a world from the wave began to rise.
Oh, who shall foretell what high emprise
Is the goal that gleams
When Italy's dreams
Spread wing and sweep into the skies?
Cæsar dreamed him a world ruled well;
Dante dreamed Heaven out of Hell;
Angelo brought us there to dwell;
And you, are you of a different birth?—
You're only a "dago,"—and "scum o' the earth"!

IV

Stay, are we doing you wrong
Calling you "scum o' the earth,"
Man of the sorrow-bowed head,
Of the features tender yet strong,—
Man of the eyes full of wisdom and mystery
Mingled with patience and dread?
Have not I known you in history,
Sorrow-bowed head?
Were you the poet-king, worth
Treasures of Ophir unpriced?
Were you the prophet, perchance, whose art
Foretold how the rabble would mock

FOR HARDENING OF THE HEART

That shepherd of spirits, ere long,
Who should gather the lambs to his heart
And tenderly feed his flock?
Man—lift that sorrow-bowed head. . . .
Behold, the face of the Christ!

The vision dies at its birth.
You're merely a butt for our mirth.
You're a "sheeny"—and therefore despised
And rejected as "scum o' the earth."

v

Countrymen, bend and invoke
Mercy for us blasphemers,
For that we spat on these marvellous folk,
Nations of darers and dreamers,
Scions of singers and seers,
Our peers, and more than our peers.
"Rabble and refuse," we name them
And "scum o' the earth," to shame them.
Mercy for us of the few, young years,
Of the culture so callow and crude,
Of the hands so grasping and rude,
The lips so ready for sneers
At the sons of our ancient more-than-peers.
Mercy for us who dare despise
Men in whose loins our Homer lies;
Mothers of men who shall bring to us
The glory of Titian, the grandeur of Huss;

Children in whose frail arms may rest
Prophets and singers and saints of the West.

Newcomers all from the eastern seas,
Help us incarnate dreams like these.
Forget, and forgive, that we did you wrong.
Help us to father a nation strong
In the comradeship of an equal birth,
In the wealth of the richest bloods of earth.

From PASSAGE TO INDIA

By Walt Whitman

Passage to India!
Lo, soul! seest thou not God's purpose from the first?
The earth to be spann'd, connected by net-work,
The people to become brothers and sisters,
The races, neighbors, to marry and to be given in marriage,
The oceans to be cross'd, the distant brought near,
The lands to be welded together.

THE MAN WITH THE HOE

By Edwin Markham

(Written after seeing Millet's World-Famous Painting of a brutalized toiler)

> God made man in His own image,
> in the image of God made He him.—Genesis.

Bowed by the weight of centuries he leans
Upon his hoe and gazes on the ground,

238 FOR HARDENING OF THE HEART

The emptiness of ages in his face,
And on his back the burden of the world.
Who made him dead to rapture and despair,
A thing that grieves not and that never hopes,
Stolid and stunned, a brother to the ox?
Who loosened and let down this brutal jaw?
Whose was the hand that slanted back this brow?
Whose breath blew out the light within this brain?

Is this the Thing the Lord God made and gave
To have dominion over sea and land;
To trace the stars and search the heavens for power;
To feel the passion of Eternity?
Is this the dream He dreamed who shaped the suns
And markt their ways upon the ancient deep?
Down all the caverns of Hell to their last gulf
There is no shape more terrible than this—
More tongued with censure of the world's blind greed—
More filled with signs and portents for the soul—
More packt with danger to the universe.

What gulfs between him and the seraphim!
Slave of the wheel of labor, what to him
Are Plato and the swing of Pleiades?
What the long reaches of the peaks of song,
The rift of dawn, the reddening of the rose?
Thru this dread shape the suffering ages look;
Time's tragedy is in that aching stoop;
Thru this dread shape humanity betrayed,

Plundered, profaned and disinherited,
Cries protest to the Judges of the World,
A protest that is also prophecy.

O masters, lords and rulers in all lands,
Is this the handiwork you give to God,
This monstrous thing distorted and soul-quencht?
How will you ever straighten up this shape;
Touch it again with immortality;
Give back the upward looking and the light;
Rebuild in it the music and the dream;
Make right the immemorial infamies,
Perfidious wrongs, immedicable woes?

O masters, lords and rulers in all lands,
How will the future reckon with this Man?
How answer his brute question in that hour
When whirlwinds of rebellion shake all shores?
How will it be with kingdoms and with kings—
With those who shaped him to the thing he is—
When this dumb Terror shall rise to judge the world,
After the silence of the centuries?

THE SECOND COMING

By Norman Gale

The Saviour came. With trembling lips
He counted Europe's battleships.
"Yet millions lack their daily bread.
So much for Calvary!" He said.

MERCY
(*From The Merchant of Venice*)

By William Shakespeare

The quality of mercy is not strain'd:
It droppeth as the gentle rain from Heaven
Upon the place beneath: it is twice bless'd;
It blesseth him that gives, and him that takes:
'Tis mightiest in the mightiest; it becomes
The thronèd monarch better than his crown:
His scepter shows the force of temporal power,
The attribute to awe and majesty,
Wherein doth sit the dread and fear of kings;
But mercy is above this sceptered sway;
It is enthronèd in the hearts of kings,
It is an attribute to God himself;
And earthly power doth then show likest God's
When mercy seasons justice.

DEDICATION

By John Erskine

When imperturbable the gentle moon
Glides above war and onslaught through the night,
When the sun burns magnificent at noon
On hate contriving horror by its light,
When man, for whom the stars were and the skies,
Turns beast to rend his fellow, fang and hoof,
Shall we not think, with what ironic eyes
Nature must look on us and stand aloof?

But not alone the sun, the moon, the stars,
Shining unharmed above man's folly move;
For us three beacons kindle one another
Which waver not with any wind of wars:
We love our children still, still them we love
Who gave us birth, and still we love each other.

AULD LANG SYNE

By Robert Burns

Should auld acquaintance be forgot,
   And never brought to min'?
Should auld acquaintance be forgot,
   And days o' auld lang syne?

CHORUS

   For auld lang syne, my dear,
     For auld lang syne,
   We'll take a cup o' kindness yet,
     For auld lang syne.

We twa hae run about the braes,
   And pu'd the gowans fine,
But we've wander'd mony a weary foot
   Sin auld lang syne.
      For auld, &c.

We twa hae paidl't i' the burn,
   From mornin sun till dine;

But seas between us braid hae roar'd
   Sin auld lang syne.
      For auld, &c.

And here's a hand, my trusty fiere,
   And gie's a hand o' thine;
And we'll tak a right guid willie waught,
   For auld lang syne.
      For auld, &c.

And surely ye'll be your pint-stowp,
   And surely I'll be mine,
And we'll tak a cup o' kindness yet
   For auld lang syne.
      For auld, &c.

OUTWITTED

By Edwin Markham

He drew a circle that shut me out—
Heretic, rebel, a thing to flout.
But Love and I had the wit to win:
We drew a circle that took him in!

THE TUFT OF FLOWERS

By Robert Frost

I went to turn the grass once after one
Who mowed it in the dew before the sun.

POEMS OF SYMPATHY

The dew was gone that made his blade so keen
Before I came to view the levelled scene.

I looked for him behind an isle of trees;
I listened for his whetstone on the breeze.

But he had gone his way, the grass all mown,
And I must be, as he had been,—alone,

"As all must be," I said within my heart,
"Whether they work together or apart."

But as I said it, swift there passed me by
On noiseless wing a bewildered butterfly,

Seeking with memories grown dim over night
Some resting flower of yesterday's delight.

And once I marked his flight go round and round,
As where some flower lay withering on the ground.

And then he flew as far as eye could see,
And then on tremulous wing came back to me.

I thought of questions that have no reply,
And would have turned to toss the grass to dry;

But he turned first, and led my eye to look
At a tall tuft of flowers beside a brook,

FOR HARDENING OF THE HEART

A leaping tongue of bloom the scythe had spared
Beside a reedy brook the scythe had bared.

I left my place to know them by their name,
Finding them butterfly-weed when I came.

The mower in the dew had loved them thus,
By leaving them to flourish, not for us,

Nor yet to draw one thought of ours to him,
But from sheer morning gladness at the brim.

The butterfly and I had lit upon,
Nevertheless, a message from the dawn,

That made me hear the wakening birds around,
And hear his long scythe whispering to the ground,

And feel a spirit kindred to my own;
So that henceforth I worked no more alone;

But glad with him, I worked as with his aid,
And weary, sought at noon with him the shade;

And dreaming, as it were, held brotherly speech
With one whose thought I had not hoped to reach.

"Men work together," I told him from the heart,
"Whether they work together or apart."

BYRON

By Joaquin Miller

In men whom men condemn as ill
I find so much of goodness still,
In men whom men pronounce divine
I find so much of sin and blot,
I do not dare to draw a line
Between the two, where God has not.

FOR MERCY, COURAGE, KINDNESS, MIRTH

By Lawrence Binyon

For Mercy, Courage, Kindness, Mirth,
There is no measure upon earth.
Nay, they wither, root and stem,
If an end be set to them.

Overbrim and overflow
If your own heart you would know.
For the spirit, born to bless,
Lives but in its own excess.

THE WORLD'S NEED

By Ella Wheeler Wilcox

So many gods, so many creeds,
   So many paths that wind and wind,
   While just the art of being kind
Is all the sad world needs.

IX

ACCELERATORS FOR SLUGGISH BLOOD

(Poems of High Voltage)

LEPANTO

By Gilbert K. Chesterton

White founts falling in the Courts of the sun,
And the Soldan of Byzantium is smiling as they run;
There is laughter like the fountains in that face of all men feared,
It stirs the forest darkness, the darkness of his beard;
It curls the blood-red crescent, the crescent of his lips;
For the inmost sea of all the earth is shaken with his ships.
They have dared the white republics up the capes of Italy,
They have dashed the Adriatic round the Lion of the Sea,
And the Pope has cast his arms abroad for agony and loss,
And called the kings of Christendom for swords about the Cross.
The cold queen of England is looking in the glass;
The shadow of the Valois is yawning at the Mass;
From evening isles fantastical rings faint the Spanish gun,
And the Lord upon the Golden Horn is laughing in the sun.

Dim drums throbbing, in the hills half heard,
Where only on a nameless throne a crownless prince has stirred,

Where, risen from a doubtful seat and half attainted stall,
The last knight of Europe takes weapons from the wall,
The last and lingering troubadour to whom the bird has sung,
That once went singing southward when all the world was young.
In that enormous silence, tiny and unafraid,
Comes up along a winding road the noise of the Crusade.
Strong gongs groaning as the guns boom far,
Don John of Austria is going to the war,
Stiff flags straining in the night-blasts cold
In the gloom black-purple, in the glint old-gold,
Torchlight crimson on the copper kettle-drums,
Then the tuckets, then the trumpets, then the cannon, and he comes.
Don John laughing in the brave beard curled,
Spurning of his stirrups like the thrones of all the world,
Holding his head up for a flag of all the free.
Love-light of Spain—hurrah!
Death-light of Africa!
Don John of Austria
Is riding to the sea.

Mahound is in his paradise above the evening star,
(*Don John of Austria is going to the war.*)

POEMS OF HIGH VOLTAGE 251

He moves a mighty turban on the timeless houri's knees,
His turban that is woven of the sunsets and the seas.
He shakes the peacock gardens as he rises from his ease,
And he strides among the tree-tops and is taller than the trees;
And his voice through all the garden is a thunder sent to bring
Black Azrael and Ariel and Ammon on the wing.
Giants and the Genii,
Multiplex of wing and eye,
Whose strong obedience broke the sky
When Solomon was king.

They rush in red and purple from the red clouds of the morn,
From the temples where the yellow gods shut up their eyes in scorn;
They rise in green robes roaring from the green hells of the sea
Where fallen skies and evil hues and eyeless creatures be,
On them the sea-valves cluster and the grey sea-forests curl,
Splashed with a splendid sickness, the sickness of the pearl;
They swell in sapphire smoke out of the blue cracks of the ground,—

They gather and they wonder and give worship to Mahound.
And he saith, "Break up the mountains where the hermit-folk can hide,
And sift the red and silver sands lest bone of saint abide,
And chase the Giaours flying night and day, not giving rest,
For that which was our trouble comes again out of the west.
We have set the seal of Solomon on all things under sun,
Of knowledge and of sorrow and endurance of things done.
But a noise is in the mountains, in the mountains, and I know
The voice that shook our palaces—four hundred years ago:
It is he that saith not 'Kismet'; it is he that knows not Fate;
It is Richard, it is Raymond, it is Godfrey at the gate!
It is he whose loss is laughter when he counts the wager worth,
Put down your feet upon him, that our peace be on the earth."
For he heard drums groaning and he heard guns jar,
(*Don John of Austria is going to the war.*)
Sudden and still—hurrah!
Bolt from Iberia!

POEMS OF HIGH VOLTAGE

Don John of Austria
Is gone by Alcalar.

St. Michael's on his Mountain in the sea-roads of the north
(*Don John of Austria is girt and going forth.*)
Where the grey seas glitter and the sharp tides shift
And the sea-folk labour and the red sails lift.
He shakes his lance of iron and he claps his wings of stone;
The noise is gone through Normandy; the noise is gone alone;
The North is full of tangled things and texts and aching eyes,
And dead is all the innocence of anger and surprise,
And Christian killeth Christian in a narrow dusty room,
And Christian dreadeth Christ that hath a newer face of doom,
And Christian hateth Mary that God kissed in Galilee,—
But Don John of Austria is riding to the sea.
Don John calling through the blast and the eclipse
Crying with the trumpet, with the trumpet of his lips,
Trumpet that sayeth *ha!*
  Domino gloria!
Don John of Austria
Is shouting to the ships.

King Philip's in his closet with the Fleece about his neck,
(*Don John of Austria is armed upon the deck.*)

The walls are hung with velvet that is black and soft as sin,
And little dwarfs creep out of it and little dwarfs creep in.
He holds a crystal phial that has colours like the moon,
He touches, and it tingles, and he trembles very soon,
And his face is as a fungus of a leprous white and grey
Like plants in the high houses that are shuttered from the day,
And death is in the phial and the end of noble work,
But Don John of Austria has fired upon the Turk.
Don John's hunting, and his hounds have bayed—
Booms away past Italy the rumour of his raid.
Gun upon gun, ha! ha!
Gun upon gun, hurrah!
Don John of Austria
Has loosed the cannonade.

The Pope was in his chapel before day or battle broke,
(*Don John of Austria is hidden in the smoke.*)
The hidden room in man's house where God sits all the year,
The secret window whence the world looks small and very dear.
He sees as in a mirror on the monstrous twilight sea
The crescent of his cruel ships whose name is mystery;
They fling great shadows foe-wards, making Cross and Castle dark,
They veil the plumèd lions on the galleys of St. Mark;

And above the ships are palaces of brown, black-bearded chiefs,
And below the ships are prisons, where with multitudinous griefs,
Christian captives sick and sunless, all a labouring race repines
Like a race in sunken cities, like a nation in the mines.
They are lost like slaves that sweat, and in the skies of morning hung
The stair-ways of the tallest gods when tyranny was young.
They are countless, voiceless, hopeless as those fallen or fleeing on
Before the high Kings' horses in the granite of Babylon.
And many a one grows witless in his quiet room in hell
Where a yellow face looks inward through the lattice of his cell,
And he finds his God forgotten, and he seeks no more a sign—
(But Don John of Austria has burst the battle-line!)
Don John pounding from the slaughter-painted poop,
Purpling all the ocean like a bloody pirate's sloop,
Scarlet running over on the silvers and the golds,
Breaking of the hatches up and bursting of the holds,
Thronging of the thousands up that labour under sea
White for bliss and blind for sun and stunned for liberty.
Vivat Hispania!
Domino Gloria!

Don John of Austria
Has set his people free!

Cervantes on his galley sets the sword back in the sheath
(*Don John of Austria rides homeward with a wreath.*)
And he sees across a weary land a straggling road in Spain,
Up which a lean and foolish knight for ever rides in vain,
And he smiles, but not as Sultans smile, and settles back the blade. . . .
(*But Don John of Austria rides home from the Crusade.*)

COMRADES

By Richard Hovey

Comrades, pour the wine to-night
For the parting is with dawn!
Oh, the clink of cups together,
With the daylight coming on!
Greet the morn
With a double horn
When strong men drink together!

Comrades, gird your swords to-night,
For the battle is with dawn!
Oh, the clash of shields together,
With the triumph coming on!

Greet the foe,
And lay him low,
When strong men fight together!

Comrades, watch the tides to-night,
For the sailing is with dawn!
Oh, to face the spray together,
With the tempest coming on!
Greet the sea
With a shout of glee,
When strong men roam together!

Comrades, give a cheer to-night,
For the dying is with dawn!
Oh, to meet the stars together,
With the silence coming on!
Greet the end
As a friend a friend,
When strong men die together!

GIVE A ROUSE

(*Cavalier Tune*)

By Robert Browning

King Charles, and who'll do him right now?
King Charles, and who's ripe for fight now?
Give a rouse: here's, in hell's despite now,
King Charles!

Who gave me the goods that went since?
Who rais'd me the house that sank once?
Who help'd me to gold I spent since?
Who found me in wine you drank once?

(Chorus)

King Charles, and who'll do him right now?
King Charles, and who's ripe for fight now?
Give a rouse: here's, in hell's despite now,
King Charles!

To whom us'd my boy George quaff else,
By the old fool's side that begot him?
For whom did he cheer and laugh else,
While Noll's damn'd troopers shot him?

(Chorus)

King Charles, and who'll do him right now?
King Charles, and who's ripe for fight now?
Give a rouse: here's, in hell's despite now,
King Charles!

THE CHARGE OF THE LIGHT BRIGADE

By Alfred Tennyson

Half a league, half a league,
Half a league onward,
All in the valley of death
Rode the six hundred.

"Forward, the Light Brigade!
Take the guns!" Nolan said;
Into the valley of Death
  Rode the six hundred.

"Forward, the Light Brigade!"
Was there a man dismayed?
Not though the soldiers knew
  Some one had blundered;
Theirs not to make reply,
Theirs not to reason why,
Theirs but to do and die;—
Into the valley of Death
  Rode the six hundred.

Cannon to right of them,
Cannon to left of them,
Cannon in front of them
  Volleyed and thundered.
Stormed at with shot and shell,
Boldly they rode and well;
Into the jaws of Death,
Into the mouth of Hell
  Rode the six hundred.

Flashed all their sabres bare,
Flashed as they turned in air,
Sabring the gunners there,
Charging an army, while

All the world wondered.
Plunged in the battery smoke,
Right through the line they broke;
Cossack and Russian
Reeled from the sabre-stroke—
 Shattered and sundered.
Then they rode back, but not—
 Not the six hundred.

Cannon to right of them,
Cannon to left of them,
Cannon behind them
 Volleyed and thundered.
Stormed at with shot and shell,
While horse and hero fell,
Those that had fought so well
Came through the jaws of Death,
Back from the mouth of Hell,
All that was left of them,
 Left of six hundred.

When can their glory fade?
O the wild charge they made!
 All the world wondered.
Honor the charge they made!
Honor the Light Brigade,
 Noble six hundred!

"HOW THEY BROUGHT THE GOOD NEWS FROM GHENT TO AIX"

[16—]

By Robert Browning

I sprang to the stirrup, and Joris, and he;
I gallop'd, Dirck gallop'd, we gallop'd all three;
"Good speed!" cried the watch, as the gate-bolts undrew;
"Speed!" echoed the wall to us galloping through;
Behind shut the postern, the lights sank to rest,
And into the midnight we gallop'd abreast.

Not a word to each other; we kept the great pace
Neck by neck, stride by stride, never changing our place;
I turn'd in my saddle and made its girths tight,
Then shorten'd each stirrup, and set the pique right,
Rebuckled the cheek-strap, chain'd slacker the bit,
Nor gallop'd less steadily Roland a whit.

'Twas moonset at starting; but while we drew near
Lokeren, the cocks crew and twilight dawn'd clear;
At Boom, a great yellow star came out to see;
At Düffeld, 'twas morning as plain as could be;
And from Mechelm church-steeple we heard the half chime,
So, Joris broke silence with, "Yet there is time!"

At Aershot, up leap'd of a sudden the sun,
And against him the cattle stood black every one,
To stare thro' the mist at us galloping past,
And I saw my stout galloper Roland at last,
With resolute shoulders, each butting away
The haze, as some bluff river headland its spray:

And his low head and crest, just one sharp ear bent back
For my voice, and the other prick'd out on his track;
And one eye's black intelligence,—ever that glance
O'er its white edge at me, his own master, askance!
And the thick heavy spume-flakes which aye and anon
His fierce lips shook upwards in galloping on.

By Hasselt, Dirck groan'd; and cried Joris "Stay spur!
Your Roos gallop'd bravely, the fault's not in her,
We'll remember at Aix"—for one heard the quick wheeze
Of her chest, saw the stretch'd neck and staggering knees,
And sunk tail, and horrible heave of the flank,
As down on her haunches she shudder'd and sank.

So, we were left galloping, Joris and I,
Past Looz and past Tongres, no cloud in the sky;
The broad sun above laugh'd a pitiless laugh,
'Neath our feet broke the brittle bright stubble like chaff;
Till over by Dalhem a dome-spire sprang white,
And "Gallop," gasped Joris, "for Aix is in sight!

'How they'll greet us!"—and all in a moment his roan
Roll'd neck and croup over, lay dead as a stone;
And there was my Roland to bear the whole weight
Of the news which alone could save Aix from her fate,
With his nostrils like pits full of blood to the brim,
And with circles of red for his eye-sockets' rim.

Then I cast loose my buffcoat, each holster let fall,
Shook off both my jack-boots, let go belt and all,
Stood up in the stirrup, lean'd, patted his ear,
Call'd my Roland his pet name, my horse without
    peer;
Clapp'd my hands, laugh'd and sang, any noise, bad or
    good,
Till at length into Aix Roland gallop'd and stood.

And all I remember is, friends flocking round
As I sat with his head 'twixt my knees on the ground;
And no voice but was praising this Roland of mine,
As I pour'd down his throat our last measure of wine,
Which (the burgesses voted by common consent)
Was no more than his due who brought good news from
    Ghent.

THE WILD JOYS OF LIVING

(*From Saul*)

By Robert Browning

Oh, the wild joys of living! the leaping from rock up
    to rock,

The strong rending of boughs from the fir-tree, the cool silver shock
Of the plunge in a pool's living water, the hunt of the bear,
And the sultriness showing the lion is couched in his lair.
And the meal, the rich dates yellowed over with gold dust divine,
And the locust-flesh steeped in the pitcher, the full draught of wine,
And the sleep in the dried river-channel where bulrushes tell
That the water was wont to go warbling so softly and well.
How good is man's life, the mere living! how fit to employ
All the heart and the soul and the senses for ever in joy!

THE ODYSSEY

By Andrew Lang

As one that for a weary space has lain
Lulled by the song of Circe and her wine
In gardens near the pale of Proserpine,
Where that Ææan isle forgets the main,
And only the low lutes of love complain,
And only shadows of wan lovers pine,
As such an one were glad to know the brine
Salt on his lips, and the large air again,—

So gladly, from the songs of modern speech
Men turn, and see the stars, and feel the free
Shrill wind beyond the close of heavy flowers,
And, through the music of the languid hours,
They hear like ocean on a western beach
The surge and thunder of the Odyssey.

KING HENRY BEFORE HARFLEUR

(From King Henry V)

By William Shakespeare

Once more into the breach, dear friends, once more;
Or close the wall up with our English dead.
In peace there's nothing so becomes a man
As modest stillness and humility:
But when the blast of war blows in our ears,
Then imitate the action of the tiger;
Stiffen the sinews, summon up the blood,
Disguise fair nature with hard-favour'd rage;
Then lend the eye a terrible aspect;
Let it pry through the portage of the head
Like the brass cannon; let the brow o'erwhelm it
As fearfully as doth a galled rock
O'erhang and jutty his confounded base,
Swill'd with the wild and wasteful ocean.
Now set the teeth and stretch the nostril wide,
Hold hard the breath and bend up every spirit
To his full height. On, on, you noblest English,
Whose blood is fet from fathers of war-proof!

Fathers that, like so many Alexanders,
Have in these parts from morn till even fought
And sheathed their swords for lack of argument:
Dishonor not your mothers; now attest
That those whom you call'd fathers did beget you.
Be copy now to men of grosser blood,
And teach them how to war. And you, good yeomen
Whose limbs were made in England, show us here
The mettle of your pasture; let us swear
That you are worth your breeding; which I doubt not
For there is none of you so mean and base,
That hath not noble lustre in your eyes.
I see you stand like greyhounds in the slips,
Straining upon the start. The game's afoot:
Follow your spirit, and upon this charge
Cry "God for Harry, England, and Saint George!"

UNREST

By Don Marquis

A fierce unrest seethes at the core
    Of all existing things:
It was the eager wish to soar
    That gave the gods their wings.

From what flat wastes of cosmic slime,
    And stung by what quick fire,
Sunward the restless races climb!—
    Men risen out of mire!

There throbs through all the worlds that are
    This heart-beat hot and strong
And shaken systems, star by star,
    Awake and glow in song.

But for the urge of this unrest
    These joyous spheres are mute;
But for the rebel in his breast
    Had man remained a brute.

When man's dim eyes demanded light
    The light he sought was born—
His wish, a Titan, scaled the height
    And flung him back the morn!

From deed to dream, from dream to deed,
    From daring hope to hope,
The restless wish, the instant need,
    Still lashed him up the slope!

. . . .

I sing no governed firmament,
    Cold, ordered, regular—
I sing the stinging discontent
    That leaps from star to star!

EXULTATION

By Shaemas O'Sheel

When the full-bosomed and free-limbed Spring
Roaring her rousing and lusty song

Comes along
With a swirl and swing,
Stirring the blood with the wind of her wing,
It is well to be out where the road is long,
It is well to be where the waters sing,
And the green things start
From the old earth's heart,
And the birds are twitt'ring by twos apart;
For that is the time when life is strong,
Stronger than death or anything,
That is when life is a lusty song
On the lips of exultant Spring!

From SURSUM CORDA

By Edith M. Thomas

Up and rejoice, and know thou hast matter for revel,
   my heart!
Up and rejoice, not heeding if drawn or undrawn be
   the dart
Last winged by the Archer whose quiver is full for
   sweeter than thou,
That yet will sing out of the dust when the ultimate
   arrow shall bow. . . .
Now thou couldst bless and godspeed, without bitter-
   ness bred in thine heart,
Loves that outworn and time-wasted were fain from
   thy lodge to depart.

Though dulled by their passing, thy faith, like a flower upfolded by night,
New kindness should quicken again, as a flower feels the touch of new light.
Ay, now thou couldst love, undefeated, with ardor instinct from pure Love—
Warmed by a sun in the heavens that knows not beneath nor above,
Nor distance its patience to weary, nor substance unpierced by its ray. . . .
Now couldst thou pity and smile where once but the scourge thou wouldst lay;
Now to thyself couldst show mercy, and up from all penance arise,
Knowing there runneth abroad that chastening Flame from the skies. . . .

Doubt not thou hast matter for revel; for once thou wouldst cage thee in steel,
And, wounded, wouldst seek out the balm and the cordial cunning to heal.
But now thou hast knowledge more sovran, more kind, than leechcraft can wield:
Never Design sent thee forth to be safe from the scath of the field,
But bade thee stand bare in the midst, and offer free way to all scath
Piercing thee inly—so, only, might Song have an outgoing path. . . .

But now 'tis not thine to bestow—to abide—or be
  known in thy place;
Withdraweth the voice into Silence, dissolveth the
  form and the face.
Death—Life—thou discernest; enlarged as thou art
  thy ground thou must shift:
Love over-liveth. Throb thou forth quickly. Heart
  be uplift!

THE WILD RIDE

By Louise Imogen Guiney

I hear in my heart, I hear in its ominous pulses,
All day, on the road, the hoofs of invisible horses;
All night, from their stalls, the importunate tramping
  and neighing.

Let cowards and laggards fall back! but alert to the
  saddle,
Straight, grim, and abreast, go the weather-worn, gal-
  loping legion,
With a stirrup-cup each to the lily of women that
  loves him.

The trail is through dolor and dread, over crags and
  morasses;
There are shapes by the way, there are things that
  appal or entice us:
What odds? We are knights, and our souls are but
  bent on the riding.

I hear in my heart, I hear in its ominous pulses,
All day, on the road, the hoofs of invisible horses;
All night, from their stalls, the importunate tramping
  and neighing.

We spur to a land of no name, out-racing the storm-
  wind;
We leap to the infinite dark, like the sparks from the
  anvil.
Thou leadest, O God! All's well with Thy troopers
  that follow.

℞ X

SEDATIVES FOR IMPATIENCE

(Poems of Reassurance)

WAITING

By John Burroughs

Serene, I fold my hands and wait,
   Nor care for wind, or tide, or sea;
I rave no more 'gainst time or fate,
   For, lo! my own shall come to me.

I stay my haste, I make delays,
   For what avails this eager pace?
I stand amid the eternal ways,
   And what is mine shall know my face.

Asleep, awake, by night or day,
   The friends I seek are seeking me;
No wind can drive my bark astray,
   Nor change the tide of destiny.

What matter if I stand alone?
   I wait with joy the coming years;
My heart shall reap where it has sown,
   And garner up its fruit of tears.

The waters know their own and draw
   The brook that springs in yonder height;
So flows the good with equal law
   Unto the soul of pure delight.

The stars come nightly to the sky;
  The tidal wave unto the sea;
Nor time, nor space, nor deep, nor high,
  Can keep my own away from me.

ENVOY

By Bliss Carman

Have little care that Life is brief,
And less that Art is long.
Success is in the silences
Though Fame is in the song.

ON HIS BLINDNESS

By John Milton

When I consider how my light is spent,
  E're half my days, in this dark world and wide,
  And that one Talent which is death to hide,
Lodg'd with me useless, though my Soul more bent
To serve therewith my Maker, and present
  My true account, least he returning chide,
  Doth God exact day-labour, light deny'd,
I fondly ask; But patience to prevent
That murmur, soon replies, God doth not need
  Either man's work or his own gifts, who best
    Bear his milde yoak, they serve him best, his State
Is Kingly. Thousands at his bidding speed
  And post o're Land and Ocean without rest:
    They also serve who only stand and waite.

WORK

By Elizabeth Barrett Browning

What are we set on earth for? Say, to toil;
  Nor seek to leave thy tending of the vines
  For all the heat o' the day, till it declines,
And Death's mild curfew shall from work assoil.
God did anoint thee with His odorous oil,
  To wrestle, not to reign; and He assigns
  All thy tears over, like pure crystallines,
For younger fellow-workers of the soil
To wear for amulets. So others shall
  Take patience, labour, to their heart and hand,
    From thy hand and thy heart and thy brave cheer,
And God's grace fructify through thee to all.
  The least flower with a brimming cup may stand,
    And share its dew-drop with another near.

A TREASURE HOUSE

By M. A. DeWolfe Howe

The poet's song, the painter's art,
Are richest when they tell but part;

We hear the sweetest player, and thrill
With dreams of music sweeter still;

The spring's first brightness is so dear
Because we feel the summer near:—

Shall I not love my love the more
For keeping wealths of love in store?

FOUND ON AN ENGLISH SUN DIAL
(From the Latin)

Time flies,
Suns rise
And shadows fall.
Let time go by.
Love is forever over all.

THE ARROW AND THE SONG

By Henry Wadsworth Longfellow

I shot an arrow into the air,
It fell to earth, I knew not where;
For, so swiftly it flew, the sight
Could not follow it in its flight.

I breathed a song into the air,
It fell to earth, I knew not where;
For who has sight so keen and strong
That it can follow the flight of song?

Long, long afterward, in an oak
I found the arrow, still unbroke;
And the song, from beginning to end,
I found again in the heart of a friend.

From THE WORD AT ST. KAVIN'S

By Bliss Carman

Therefore, my friends, I say
  Back to the fair sweet way
Our Mother Nature taught us long ago,—
The large primeval mood,
Leisure and amplitude,
The dignity of patience strong and slow.

Let us go in once more
  By some blue mountain door,
And hold communion with the forest leaves;
Where long ago we trod
The Ghost House of the God,
Through orange dawns and amethystine eves!

THE RECOMPENSE [1]

By Anna Wickham

Of every step I took in pain
I had some gain.
Of every night of blind excess
I had reward of half-dead idleness.
Back to the lone road
With the old load!
But rest at night is sweet
To wounded feet.
And when the day is long,
There is miraculous reward of song.

[1] From "The Contemplative Quarry" by Anna Wickham, copyright, 1921, by Harcourt, Brace and Company, Inc.

From SAINT PAUL

By F. W. H. Myers

God who, whatever frenzy of our fretting,
　Vexeth sad life to spoil and to destroy,
Lendeth an hour for peace and for forgetting,
　Setteth in pain the jewel of His joy.

TO A FRIEND

Chafing at Enforced Idleness from Interrupted Health

By William Watson

Soon may the edict lapse, that on you lays
This dire compulsion of infertile days,
This hardest penal toil, reluctant rest!
Meanwhile I count you eminently blest,
Happy from labours heretofore well done,
Happy in tasks auspiciously begun.
For they are blest that have not much to rue—
That have not oft mis-heard the prompter's cue,
Stammered and stumbled and the wrong parts played,
And life a Tragedy of Errors made.

"WITH WHOM IS NO VARIABLENESS, NEITHER SHADOW OF TURNING"

By Arthur Hugh Clough

It fortifies my soul to know
　That, though I perish, Truth is so:

That, howsoe'er I stray and range,
Whate'er I do, Thou dost not change.
I steadier step when I recall
That, if I slip Thou dost not fall.

MAGNA EST VERITAS

By Coventry Patmore

Here, in this little Bay,
Full of tumultuous life and great repose,
Where, twice a day,
The purposeless, glad ocean comes and goes,
Under high cliffs, and far from the huge town,
I sit me down.
For want of me the world's course will not fail;
When all its work is done, the lie shall rot;
The truth is great, and shall prevail,
When none cares whether it prevail or not.

℞ XI

BEAUTY'S WINE

(A Specific for Ugliness)

ODE TO A NIGHTINGALE

By John Keats

My heart aches, and a drowsy numbness pains
    My sense, as though of hemlock I had drunk,
Or emptied some dull opiate to the drains
    One minute past, and Lethe-wards had sunk:
'Tis not through envy of thy happy lot,
    But being too happy in thy happiness,
        That thou, light-wingèd Dryad of the trees,
            In some melodious plot
    Of beechen green, and shadows numberless,
        Singest of summer in full-throated ease.

O for a draught of vintage! that hath been
    Cool'd a long age in the deep-delvèd earth,
Tasting of Flora and the country-green,
    Dance, and Provençal song, and sunburnt mirth!
O for a beaker full of the warm South!
    Full of the true, the blushful Hippocrene,
        With beaded bubbles winking at the brim,
            And purple-stainèd mouth;
    That I might drink, and leave the world unseen,
        And with thee fade away into the forest dim:

Fade far away, dissolve, and quite forget
    What thou among the leaves hast never known,

BEAUTY'S WINE

The weariness, the fever, and the fret
  Here, where men sit and hear each other groan;
Where palsy shakes a few, sad, last grey hairs,
  Where youth grows pale, and spectre-thin, and dies;
    Where but to think is to be full of sorrow
      And leaden-eyed despairs;
    Where beauty cannot keep her lustrous eyes,
      Or new Love pine at them beyond to-morrow.

Away! away! for I will fly to thee,
  Not charioted by Bacchus and his pards,
But on the viewless wings of Poesy,
  Though the dull brain perplexes and retards:
Already with thee! tender is the night,
  And haply the Queen-Moon is on her throne,
    Cluster'd around by all her starry Fays;
      But here there is no light,
    Save what from heaven is with the breezes blown
      Through verdurous glooms and winding mossy ways.

I cannot see what flowers are at my feet,
  Nor what soft incense hangs upon the boughs,
But, in embalmèd darkness, guess each sweet
  Wherewith the seasonable month endows
The grass, the thicket, and the fruit-tree wild;
  White hawthorn, and the pastoral eglantine;
    Fast-fading violets cover'd up in leaves;
      And mid-May's eldest child,
    The coming musk-rose, full of dewy wine,
      The murmurous haunt of flies on summer eves.

A SPECIFIC FOR UGLINESS

Darkling I listen; and for many a time
 I have been half in love with easeful Death,
Call'd him soft names in many a musèd rhyme,
 To take into the air my quiet breath;
Now more than ever seems it rich to die,
 To cease upon the midnight with no pain,
  While thou art pouring forth thy soul abroad
   In such an ecstasy!
 Still wouldst thou sing, and I have ears in vain—
  To thy high requiem become a sod.

Thou wast not born for death, immortal Bird!
 No hungry generations tread thee down;
The voice I hear this passing night was heard
 In ancient days by emperor and clown:
Perhaps the self-same song that found a path
 Through the sad heart of Ruth, when, sick for home,
  She stood in tears amid the alien corn;
   The same that ofttimes hath
 Charm'd magic casements, opening on the foam
  Of perilous seas, in faery lands forlorn.

Forlorn! the very word is like a bell
 To toll me back from thee to my sole self!
Adieu! the fancy cannot cheat so well
 As she is famed to do, deceiving elf.
Adieu! adieu! thy plaintive anthem fades
 Past the near meadows, over the still stream,
  Up the hill-side; and now 'tis buried deep
   In the next valley-glades:

Was it a vision, or a waking dream?
Fled is that music:—do I wake or sleep?

SONNET

By William Shakespeare

When, in disgrace with Fortune and men's eyes,
I all alone beweep my outcast state,
And trouble deaf heaven with my bootless cries,
And look upon myself and curse my fate,
Wishing me like to one more rich in hope,
Featured like him, like him with friends possest,
Desiring this man's art and that man's scope,
With what I most enjoy contented least;
Yet in these thoughts myself almost despising—
Haply I think on thee: and then my state,
Like to the Lark at break of day arising
From sullen earth, sings hymns at Heaven's gate;
For thy sweet love rememb'red such wealth brings
That then I scorn to change my fate with Kings.

TO HELEN

By Edgar Allan Poe

Helen, thy beauty is to me
  Like those Nicæan barks of yore,
That gently, o'er a perfumed sea,
  The weary, wayworn wanderer bore
  To his own native shore.

A SPECIFIC FOR UGLINESS

On desperate seas long wont to roam,
  Thy hyacinth hair, thy classic face,
Thy Naiad airs, have brought me home
  To the glory that was Greece
  And the grandeur that was Rome.

Lo! in yon brilliant window-niche
  How statue-like I see thee stand,
The agate lamp within thy hand!
  Ah, Psyche, from the regions which
  Are Holy Land!

TO ——

By Percy Bysshe Shelley

One word is too often profaned
  For me to profane it;
One feeling too falsely disdained
  For thee to disdain it;
One hope is too like despair
  For prudence to smother;
And pity from thee more dear
  Than that from another.

I can give not what men call love:
  But wilt thou accept not
The worship the heart lifts above
  And the heavens reject not,

The desire of the moth for the star,
  Of the night for the morrow,
The devotion to something afar
  From the sphere of our sorrow?

SONG

By Robert Burns

O my Luve's like a red, red rose
  That's newly sprung in June:
O my Luve's like the melodie
  That's sweetly play'd in tune.

As fair art thou, my bonnie lass,
  So deep in luve am I:
And I will luve thee still, my dear,
  Till a' the seas gang dry:

Till a' the seas gang dry, my dear,
  And the rocks melt wi' the sun;
I will luve thee still, my dear,
  While the sands o' life shall run.

And fare thee weel, my only Luve!
  And fare thee weel awhile!
And I will come again, my Luve,
  Tho' it were ten thousand mile.

A SPECIFIC FOR UGLINESS

From IL PENSEROSO

By John Milton

But let my due feet never fail,
To walk the studious Cloysters pale,
And love the high embowèd Roof,
With antick Pillars massy proof,
And storied Windows richly dight,
Casting a dimm religious light.
There let the pealing Organ blow,
To the full voic'd Quire below,
In Service high, and Anthems cleer,
As may with sweetnes, through mine ear,
Dissolve me into extasies,
And bring all Heav'n before mine eyes.

From LYCIDAS

By John Milton

Alas! What boots it with uncessant care
To tend the homely slighted Shepherd's trade,
And strictly meditate the thankles Muse,
Were it not better don as others use,
To sport with Amaryllis in the shade,
Or with the tangles of Neæra's hair?
Fame is the spur that the clear spirit doth raise
(That last infirmity of Noble mind)
To scorn delights, and live laborious dayes;

But the fair guerdon when we hope to find,
And think to burst out into sudden blaze,
Comes the blind Fury with th'abhorrèd shears,
And slits the thin spun life. But not the praise,
Phœbus repli'd, and touched my trembling ears;
Fame is no plant that grows on mortal soil,
Nor in the glistering foil
Set off to th'world, nor in broad rumour lies,
But lives and spreads abroad by those pure eyes,
And perfet witnes of all judging Jove;
As he pronounces lastly on each deed,
Of so much fame in Heav'n expect thy meed.

From the Paraphrase of THE RUBÁIYÁT OF OMAR KHAYYÁM

By Edward FitzGerald

I

A book of verses underneath the bough,
A jug of wine, a loaf of bread—and thou
  Beside me singing in the wilderness—
O, wilderness were Paradise enow!

Some for the glories of this world; and some
Sigh for the Prophet's Paradise to come;
  Ah, take the cash, and let the credit go,
Nor heed the rumble of a distant drum!

Look to the blowing Rose about us—"Lo,
Laughing," she says, "into the world I blow,

A SPECIFIC FOR UGLINESS

At once the silken tassel of my purse
Tear, and its treasure on the garden throw."

And those who husbanded the golden grain,
And those who flung it to the winds like rain,
  Alike to no such aureate earth are turn'd
As, buried once, men want dug up again.

The worldly hope men set their hearts upon
Turns ashes—or it prospers; and anon,
  Like snow upon the desert's dusty face,
Lighting a little hour or two—was gone.

Think, in this batter'd caravanserai
Whose portals are alternate Night and Day,
  How Sultán after Sultán with his pomp
Abode his destin'd hour, and went his way.

They say the lion and the lizard keep
The courts where Jamshyd gloried and drank deep:
  And Bahrám, that great hunter—the wild ass
Stamps o'er his head, but cannot break his sleep.

I sometimes think that never blows so red
The rose as where some buried Cæsar bled;
  That every hyacinth the garden wears
Dropp'd in her lap from some once lovely head.

And this reviving herb whose tender green
Fledges the river-lip on which we lean—
  Ah, lean upon it lightly! for who knows
From what once lovely lip it springs unseen!

BEAUTY'S WINE

Ah, my Beloved, fill the cup that clears
To-day of past regrets and future fears:
  To-morrow!—Why to-morrow I may be
Myself with Yesterday's sev'n thousand years.

For some we lov'd, the loveliest and the best
That from his vintage rolling Time has prest,
  Have drunk their cup a round or two before,
And one by one crept silently to rest.

And we, that now make merry in the room
They left, and Summer dresses in new bloom,
  Ourselves must we beneath the couch of earth
Descend—ourselves to make a couch—for whom?

Ah, make the most of what we yet may spend,
Before we too into the dust descend;
  Dust into dust, and under dust, to lie,
Sans wine, sans song, sans singer, and—sans end!

II

And if the wine you drink, the lip you press
End in what all begins and ends in—Yes;
  Think then you are To-day what Yesterday
You were—To-morrow you shall not be less.

So when the Angel of the darker drink
At last shall find you by the river-brink,
  And, offering his cup, invite your Soul
Forth to your lips to quaff—you shall not shrink.

A SPECIFIC FOR UGLINESS

Why, if the Soul can fling the dust aside,
And naked on the air of Heaven ride,
   Wer't not a shame—wer't not a shame for him
In this clay carcase crippled to abide?

'Tis but a tent where takes his one-day's rest
A Sultán to the realm of Death addrest;
   The Sultán rises, and the dark Ferrásh
Strikes, and prepares it for another guest.

And fear not lest existence closing your
Account, and mine, should know the like no more;
   The Eternal Sáki from that bowl has pour'd
Millions of bubbles like us, and will pour. . . .

III

Yet ah, that Spring should vanish with the rose!
That Youth's sweet-scented manuscript should close!
   The nightingale that in the branches sang,
Ah whence and whither flown again, who knows!

Would but the desert of the fountain yield
One glimpse—if dimly, yet indeed, reveal'd,
   To which the fainting traveller might spring,
As springs the trampled herbage of the field! . . .

Ah Love! could you and I with Him conspire
To grasp this sorry scheme of things entire,
   Would not we shatter it to bits—and then
Re-mould it nearer to the heart's desire!

Yon rising moon that looks for us again—
How oft hereafter will she wax and wane;
  How oft hereafter rising look for us
Through this same garden—and for *one* in vain!

And when like her, oh Sáki, you shall pass
Among the guests star-scatter'd on the grass,
  And in your blissful errand reach the spot
Where I made one—turn down an empty glass!

TEARS, IDLE TEARS

By Alfred Tennyson

Tears, idle tears, I know not what they mean,
Tears from the depths of some divine despair
Rise in the heart, and gather to the eyes,
In looking on the happy Autumn-fields,
And thinking of the days that are no more.

Fresh as the first beam glittering on a sail,
That brings our friends up from the underworld,
Sad as the last which reddens over one
That sinks with all we love below the verge;
So sad, so fresh, the days that are no more.

Ah, sad and strange as in dark summer dawns
The earliest pipe of half-awaken'd birds
To dying ears, when unto dying eyes
The casement slowly grows a glimmering square;
So sad, so strange, the days that are no more.

Dear as remembered kisses after death,
And sweet as those by hopeless fancy feign'd
On lips that are for others; deep as love,
Deep as first love, and wild with all regret;
O Death in Life, the days that are no more.

From THE EVE OF SAINT AGNES

By John Keats

A casement high and triple-arched there was,
All garlanded with carven imageries
Of fruits, and flowers, and bunches of knotgrass,
And diamonded with panes of quaint device,
Innumerable of stains and splendid dyes,
As are the tiger-moth's deep-damasked wings;
And in the midst, 'mong thousand heraldries,
And twilight saints, and dim emblazonings,
A shielded scutcheon blushed with blood of queens and
    kings.

Full on this casement shone the wintry moon,
And threw warm gules on Madeline's fair breast,
As down she knelt for Heaven's grace and boon;
Rose-bloom fell on her hands, together pressed,
And on her silver cross soft amethyst,
And on her hair a glory, like a saint;
She seemed a splendid angel, newly dressed,
Save wings, for Heaven—Porphyro grew faint—
She knelt so pure a thing, so free from mortal taint.

MOONLIGHT MUSIC

(*From The Merchant of Venice*)
BY WILLIAM SHAKESPEARE

How sweet the moonlight sleeps upon this bank!
Here will we sit, and let the sounds of music
Creep in our ears; soft stillness and the night
Become the touches of sweet harmony.
Sit, Jessica: Look how the floor of heaven
Is thick inlaid with patines of bright gold;
There's not the smallest orb, which thou behold'st,
But in his motion like an angel sings,
Still quiring to the young-eyed cherubins!
Such harmony is in immortal souls;
But, whilst this muddy vesture of decay
Doth grossly close it in, we cannot hear it.

SUCH STUFF AS DREAMS

(*From The Tempest*)
BY WILLIAM SHAKESPEARE

These our actors,
As I foretold you, were all spirits and
Are melted into air, into thin air:
And, like the baseless fabric of this vision,
The cloud-capp'd towers, the gorgeous palaces,
The solemn temples, the great globe itself,
Yea, all which it inherit, shall dissolve

And, like this insubstantial pageant faded,
Leave not a rack behind. We are such stuff
As dreams are made on, and our little life
Is rounded with a sleep.

MUTABILITY

By William Wordsworth

From low to high doth dissolution climb,
  And sink from high to low, along a scale
  Of awful notes, whose concord shall not fail;
A musical but melancholy chime,
Which they can hear who meddle not with crime,
  Nor avarice, nor over-anxious care.
  Truth fails not; but her outward forms that bear
The longest date do melt like frosty rime,
That in the morning whiten'd hill and plain
  And is no more; drop like the tower sublime
  Of yesterday, which royally did wear
His crown of weeds, but could not even sustain
    Some casual shout that broke the silent air
Or the unimaginable touch of Time.

ODE TO A GRECIAN URN

By John Keats

Thou still unravished bride of quietness!
  Thou foster-child of silence and slow time!
Sylvan historian, who canst thus express
  A flowery tale more sweetly than our rhyme;

What leaf-fringed legend haunts about thy shape
Of deities, or mortals, or of both,
   In Tempe or the vales of Arcady?
What men or gods are these? What maidens loth?
What mad pursuit? What struggles to escape?
   What pipes and timbrels? What wild ecstasy?

Heard melodies are sweet, but those unheard
   Are sweeter; therefore ye soft pipes, play on—
Not to the sensual ear, but more endeared,
   Pipe to the spirit ditties of no tone!
Fair youth beneath the trees, thou canst not leave
Thy song, nor even can those trees be bare;
   Bold lover, never, never canst thou kiss
Though winning near the goal, yet do not grieve—
   She cannot fade, though thou hast not thy bliss,
Forever wilt thou love and she be fair!

Ah, happy, happy boughs! that cannot shed
   Your leaves, nor ever bid the spring adieu;
And happy melodist, unwearied,
   Forever piping songs forever new;
More happy love! More happy, happy love!
   Forever warm and still to be enjoyed,
Forever panting and forever young;
All breathing human passion far above,
   That leaves a heart high sorrowful and cloyed,
A burning forehead and a parching tongue.

Who are these coming to the sacrifice?
   To what green altar, O mysterious priest,

A SPECIFIC FOR UGLINESS

Lead'st thou that heifer lowing at the skies,
   And all her silken flanks with garlands drest?
What little town by river or sea-shore,
   Or mountain-built with peaceful citadel,
Is emptied of her folk, this pious morn?
And, little town, thy streets forevermore
   Will silent be; and not a soul to tell
Why thou art desolate, will e'er return.

O Attic shape! Fair attitude! with brede
   Of marble men and maidens overwrought,
With forest branches and the trodden weed!
   Thou, silent form, dost tease us out of thought
As doth eternity! Cold pastoral!
When old age shall this generation waste,
   Thou shalt remain in midst of other woe
Than ours, a friend to man, to whom thou say'st,
"Beauty is truth, truth, beauty,—that is all
   Ye know on earth, and all ye need to know!"

℞ XII

FOR TIMES WHEN "THE WORLD IS TOO MUCH WITH US"

(Antidotes for the Strenuous Life)

THE WORLD

By William Wordsworth

The world is too much with us; late and soon,
   Getting and spending, we lay waste our powers:
   Little we see in Nature that is ours;
We have given our hearts away, a sordid boon!
This sea that bares her bosom to the moon;
   The winds that will be howling at all hours,
   And are up-gather'd now like sleeping flowers;
For this, for everything, we are out of tune;
It moves us not.—Great God! I'd rather be
   A Pagan suckled in a creed outworn;
So might I, standing on this pleasant lea,
   Have glimpses that would make me less forlorn;
Have sight of Proteus rising from the sea;
   Or hear old Triton blow his wreathèd horn.

LEISURE

By William H. Davies

What is this life if, full of care,
We have no time to stand and stare?

No time to stand beneath the boughs
And stare as long as sheep or cows.

No time to see, when woods we pass,
Where squirrels hide their nuts in grass.

No time to see, in broad daylight,
Streams full of stars, like skies at night.

No time to turn at Beauty's glance,
And watch her feet, how they can dance.

No time to wait till her mouth can
Enrich that smile her eyes began.

A poor life this if, full of care,
We have no time to stand and stare.

SIMPLICITY

By Emily Dickinson

How happy is the little stone
That rambles in the road alone,
And doesn't care about careers,
And exigencies never fears;
Whose coat of elemental brown
A passing universe put on;
And independent as the sun,
Associates or glows alone,
Fulfilling absolute decree
In casual simplicity.

NATURE CURE

By Jean Starr Untermeyer

Tell it again in stronger tones
And make your meaning plain:
White cliff, that stabs the water's side
Without the crease of pain.

You gallant maple, teasing birch,
And ruffled, stately pine,
There is a sturdy sap in you—
Share it, let it be mine.

Resistless grass, to every wind
And every scuffling tread,
You yield and bend a patient back.
So let me bow my head.

And you, dear lake, whose candid gaze
Resists my importunate soul,
You hide a secret in your depths—
Deliver it to me whole.

Invite me in and let me work
In that great pattern, planned
In beauty I must kneel before
But cannot understand.

BALLADE TO THEOCRITUS, IN WINTER

ἐσορῶν τὰν Σικελὰν ἐς ἅλα
Id. viii, 56.

By Andrew Lang

Ah! leave the smoke, the wealth, the roar
Of London, leave the bustling street,
For still, by the Sicilian shore,
The murmur of the Muse is sweet.
Still, still, the suns of summer greet
The mountain-grave of Helikê,
And shepherds still their songs repeat
Where breaks the blue Sicilian sea.

What though they worship Pan no more,
That guarded once the shepherd's seat,
They chatter of their rustic lore,
They watch the wind among the wheat;
Cicalas chirp, the young lambs bleat,
Where whispers pine to cypress tree;
They count the waves that idly beat
Where breaks the blue Sicilian sea.

Theocritus! thou canst restore
The pleasant years, and over-fleet;
With thee we live as men of yore,
We rest where running waters meet:
And then we turn unwilling feet
And seek the world—so must it be—

We may not linger in the heat
Where breaks the blue Sicilian sea!

ENVOY

Master,—when rain, and snow, and sleet
And northern winds are wild, to thee
We come, we rest in thy retreat,
Where breaks the blue Sicilian sea!

CLEAR AND COOL

By Charles Kingsley

Clear and cool, clear and cool,
By laughing shallow, and dreaming pool;
Cool and clear, cool and clear,
By shining shingle and foaming weir;
Under the crag where the ouzel sings,
And the ivied wall where the church-bell rings;
Undefiled for the undefiled;
Play by me, bathe in me, mother and child.

Dank and foul, dank and foul,
By the smoky town in its murky cowl;
Foul and dank, foul and dank,
By wharf and sewer and slimy bank;
Darker and darker the further I go,
Baser and baser the richer I grow;
Who dare sport with the sin-defiled?
Shrink from me, turn from me, mother and child.

Strong and free, strong and free;
The floodgates are open, away to the sea.
Free and strong, free and strong,
Cleansing my streams as I hurry along
To the golden sands and the leaping bar,
And the taintless tide that awaits me afar,
As I lose myself in the infinite main,
Like a soul that has sinned and is pardoned again.
Undefiled, for the undefiled;
Play by me, bathe in me, mother and child.

WHERE NONE INTRUDES

By Lord Byron

There is a pleasure in the pathless woods,
　There is a rapture on the lonely shore,
There is society, where none intrudes,
　By the deep sea, and music in its roar:
I love not man the less, but Nature more,
　From these our interviews; in which I steal
From all I may be, or have been before,
　To mingle with the universe, and feel
What I can ne'er express, yet cannot all conceal.

THE MARSHES OF GLYNN

By Sidney Lanier

Glooms of the live-oaks, beautiful-braided and woven
With intricate shades of the vines that myriad-cloven
Clamber the forks of the multiform boughs,—

> Emerald twilights,—
> Virginal shy lights,

Wrought of the leaves to allure to the whisper of vows,
When lovers pace timidly down through the green
> colonnades
Of the dim sweet woods, of the dear dark woods,
> Of the heavenly woods and glades,
That run to the radiant marginal sand-beach within
> The wide sea-marshes of Glynn;—

Beautiful glooms, soft dusks in the noonday fire,—
Wildwood privacies, closets of lone desire,
Chamber from chamber parted with wavering arras
> of leaves,—
Cells for the passionate pleasure of prayer to the soul
> that grieves,
Pure with a sense of the passing of saints through the
> wood,
Cool for the dutiful weighing of ill with good;—

O braided dusks of the oak and woven shades of the
> vine,
While the riotous noonday sun of the June-day long
> did shine
Ye held me fast in your heart and I held you fast in
> mine;
But now when the noon is no more, and riot is rest,
And the sun is a-wait at the ponderous gate of the West,
And the slant yellow beam down the wood-aisle doth
> seem

Like a lane into heaven that leads from a dream,—
Ay, now, when my soul all day hath drunken the soul of the oak,
And my heart is at ease from men, and the wearisome sound of the stroke
  Of the scythe of time and the trowel of trade is low,
  And belief overmasters doubt, and I know that I know,
  And my spirit is grown to a lordly great compass within,
That the length and the breadth and the sweep of the marshes of Glynn
Will work me no fear like the fear they have wrought me of yore
When length was fatigue, and when breadth was but bitterness sore,
And when terror and shrinking and dreary unnamable pain
Drew over me out of the merciless miles of the plain,—

Oh, now, unafraid, I am fain to face
  The vast sweet visage of space.
To the edge of the wood I am drawn, I am drawn,
Where the gray beach glimmering runs, as a belt of the dawn,
  For a mete and a mark
  To the forest-dark:—
         So:
Affable live-oak, leaning low,—
Thus—with your favor—soft, with a reverent hand,

ANTIDOTES FOR THE STRENUOUS LIFE

(Not lightly touching your person, Lord of the land!)
Bending your beauty aside, with a step I stand
On the firm-packed sand,
              Free
By a world of marsh that borders a world of sea.

  Sinuous southward and sinuous northward the shimmering band
    Of the sand-beach fastens the fringe of the marsh to the folds of the land.
  Inward and outward to northward and southward the beach-lines linger and curl
  As a silver-wrought garment that clings to and follows the firm sweet limbs of a girl.
  Vanishing, swerving, evermore curving again into sight,
  Softly the sand-beach wavers away to a dim gray looping of light.
  And what if behind me to westward the wall of the woods stands high?
  The world lies east: how ample, the marsh and the sea and the sky!
  A league and a league of marsh-grass, waist-high, broad in the blade,
  Green, and all of a height, and unflecked with a light or a shade,
  Stretch leisurely off, in a pleasant plain,
  To the terminal blue of the main.

Oh, what is abroad in the marsh and the terminal sea?
  Somehow my soul seems suddenly free

TIMES WHEN "WORLD IS WITH US"

From the weighing of fate and the sad discussion of sin,
By the length and the breadth and the sweep of the marshes of Glynn.

Ye marshes, how candid and simple and nothing-withholding and free
Ye publish yourselves to the sky and offer yourselves to the sea!
Tolerant plains, that suffer the sea and the rains and the sun,
Ye spread and span like the catholic man who hath mightily won
God out of knowledge and good out of infinite pain
And sight out of blindness and purity out of a stain.

As the marsh-hen secretly builds on the watery sod,
Behold I will build me a nest on the greatness of God:
I will fly in the greatness of God as the marsh-hen flies
In the freedom that fills all the space 'twixt the marsh and the skies:
By so many roots as the marsh-grass sends in the sod
I will heartily lay me a-hold on the greatness of God:
Oh, like to the greatness of God is the greatness within
The range of the marshes, the liberal marshes of Glynn.

And the sea lends large, as the marsh: lo, out of his plenty the sea
Pours fast: full soon the time of the flood-tide must be:

Look how the grace of the sea doth go
About and about through the intricate channels that
 flow
 Here and there,
 Everywhere,
Till his waters have flooded the uttermost creeks and
 the low-lying lanes,
And the marsh is meshed with a million veins,
That like as with rosy and silvery essences flow
 In the rose-and-silver evening glow.
 Farewell, my lord Sun!
The creeks overflow: a thousand rivulets run
'Twixt the roots of the sod; the blades of the marsh-
 grass stir;
Passeth a hurrying sound of wings that westward whirr;
Passeth, and all is still; and the currents cease to run;
And the sea and the marsh are one.

How still the plains of the waters be!
The tide is in his ecstasy;
The tide is at his highest height;
 And it is night.

And now from the Vast of the Lord will the waters of
 sleep
Roll in on the souls of men,
But who will reveal to our waking ken
The forms that swim and the shapes that creep
 Under the waters of sleep?

A CALIFORNIA VIGNETTE

(*From Tamar*)

By Robinson Jeffers

        Old cypresses
The sailor wind works into deep-sea knots
A thousand years; age-reddened granite
That was the world's cradle and crumbles apieces
Now that we're all grown up, breaks out at the roots;
And underneath it the old gray-granite strength
Is neither glad nor sorry to take the seas
Of all the storms forever and stand as firmly
As when the red hawk wings of the first dawn
Streamed up the sky over it: there is one more beautiful thing,
Water that owns the north and west and south
And is all colors and never is all quiet,
And the fogs are its breath and float along the branches of the cypresses.
And I forgot the coals of ruby lichen
That glow in the fog on the old twigs.

IN THE WOOD

By Sara Teasdale

I heard the waterfall rejoice,
   Singing like a choir,
I saw the sun flash out of it
   Azure and amber fire.

The earth was like an open flower
   Enamelled and arrayed,
The path I took to find its heart
   Fluttered with sun and shade.

And while earth lured me, gently, gently,
   Happy and all alone,
Suddenly a heavy snake
   Reared black upon a stone.

ENGLAND AND SWITZERLAND, 1802

By William Wordsworth

Two voices are there; one is of the Sea,
   One of the Mountains; each a mighty voice:
   In both from age to age thou didst rejoice,
They were thy chosen music, Liberty!
There came a tyrant, and with holy glee
   Thou fought'st against him,—but hast vainly striven:
   Thou from thy Alpine holds at length art driven,
Where not a torrent murmurs heard by thee.

—Of one deep bliss thine ear hath been bereft;
Then cleave, O cleave to that which still is left—
  For, high-soul'd Maid, what sorrow would it be
    That Mountain floods should thunder as before
    And Ocean bellow from his rocky shore,
  And neither awful Voice be heard by Thee!

THE INVITATION

By Percy Bysshe Shelley

Best and brightest, come away!
Fairer far than this fair Day,
Which, like thee to those in sorrow,
Comes to bid a sweet good-morrow
To the rough Year just awake
In its cradle on the brake.
The brightest hour of unborn Spring,
Through the winter wandering,
Found, it seems, the halcyon Morn
To hoar February born.
Bending from heaven, in azure mirth,
It kiss'd the forehead of the Earth;
And smiled upon the silent sea;
And bade the frozen streams be free;
And waked to music all their fountains;
And breathed upon the frozen mountains;
And like a prophetess of May
Strew'd flowers upon the barren way,
Making the wintry world appear
Like one on whom thou smilest, dear.

ANTIDOTES FOR THE STRENUOUS LIFE

Away, away, from men and towns,
To the wild wood and the downs—
To the silent wilderness
Where the soul need not repress
Its music lest it should not find
An echo in another's mind,
While the touch of Nature's art
Harmonizes heart to heart.
I leave this notice on my door
For each accustom'd visitor:—
"I am gone into the fields
To take what this sweet hour yields.
Reflections, you may come to-morrow;
Sit by the fireside with Sorrow.
You with the unpaid bill, Despair,—
You tiresome verse-reciter, Care,—
I will pay you in the grave,—
Death will listen to your stave.
Expectation too, be off!
To-day is for itself enough.
Hope, in pity, mock not Woe
With smiles, nor follow where I go;
Long having lived on your sweet food,
At length I find one moment's good
After long pain: with all your love,
This you never told me of."

Radiant Sister of the Day,
Awake! arise! and come away!
To the wild woods and the plains;

And the pools where winter rains
Image all their roofs of leaves;
Where the pine its garland weaves
Of sapless green and ivy dun
Round stems that never kiss the sun;
Where the lawns and pastures be,
And the sandhills of the sea;
When the melting hoar-frost wets
The daisy-star that never sets,
And wind-flowers, and violets
Which yet join not scent to hue,
Crown the pale year weak and new;
When the night is left behind
In the deep east, dun and blind,
And the blue noon is over us,
And the multitudinous
Billows murmur at our feet
Where the earth and ocean meet,
And all things seem only one
In the universal sun.

ON A SUBWAY EXPRESS

By Chester Firkins

I, who have lost the stars, the sod,
  For chilling pave and cheerless light,
Have made my meeting-place with God
  A new and nether Night—

ANTIDOTES FOR THE STRENUOUS LIFE

Have found a fane where thunder fills
    Loud caverns, tremulous;—and these
Atone me for my reverend hills
    And moonlit silences.

A figment in the crowded dark,
    Where men sit muted by the roar,
I ride upon the whirring Spark
    Beneath the city's floor.

In this dim firmament, the stars
    Whirl by in blazing files and tiers;
Kin meteors graze our flying bars,
    Amid the spinning spheres.

Speed! speed! until the quivering rails
    Flash silver where the head-light gleams,
As when on lakes the Moon impales
    The waves upon its beams.

Life throbs about me, yet I stand
    Outgazing on majestic Power;
Death rides with me, on either hand,
    In my communion hour.

You that 'neath country skies can pray,
    Scoff not at me—the city clod;—
My only respite of the Day
    Is this wild ride—with God.

SONG OF THE OPEN COUNTRY

By Dorothy Parker

*When lights are low, and the day has died,
I sit and dream of the countryside.*

Where sky meets earth at the meadow's end,
　I dream of a clean and wind-swept space
Where each tall tree is a stanch old friend,
　And each frail bud turns a trusting face.
A purling brook, with each purl a pray'r,
　To the bending grass its secret tells;
While, softly borne on the scented air,
　Comes the far-off chime of chapel bells.

A tiny cottage I seem to see,
　In its quaint old garden set apart;
And a Sabbath calm steals over me,
　While peace dwells deep in my brooding heart.

*And I thank whatever gods look down
That I am living right here in town.*

DISCOVERY

By Hermann Hagedorn

Out of the Eden of my love,
　The little house so lean and spent,
The little room where, like a dove,

Under the rafters lives my love,
  Back to the bustling world I went.

I wandered down the dusty street,
  Men jostled there and wept and swore,
But in the throbbing and the beat,
The Babel of the feverish street,
  Was something that was not before.

Deep into each pale, passing face
  I gazed in wonder. What strange gleam
Had in this gray and sordid place
Clothed as with glory each pale face,
  And lit dim eyes with dream?

Like an explorer, midst those eyes,
  By unimagined deeps I trod;
And, lo! where yesterday were lies
And lusts in those world-hardened eyes,
  I saw the stars of God.

WALLS

By Marjorie Meeker

Ask me why I peer
  Through such a narrow cranny—
I say that sky from here
  Is better than not any.

The walls that shut me in
  No mind can make immortal;

My harder will shall win
  The yet unthought-of portal.

Ask why I take root
  Where nothing green is growing—
I say that seed and shoot
  Follow the mad wind's sowing;

But where these live roots turn
  And thrust, no wall may block:
Tendril of frailest fern
  Can split a rock.

SOLITUDE

By William Allingham

Solitude is very sad,
Too much company twice as bad.

THE ESCAPE

By Lee Wilson Dodd

Out from the whirl of factional unrest,
Out from the city clamor and spent steam
Of speculative scheme and counter-scheme,
Out from the curdling spume, the very crest
Of time's froth-feathered wave, I spring—and seem
At once in a far land my heart loves best:
A land of sheltered valleys, a green nest
For the wise leisure of luxurious dream.

There, a familiar native, I frequent
The shade of ancient ilexes, or pass
A rippling shadow over rippling grass,
Or leap unharmed down some sheer, swift descent,
A light-foot Mercury; or else I lie
Like a still lake hoarding the azure sky.

UP! UP! MY FRIEND

By William Wordsworth

Up! up! my friend, and quit your books,
Or surely you'll grow double.
Up! up! my friend, and clear your looks;
Why all this toil and trouble?

The sun, above the mountain's head,
A freshening lustre mellow
Through all the long green fields has spread,
His first sweet evening yellow.

Books! 'tis a dull and endless strife:
Come, hear the woodland linnet,
How sweet his music! on my life
There's more of wisdom in it.

And hark! how blithe the throstle sings!
He, too, is no mean preacher:
Come forth into the light of things,
Let Nature be your teacher.

She has a world of ready wealth
Our minds and hearts to bless—
Spontaneous wisdom breathed by health,
Truth breathed by cheerfulness.

One impulse from a vernal wood
May teach you more of man,
Of moral evil and of good
Than all the sages can.

Sweet is the lore which Nature brings;
Our meddling intellect
Mis-shapes the beauteous forms of things:—
We murder to dissect.

Enough of science and of art;
Close up these barren leaves:
Come forth, and bring with you a heart
That watches and receives.

THERE IS STRENGTH IN THE SOIL

By Arthur Stringer

There is strength in the soil;
In the earth there is laughter and youth.
There is solace and hope in the upturned loam.
And lo, I shall plant my soul in it here like a seed!
And forth it shall come to me as a flower of song;

For I know it is good to get back to the earth
That is orderly, placid, all-patient!
It is good to know how quiet
And noncommittal it breathes,
This ample and opulent bosom
That must some day nurse us all!

A BALLAD OF TREES AND THE MASTER

By Sidney Lanier

Into the woods my Master went,
Clean forspent, forspent.
Into the woods my Master came,
Forspent with love and shame.
But the olives they were not blind to Him;
The little gray leaves were kind to Him;
The thorn-tree had a mind to Him
When into the woods He came.

Out of the woods my Master went,
And He was well content.
Out of the woods my Master came,
Content with death and shame.
When Death and Shame would woo Him last,
From under the trees they drew Him last:
'Twas on a tree they slew Him—last,
When out of the woods He came.

BEFORE DAWN IN THE WOOD

By Marguerite Wilkinson

Upon our eyelids, dear, the dew will lie,
  And on the roughened meshes of our hair,
While little feet make bold to scurry by
  And half-notes shrilly cut the quickened air.

Our clean, hard bodies, on the clean, hard ground
  Will vaguely feel that they are full of power,
And they will stir, and stretch, and look around,
  Loving the early, chill, half-lighted hour.

Loving the voices in the shadowed trees,
  Loving the feet that stir the blossoming grass—
Oh, always we have known such things as these,
  And knowing, can we love and let them pass?

ESCAPE

By James Rorty

I

THE POOL

I have come far for this cleansing;
Now I shall not hurry.
The city had tied a great stone
About my neck.
I drop it—so!
Now I can see the mountain.

I leave this soiled bundle of bitterness
In the reeds by the brink.
Now
I stand free and naked to the evening.
Hearken, O Sun,
Staring so hard at me through the balsams—you who fuse
Earth, air and water in a golden calm—
I am not strange;
I too am beautiful;
I have not forgotten—
Plunge!
See, O Sun,
The first man laughs among the fishes.

II

THE MOUNTAIN

Will you be quiet, my friends—will you gather close, you who strive so hard to do, and do?
See, I bring you gifts of silence, and cool snows.
I tell you of tall pines, erect and motionless, pointing at the sky.
I deal treacherously with your desires. I bleach your hearts. I confront your troubled faces with the old faces of the rocks.
I give your strained ears only silence, and the zoom of the night hawk.
I take the greed of the merchant, the pride of the

soldier, the terror of the driven worker, and drop
them one by one into the lake.
Will you be quiet, my friends—will you gather close
you who strive so hard to do, and do?
See, I bring you gifts of silence, and cool snows.

FLOOD TIDE [1]

By Hermann Hagedorn

Such quiet gray and green! Such peaceful farms!
No whistle here, no horn, no clamorous swarms!
Only the bay's low rippling on the beach,
The spruce's murmuring, the reed's faint speech.
Oh, sweet and moody twilight, it is good
For starving eyes and ears to find such food!
Good for the slack spine, or the quavering knee,
Good for the frightened heart to scent the sea.
Oh, dark, slow waters, creeping up these meadows,
Resistless, punctual, and mute as shadows,
What spirit, smarting, choked with dust and bruised,
Lashed by the jealous hours, by tongues confused,
Stunted by small dreams, would not thrill to see,
Once more, this pulse-beat of infinity?

MY NOSEGAYS ARE FOR CAPTIVES

By Emily Dickinson

My nosegays are for captives;
Dim, long-expectant eyes,

[1] Copyrighted 1925, by Doubleday, Page & Co.

Fingers denied the plucking,
  Patient till paradise.

To such, if they should whisper
  Of morning and the moor,
They bear no other errand,
  And I, no other prayer.

THE CREED OF THE WOOD

By Katharine Lee Bates

A whiff of forest scent,
Balsam and fern,
Won from dreary mood
My heart's return,
From its discontent,
Joy's run-away,
To the sweet, wise wood
And the laughing day.

Simple as dew and gleam
Is the creed of the wood!
The Beautiful gave us life,
And life is good.
Be the world but a dream,
Let the world go shod
With peace, not strife,
For the Dreamer is God.

"WITH PIPE AND FLUTE"
(*To Edmund Gosse*)
By Austin Dobson

With pipe and flute the rustic Pan
Of old made music sweet for man;
  And wonder hushed the warbling bird,
  And closer drew the calm-eyed herd,—
The rolling river slowlier ran.

Ah! would,—ah! would, a little span,
Some air of Arcady could fan
  This age of ours, too seldom stirred
          With pipe and flute!

But now for gold we plot and plan;
And from Beersheba unto Dan,
  Apollo's self might pass unheard,
  Or find the night-jar's note preferred;—
Not so it fared, when time began,
          With pipe and flute!

HOMESICK IN ENGLAND
By Robert Haven Schauffler

I love the glamour of English towns,
The abbeys and castles and blossoming downs,

Shakespeare's cottage, Westminster, vast
With organ notes from the dominant past,

ANTIDOTES FOR THE STRENUOUS LIFE

And English people and English beer;—
But still it is Maine I'm missing here.

I long for the sparkle and foam and dash
Of the rollicking, headlong Allagash

Where the silk fawn feeds and the eagle flies
Twenty leagues from the rails and ties.

Crushed balsam bark with the spicy smell
When the mad stream juggles the wood pellmell,

And the feel of your canthook, strangely alive,
As you shepherd the rear of the great log drive.

The lonely shores of Sourdnahunk
Where the young mink wrestle like kittens, drunk

With the heady sun and the sparkling air,
And the shy bear lurks in his shadowy lair.

Where the fierce two-pounder lustily tackles
The little green fly with the little brown hackles.

I miss the pull of my three stone pack,
And the uncut forests without a track

Where compass and map and Katahdin's peak
Are all the guides that I care to seek,

And all the companions I care to choose
Are the fox and the deer and the haughty moose;

Till I stumble on some crude trapper's den
And he shows me the kindness of primitive men,

And, after a feast of Adam's ale,
Trout and partridge and beaver tail,

The birch fire gleams on the forest walls
While my Homeric host recalls

How he swamped in white water near Roarin' Rocks
And lost that wonderful silver fox. . . .

Yes, I love the glamour of English towns,
The abbeys and castles and blossoming downs

And the scent of an English country lane,—
But none of these can make up for Maine!

THE HILL-BORN

By Maxwell Struthers Burt

You who are born of the hills,
Hill-bred, lover of hills,
Though the world may not treat you aright,
Though your soul be aweary with ills:
This will you know above other men,
In the hills you will find your peace again.

You who were nursed on the heights,
Hill-bred, lover of skies,
Though your love and your hope and your heart,
Though your trust be hurt till it dies:
This will you know above other men,
In the hills you will find your faith again.

You who are brave from the winds,
Hill-bred, lover of winds,
Though the God whom you know seems dim,
Seems lost in a mist that blinds:
This will you know above other men,
In the hills you will find your God again.

THE BROOK

By Alfred Tennyson

I come from haunts of coot and hern,
   I make a sudden sally,
And sparkle out among the fern,
   To bicker down a valley.

By thirty hills I hurry down,
   Or slip between the ridges;
By twenty thorps, a little town,
   And half a hundred bridges.

I chatter over stony ways,
   In little sharps and trebles,

I bubble into eddying bays,
  I babble on the pebbles.

With many a curve my banks I fret,
  By many a field and fallow,
And many a fairy foreland set
  With willow-weed and mallow.

I chatter, chatter, as I flow
  To join the brimming river;
For men may come and men may go,
  But I go on forever.

I wind about, and in and out,
  With here a blossom sailing,
And here and there a lusty trout,
  And here and there a grayling,

And here and there a foamy flake
  Upon me, as I travel,
With many a silvery waterbreak
  Above the golden gravel.

I steal by lawns and grassy plots,
  I slide by hazel covers;
I move the sweet forget-me-nots
  That grow for happy lovers.

<u>I slip, I slide, I gloom. I glance,</u>
  Among my skimming swallows;

I make the netted sunbeams dance
  Against my sandy shallows.

I murmur under moon and stars
  In brambly wildernesses;
I linger by my shingly bars;
  I loiter round my cresses.

And out again I curve and flow
  To join the brimming river,
For men may come and men may go,
  But I go on forever.

From THE DEEP

By Gladys Cromwell

. . . Where floating shapes of stars and leaves
Are free to dwell,
And feel the quietude of Life's
Eternal spell.

I must have peace, and so in some
Dark peace I trust,
Where thoughts like stars and leafage can
Be spun from dust.

MY GARDEN

By Thomas Edward Brown

A garden is a lovesome thing, God wot!
Rose plot,

    Fringed pool,
Fern'd grot—
    The veriest school
    Of peace; and yet the fool
Contends that God is not—
Not God! in gardens! when the eve is cool?
    Nay, but I have a sign;
    'Tis very sure God walks in mine.

COUPLET

By William Blake

Great things are done when men and mountains meet;
These are not done by jostling in the street.

VOICES [1]

By Louis Untermeyer

All day with anxious heart and wondering ear
  I listened to the city; heard the ground
  Echo with human thunder, and the sound
Go reeling down the streets and disappear.
The headlong hours, in their wild career,
  Shouted and sang until the world was drowned
  With babel-voices, each one more profound. . . .
All day it surged—but nothing could I hear.

That night the country never seemed so still;
  The trees and grasses spoke without a word

[1] From "Challenge" by Louis Untermeyer, by permission of Harcourt, Brace & Company, Inc., holders of the copyright.

To stars that brushed them with their silver wings.
Together with the moon I climbed the hill,
And, in the very heart of Silence, heard
The speech and music of immortal things.

IN ROMNEY MARSH

By John Davidson

As I went down to Dymchurch Wall,
  I heard the South sing o'er the land;
I saw the yellow sunlight fall
  On knolls where Norman churches stand.

And ringing shrilly, taut and lithe,
  Within the wind a core of sound,
The wire from Romney town to Hythe
  Alone its airy journey wound.

A veil of purple vapor flowed
  And trailed its fringe along the Straits;
The upper air like sapphire glowed;
  The roses filled heaven's central gates.

Masts in the offing wagged their tops;
  The swinging waves pealed on the shore;
The saffron beach, all diamond drops
  And beads of surge, prolonged the roar.

As I came up from Dymchurch Wall,
  I saw above the Down's low crest

The crimson bands of sunset fall,
  Flicker and fade from out the west.

Night sank; like flashes of silver fire
  The stars in one great shower came down;
Shrill blew the wind; and shrill the wire
  Rang out from Hythe to Romney town.

The darkly shining salt sea drops
  Streamed as the waves clashed on the shore;
The beach, with all its organ stops
  Pealing again, prolonged the roar.

THE DAFFODILS

By William Wordsworth

I wandered lonely as a cloud
That floats on high o'er vales and hills,
When all at once I saw a crowd,
A host of golden daffodils;
Beside the lake, beneath the trees,
Fluttering and dancing in the breeze.

Continuous as the stars that shine
And twinkle on the Milky Way,
They stretched in never-ending line
Along the margin of the bay;
Ten thousand saw I at a glance,
Tossing their heads in sprightly dance.

The waves beside them danced; but they
Outdid the sparkling waves in glee;
A poet could not but be gay
In such a jocund company;
I gazed—and gazed—but little thought
What wealth the show to me had brought.

For oft when on my couch I lie
In vacant or in pensive mood,
They flash upon that inward eye
Which is the bliss of solitude;
And then my heart with pleasure fills,
And dances with the daffodils.

From LINES COMPOSED A FEW MILES ABOVE TINTERN ABBEY

By William Wordsworth

. . . For I have learned
To look on nature, not as in the hour
Of thoughtless youth; but hearing oftentimes
The still, sad music of humanity,
Nor harsh nor grating, though of ample power
To chasten and subdue. And I have felt
A presence that disturbs me with the joy
Of elevated thoughts; a sense sublime
Of something far more deeply interfused,
Whose dwelling is the light of setting suns,
And the round ocean and the living air,
And the blue sky, and in the mind of man

A motion and a spirit, that impels
All thinking things, all objects of all thought,
And rolls through all things. Therefore am I still
A lover of the meadows and the woods,
And mountains; and of all that we behold
From this green earth; of all the mighty world
Of eye, and ear,—both what they half create,
And what perceive; well pleased to recognise
In nature and the language of the sense,
The anchor of my purest thoughts, the nurse,
The guide, the guardian of my heart, and soul
Of all my moral being.

SONNET

By John Keats

To one who has been long in city pent
'Tis very sweet to look into the fair
And open face of heaven, to breathe a prayer
Full in the smile of the blue firmament.
Who is more happy, when, with heart's content,
Fatigued he sinks into some pleasant lair
Of wavy grass, and reads a debonair
And gentle tale of love and languishment?
Returning home at evening, with an ear
Catching the notes of Philomel, an eye
Watching the sailing cloudlet's bright career,
He mourns that day so soon has glided by,
Even like the passage of an angel's tear
That falls through the clear ether silently.

THE LAKE ISLE OF INNISFREE
By William Butler Yeats

I will arise and go now, and go to Innisfree,
And a small cabin build there, of clay and wattles made;
Nine bean rows will I have there, a hive for the honey bee,
And live alone in the bee-loud glade.

And I shall have some peace there, for peace comes dropping slow,
Dropping from the veils of the morning to where the cricket sings;
There midnight's all a-glimmer, and noon a purple glow,
And evening full of the linnet's wings.

I will arise and go now, for always night and day
I hear lake water lapping with low sounds by the shore;
While I stand on the roadway, or on the pavements gray,
I hear it in the deep heart's core.

℞ XIII

"PILLS TO PURGE MELANCHOLY"
(Poems of Cheer)

LAUGH AND BE MERRY

By John Masefield

Laugh and be merry; remember, better the world with a song,
Better the world with a blow in the teeth of a wrong.
Laugh, for the time is brief, a thread the length of a span.
Laugh and be proud to belong to the old proud pageant of man.

Laugh and be merry; remember, in olden time,
God made Heaven and Earth for joy He took in a rime,
Made them, and filled them full with the strong red wine of His mirth,
The splendid joy of the stars, the joy of the earth.

So we must laugh and drink from the deep blue cup of the sky,
Join the jubilant song of the great stars sweeping by,
Laugh, and battle, and work, and drink of the wine outpoured
In the dear green earth, the sign of the joy of the Lord.

Laugh and be merry together, like brothers akin,
Guesting awhile in the rooms of a beautiful inn,

Glad till the dancing stops, and the lilt of the music ends.
Laugh till the game is played; and be you merry, my friends.

SADNESS AND JOY

By William H. Davies

I pray you, Sadness, leave me soon,
   In sweet invention thou art poor!
Thy sister, Joy, can make ten songs
   While thou art making four.

One hour with thee is sweet enough;
   But when we find the whole day gone
And no created thing is left—
   We mourn the evil done.

Thou art too slow to shape thy thoughts
   In stone, on canvas, or in song;
But Joy, being full of active heat,
   Must do some deed ere long.

Thy sighs are gentle, sweet thy tears;
   But if thou canst not help a man
To prove in substance what he feels—
   Then give me Joy, who can.

Therefore, sweet Sadness, leave me soon,
   Let thy bright sister, Joy, come more;

For she can make ten lovely songs
While thou art making four.

TO A FRIEND WHOSE WORK HAS COME TO NOTHING

By William Butler Yeats

Now all the truth is out,
Be secret and take defeat
From any brazen throat,
For how can you compete,
Being honour bred, with one
Who, were it proved he lies,
Were neither shamed in his own
Nor in his neighbours' eyes?
Bred to a harder thing
Than Triumph, turn away
And like a laughing string
Whereon mad fingers play
Amid a place of stone,
Be secret and exult,
Because of all things known
That is most difficult.

GLADNESS

By Anna Hempstead Branch

The world has brought not anything
To make me glad to-day!

The swallow had a broken wing,
And after all my journeying
There was no water in the spring—
  My friend has said me nay.
But yet somehow I needs must sing
  As on a luckier day.

Dusk falls as gray as any tear,
  There is no hope in sight!
But something in me seems so fair,
That like a star I needs must wear
A safety made of shining air
  Between me and the night.
Such inner weavings do I wear
  All fashioned of delight!

I need not for these robes of mine
  The loveliness of earth,
But happenings remote and fine
Like threads of dreams will blow and shine
In gossamer and crystalline,
  And I was glad from birth.
So even while my eyes repine,
  My heart is clothed in mirth.

OVER THE SHOULDERS AND SLOPES OF THE DUNE

By Bliss Carman

Over the shoulders and slopes of the dune
I saw the white daisies go down to the sea,

A host in the sunshine, an army in June,
The people God sends us to set our hearts free.

The bobolinks rallied them up from the dell,
The orioles whistled them out of the wood,
And all of their singing was "Earth it is well,"
    And all of their dancing was "Life, thou art good."

GOLDEN HANDS

(Author Unknown)

Golden hands,
Golden wings,
With thy fiery radiance
Scorch and consume all ills and evil,
And bring the day
That will press my heart against the heart of God.

From PSALM XCV

O come, let us sing unto the Lord:
Let us make a joyful noise to the Rock of our salvation.
Let us come before his presence with thanksgiving,
And make a joyful noise unto him with psalms.
For the Lord is a great God,
And a great King above all gods.
In his hand are the deep places of the earth:
The strength of the hills is his also.

The sea is his, and he made it:
And his hands formed the dry land.
O come, let us worship and bow down:
Let us kneel before the Lord our maker.

THE PLACE OF REST

By A. E.

The soul is its own witness and its own refuge

Unto the deep the deep heart goes,
It lays its sadness nigh the breast:
Only the Mighty Mother knows
The wounds that quiver unconfessed.

It seeks a deeper silence still;
It folds itself around with peace,
Where thoughts alike of good or ill
In quietness unfostered cease.

It feels in the unwounding vast
For comfort for its hopes and fears:
The Mighty Mother bows at last;
She listens to her children's tears.

Where the last anguish deepens—there
The fire of beauty smites through pain:
A glory moves amid despair,
The Mother takes her child again.

A BLACKBIRD SUDDENLY

By Joseph Auslander

Heaven is in my hand, and I
Touch a heart-beat of the sky,
Hearing a blackbird's cry.

Strange, beautiful, unquiet thing,
Lone flute of God, how can you sing
Winter to spring?

You have outdistanced every voice and word,
And given my spirit wings until it stirred
Like you—a bird!

ANGLER

By Isabel Fiske Conant

I go a-fishing
With a jointed rod,
In a still river
By a field of God.

Sometimes the sinker
Is a leaden grief.
Sometimes the bait is
Joy, light as a leaf.

Few the soft splashes
On a sunny day,

The circles widen mostly
When the skies are gray.

Even when returning
With no shining string,
I have watched by water
And heard the thrush sing.

THE SECRET

By Jessie B. Rittenhouse

I go in vesture spun by hands
 Upon no loom of earth,
I dwell within a shining house
 That has no walls nor hearth;

I live on food more exquisite
 Than honey of the bee,
More delicate than manna
 It falls to nourish me;

But none may see my shining house,
 Nor taste my food so rare,
And none may see my moon-spun robe
 Nor my star-powdered hair.

JOY

By Hilda Conkling

Joy is not a thing you can see.
It is what you feel when you watch waves breaking,

Or when you peer through a net of woven violet stems
In Spring grass.
It is not sunlight, not moonlight,
But a separate shining.
Joy lives behind people's eyes.

Reprinted by permission of F. A. Stokes Company, from Shoes of the Wind by Hilda Conkling, copyrighted, 1922.

From L'ALLEGRO

By John Milton

Haste thee nymph, and bring with thee
Jest and youthful Jollity,
Quips and Cranks, and wanton Wiles
Nods, and Becks, and Wreathèd Smiles
Such as hang on Hebe's cheek,
And love to live in dimple sleek;
Sport that wrinkled Care derides,
And Laughter holding both his sides.
Com, and trip it as ye go
On the light fantastick toe,
And in thy right hand lead with thee,
The Mountain Nymph, sweet Liberty;
And if I give thee honour due,
Mirth, admit me of thy crue
To live with her, and live with thee,
In unreprovèd pleasures free;
To hear the Lark begin his flight,
And singing startle the dull night,
From his watch-towre in the skies,
Till the dappled dawn doth rise;

Then to com in spight of sorrow,
And at my window bid good morrow,
Through the Sweet-Briar, or the Vine,
Or the twisted Eglantine.
While the Cock with lively din,
Scatters the rear of darknes thin,
And to the stack, or the Barn dore,
Stoutly struts his Dames before,
Oft list'ning how the Hounds and horn
Chearly rouse the slumbring morn,
From the side of som Hoar Hill,
Through the high wood echoing shrill.
Som time walking not unseen
By Hedge-row Elms, on Hillocks green,
Right against the Eastern gate,
Wher the great Sun begins his state,
Rob'd in flames, and Amber light,
The clouds in thousand Liveries dight.
While the Plowman neer at hand,
Whistles ore the Furrow'd Land,
And the Milkmaid singeth blithe,
And the Mower whets his sithe,
And every Shepherd tells his tale
Under the Hawthorn in the dale. . . .
Som times with secure delight
The up-land Hamlets will invite,
When the merry Bells ring round,
And the jocond rebecks sound
To many a youth, and many a maid,
Dancing in the Chequer'd shade;

And young and old com forth to play
On a Sunshine Holyday. . . .
   Towred Cities please us then,
And the busie humm of men,
Where throngs of Knights and Barons bold,
In weeds of Peace high triumphs hold,
With store of Ladies, whose bright eies
Rain influence, and judge the prise
Of Wit, or Arms, while both contend
To win her Grace, whom all commend.
There let Hymen oft appear
In Saffron robe, with Taper clear,
And pomp, and feast, and revelry,
With mask, and antique Pageantry,
Such sights as youthfull Poets dream
On Summer eeves by haunted stream.
Then to the well-trod stage anon,
If Jonsons learnèd Sock be on,
Or sweetest Shakespear fancies childe,
Warble his native Wood-notes wilde,
And ever against eating Cares,
Lap me in soft Lydian Aires,
Married to immortal verse
Such as the meeting soul may pierce
In notes, with many a winding bout
Of linckèd sweetnes long drawn out,
With wanton heed, and giddy cunning,
The melting voice through mazes running;
Untwisting all the chains that ty
The hidden soul of harmony.

That Orpheus self may heave his head
From golden slumber on a bed
Of heapt Elysian flowres, and hear
Such streins as would have won the ear
Of Pluto, to have quite set free
His half regain'd Eurydice.
These delights, if thou canst give,
Mirth with thee, I mean to live.

JENNY KISSED ME

By Leigh Hunt

Jenny kissed me when we met,
  Jumping from the chair she sat in;
Time, you thief, who love to get
  Sweets into your list, put that in!
Say I'm weary, say I'm sad,
  Say that health and wealth have missed me,
Say I'm growing old, but add,
  Jenny kissed me.

VILLANELLE, WITH STEVENSON'S ASSISTANCE

By Franklin P. Adams

The world is so full of a number of things
  Like music and pictures and statues and plays,
I'm sure we should all be as happy as kings.

We've winters and summers and autumns and springs,
  We've Aprils and Augusts, Octobers and Mays—
The world is so full of a number of things.

Though minor the key of my lyrical strings,
  I change it to major when pæaning praise:
I'm sure we should all be as happy as kings.

Each morning a myriad wonderments brings,
  Each evening a myriad marvels conveys,
The world is so full of a number of things.

With pansies and roses and pendants and rings,
  With purples and yellows and scarlets and grays,
I'm sure we should all be as happy as kings.

So pardon a bard if he carelessly sings
  A solo indorsing these Beautiful Days—
The world is so full of a number of things,
I'm sure we should all be as happy as kings.

COMMUNION

By Sophie Jewett

Dusk of a lowering evening,
  Chill of a northern zone,
Pitiful press of worn faces,
  And an exiled heart alone.

Warm, as with sun of the tropic,
  Keen, as with salt of the sea,
Sweet, as with breath of blown roses,
  Cometh thy thought to me.

WHEN YOU ARE OLD

By William Butler Yeats

When you are old and gray and full of sleep
  And nodding by the fire, take down this book,
  And slowly read, and dream of the soft look
Your eyes had once, and of their shadows deep;

How many loved your moments of glad grace,
  And loved your beauty with love false or true;
  But one man loved the pilgrim soul in you,
And loved the sorrows of your changing face.

And bending down beside the glowing bars,
  Murmur, a little sadly, how love fled
  And paced upon the mountains overhead,
And hid his face amid a crowd of stars.

From THE DEATH SONG

in The Masque of Taliesin

By Richard Hovey

Man from his blindness attaining the succor of sight,
  God from his glory descends to the shape we can see;

Life, like a moon, is a radiant pearl in the night
  Thrilled with his beauty to beacon o'er forest and
    sea;
Life, like a sacrifice laid on the altar, delight
  Kindles as flame from the air to be fire at its core!
Joy, joy, joy in the deep and the height!
  Joy in the holiest, joy evermore, evermore!

THE OPTIMIST

By Graham R. Tomson

Heed not the folk who sing or say
  In sonnet sad or sermon chill,
"Alas! alack! and well-a-day!
  This round world's but a bitter pill!"
  Poor porcupines of fretful quill!
Sometimes we quarrel with our lot:
  We, too, are sad and careful—still,
We'd rather be alive than not.

What though we wish the cats at play
  Would some one else's garden till;
Though Sophonisba drop the tray
  And all our worshipped Worcester spill,
  Though neighbours "practice" loud and shrill,
Though May be cold and June be hot,
  Though April freeze and August grill,—
We'd rather be alive than not.

And, sometimes, on a summer's day
  To self and every mortal ill

We give the slip, we steal away,
  To lie beside some sedgy rill;
  The darkening years, the cares that kill,
A little while are well forgot;
  Deep in the broom upon the hill
We'd rather be alive than not.

Pistol, with oaths didst thou fulfil
  The task thy braggart tongue begot.
We eat our leek with better will,
  We'd rather be alive than not.

A LITTLE SONG OF LIFE

By Lizette Woodworth Reese

Glad that I live am I;
That the sky is blue;
Glad for the country lanes,
And the fall of dew.

After the sun the rain
After the rain the sun;
This is the way of life,
Till the work be done.

All that we need to do,
Be we low or high,
Is to see that we grow
Nearer the sky.

From PSALM CIII

By David

Bless the Lord, O my soul:
And all that is within me, bless his holy name.
Bless the Lord, O my soul,
And forget not all his benefits:
Who forgiveth all thine iniquities;
Who healeth all thy diseases;
Who redeemeth thy life from destruction;
Who crowneth thee with lovingkindness and tender
    mercies;
Who satisfieth thy mouth with good things;
So that thy youth is renewed like the eagle's. . . .
He hath not dealt with us after our sins;
Nor rewarded us according to our iniquities.
For as the heaven is high above the earth,
So great is his mercy toward them that fear him.
As far as the east is from the west,
So far hath he removed our transgressions from us.
Like as a father pitieth his children,
So the Lord pitieth them that fear him.
For he knoweth our frame;
He remembereth that we are dust.
As for man, his days are as grass:
As a flower of the field, so he flourisheth.
For the wind passeth over it, and it is gone;

And the place thereof shall know it no more.
But the mercy of the Lord is from everlasting to ever
 lasting
Upon them that fear him,
And his righteousness unto children's children. . . .
Bless the Lord, all his works in all places of his do
 minion:
Bless the Lord, O my soul.

℞ XIV

ANODYNES FOR SORROW

(To be Taken in the Hour of Great Need)

INVICTUS

By William Ernest Henley

Out of the night that covers me,
　Black as the pit from pole to pole,
I thank whatever gods may be
　For my unconquerable soul.

In the fell clutch of circumstance
　I have not winced nor cried aloud.
Under the bludgeonings of chance
　My head is bloody, but unbow'd.

Beyond this place of wrath and tears
　Looms but the Horror of the shade,
And yet the menace of the years
　Finds and shall find me unafraid.

It matters not how strait the gate,
　How charged with punishments the scroll,
I am the master of my fate:
　I am the captain of my soul.

IF SO TOMORROW SAVES

By Christina Rossetti

Heaven overarches earth and sea,
　Earth-sadness and sea-bitterness.

Heaven overarches you and me:
A little while and we shall be—
Please God—where there is no more sea
  Nor barren wilderness.

Heaven overarches you and me,
  And all earth's gardens and her graves.
Look up with me, until we see
The day break and the shadows flee.
What though to-night wrecks you and me
  If so to-morrow saves?

THE BALANCE

By George Sterling

Let us be just with life. Although it bear
  A thousand thorns for every perfect rose,
  And though the happy day have mournful close,
Slumber awaits to house the mind from care.
Howe'er the shoe pinch, still must we compare
  Unnumbered friends with so infrequent foes.
  The path we know—its end what traveller knows?
Appraising life, let us at least be fair.

Whose memory but holds the blinding bliss
Of love's high-noon and paradisal kiss?
  Say not, in hours when deepening shadows fall,
    That life is ill, but leave the pain unsaid,
    Knowing that in those gracious moments fled
  The far and mighty joy repaid for all.

ILLUSION

By Nevah Trebor

Sundown is but the mortal eye's confusion,
  Like death, the great illusion.

The spirit whose corporeal ember chills
  Is bright on farther hills.

Bird-man, fly westward with the westering light,--
  Would you outdistance Night.

THE WIND OF SORROW

By Henry Van Dyke

The fire of love was burning, yet so low
  That in the peaceful dark it made no rays,
  And in the light of perfect-placid days
The ashes hid the smouldering embers' glow.
Vainly, for love's delight, we sought to throw
  New pleasures on the pyre to make it blaze:
  In life's calm air and tranquil-prosperous ways
We missed the radiant heat of long ago.

Then in the night, a night of sad alarms,
  Bitter with pain and black with fog of fears
That drove us trembling to each other's arms,
  Across the gulf of darkness and salt tears

Into life's calm the wind of sorrow came,
And fanned the fire of love to clearest flame.

VICTORY IN DEFEAT

By Edwin Markham

Defeat may serve as well as victory
To shake the soul and let the glory out.
When the great oak is straining in the wind,
The boughs drink in new beauty, and the trunk
Sends down a deeper root on the windward side.
Only the soul that knows the mighty grief
Can know the mighty rapture. Sorrows come
To stretch out spaces in the heart for joy.

SONGS OF JOY

By William H. Davies

Sing out, my Soul, thy songs of joy;
   Such as a happy bird will sing
Beneath a Rainbow's lovely arch
   In early spring.

Think not of Death in thy young days;
   Why shouldst thou that grim tyrant fear,
And fear him not when thou art old,
   And he is near.

FOR THE HOUR OF GREAT NEED

Strive not for gold, for greedy fools
   Measure themselves by poor men never;
Their standard still being richer men,
   Makes them poor ever.

Train up thy mind to feel content,
   What matters then how low thy store?
What we enjoy, and not possess,
   Makes rich or poor.

Filled with sweet thought, then happy I
   Take not my state from others' eyes;
What's in my mind—not on my flesh
   Or theirs—I prize.

Sing, happy Soul, thy songs of joy;
   Such as a Brook sings in the wood,
That all night has been strengthened by
   Heaven's purer flood.

PIPPA'S SONG

By Robert Browning

The year's at the spring,
And day's at the morn;
Morning's at seven;
The hill-side's dew-pearl'd;
The lark's on the wing;
The snail's on the thorn;
God's in His heaven—
All's right with the world!

IDLE TO GRIEVE

By Duncan Campbell Scott

Idle to grieve when the stars are clear above me,
When the bright waters bubble in the spring,
Idle to grieve when there are storms to prove me
And birds that seek me out to come and sing.

Idle to grieve, the light is on the highway,
There are the mountain meadows to achieve,
Beyond in the pass the airy heights are my way,
Idle to grieve, glad heart, idle to grieve.

DUET

(*I sing with myself*)

By Leonora Speyer

Out of my sorrow
I'll build a stair,
And every to-morrow
Will climb to me there—

>   *With ashes of yesterday
>   In its hair.*

My fortune is made
Of a stab in the side,
My debts are paid
In pennies of pride—

> *Unminted coins*
> *In a heart I hide.*

The stones that I eat
Are ripe for my needs,
My cup is complete
With the dregs of deeds—

> *Clear are the notes*
> *Of my broken reeds.*

I carry my pack
Of aches and stings,
Light with the lack
Of all good things—

> *But not on my back,*
> *Because of my wings!*

COMFORT

By Margaret French Patton

If grief should come to me
Like a big wind bringing the rain,
Or if sorrow should cramp my heart
With its pain,

I know where my heart would turn,
As a battered flower to the sun,—

To your face—with its wrinkled smile—
And its fun.

THE MINISTERING SPIRITS

By Edmund Spenser

How oft do they their silver bowers leave,
To come to succour us that succour want!
How oft do they with golden pineons cleave
The flitting skyes, like flying Pursuivant,
Against fowle feendes to ayd us militant!
They for us fight, they watch and dewly ward,
And their bright Squadrons round about us plant;
And all for love, and nothing for reward.
O! why should hevenly God to men have such regard?

I LOVE THE FRIENDLY FACES OF OLD SORROWS

By Karle Wilson Baker

I love the friendly faces of old Sorrows;
I have no secrets that they do not know.
They are so old, I think they have forgotten
What bitter words were spoken, long ago.

I hate the cold, stern faces of new Sorrows
Who stand and watch, and catch me all alone.
I should be braver if I could remember
How different the older ones have grown.

TEARS

By Elizabeth Barrett Browning

Thank God, bless God, all ye who suffer not
More grief than ye can weep for. That is well—
That is light grieving! lighter, none befell
Since Adam forfeited the primal lot.
Tears! what are tears? The babe weeps in its cot,
The mother singing; at her marriage-bell
The bride weeps, and before the oracle
Of high-faned hills the poet has forgot
Such moisture on his cheeks. Thank God for grace,
Ye who weep only! If, as some have done,
Ye grope tear-blinded in a desert place
And touch but tombs,—look up! those tears will run
Soon in long rivers down the lifted face,
And leave the vision clear for stars and sun.

TEARS

By Lizette Woodworth Reese

When I consider Life and its few years—
A wisp of fog betwixt us and the sun;
A call to battle, and the battle done
Ere the last echo dies within our ears;
A rose choked in the grass; an hour of fears;
The gusts that past a darkening shore do beat;
The burst of music down an unlistening street,—
I wonder at the idleness of tears.
Ye old, old dead, and ye of yesternight,

Chieftains, and bards, and keepers of the sheep,
By every cup of sorrow that you had,
Loose me from tears, and make me see aright
How each hath back what once he stayed to weep:
Homer his sight, David his little lad!

PANDORA'S SONG

(*From the Fire-Bringer*)

By William Vaughn Moody

Of wounds and sore defeat
I made my battle stay;
Winged sandals for my feet
I wove of my delay;
Of weariness and fear
I made my shouting spear;
Of loss, and doubt and dread,
And swift oncoming doom,
I made a helmet for my head
And a floating plume.
From the shutting mist of death,
From the failure of the breath,
I made a battle-horn to blow
Across the vales of overthrow.
O hearken, love, the battle-horn!
The triumph clear, the silver scorn!
O hearken where the echoes bring,
Down the grey disastrous morn,
Laughter and rallying.

AUTHOR'S INDEX

Adams, Franklin P.	The Rich Man	76
	"Such Stuff as Dreams"	78
	Villanelle, with Stevenson's Assistance	358
A. E.	Hope in Failure	13
	The Place of Rest	352
Aldrich, Thomas Bailey	Enamoured Architect of Airy Rhyme	26
Allen, Hervey	We	106
Allingham, William	Solitude	324
Arnold, Matthew	Immortality	40
	On the Death of a Favourite Canary	210
	From A Summer Night	154
Auslander, Joseph	A Blackbird Suddenly	353
Baker, Karle Wilson	Courage	37
	I Love the Friendly Faces of Old Sorrows	374
Bates, Arlo	The Pool of Sleep	132
Bates, Katharine Lee	The Creed of the Wood	331
Belloc, Hilaire	The Night	120
Benét, William Rose	The Falconer of God	174
	His Ally	36
Benét, Stephen Vincent	Portrait of a Boy	173
Benson, E. F.	Prayer	22
Binyon, Lawrence	For Mercy, Courage, Kindness, Mirth	245
Blake, William	Couplet	338
	The Tiger	183
Blount, Edward Augustus, Jr.	A Crew Poem	82
Branch, Anna Hempstead	Gladness	349
	So I May Feel the Hands of God	208

377

AUTHOR'S INDEX

Author	Title	Page
Brontë, Emily	Last Lines	10
	The Old Stoic	39
Brown, Thomas Edward	My Garden	332
Browning, Elizabeth Barrett	Tears	375
	Work	277
Browning, Robert	From Apparent Failure	24
	Epilogue to Asolando	12
	Give a Rouse	257
	"How They Brought the Good News from Ghent to Aix"	261
	My Star	180
	Pippa's Song	371
	Prospice	9
	The Wild Joys of Living	263
Bunner, Henry Cuyler	A Pitcher of Mignonette	220
Burns, Robert	Auld Lang Syne	241
	Song	290
Burroughs, John	Waiting	275
Burt, Maxwell Struthers	The Hill-Born	334
Byron	Where None Intrudes	310
Calverley, Charles Stuart	Ballad	77
Carman, Bliss	Envoy	276
	Over the Shoulders and Slopes of the Dune	350
	From The Word at St. Kavin's	279
Carroll, Lewis	Father William	85
	Poeta Fit, Non Nascitur	70
Chesterton, Gilbert K.	Lepanto	249
Cleghorn, Sarah N.	"An Air of Coolness Plays upon His Face"	154
	The Anodyne	163
	For Sleep When Overtired or Worried	118
	O Altitudo!	6
	To Safeguard the Heart from Hardness	213
Clough, Arthur Hugh	Say Not the Struggle Naught Availeth	28

AUTHOR'S INDEX

Clough, Arthur Hugh	"With Whom Is No Variableness, Neither Shadow of Turning"	280
Coleridge, Samuel Taylor	Kubla Khan	167
	From The Rime of the Ancient Mariner	212
Conant, Isabel Fiske	Angler	353
	Kind Sleep	117
Cone, Helen Gray	The Spark	207
Conkling, Grace Hazard	A Child's Song Overheard	169
Conkling, Hilda	Joy	354
Cowper, William	On One Ignorant and Arrogant	147
Cromwell, Gladys	From The Deep	337
Crosby, Ernest	From Town Pictures	225
David	From Psalm XIX	140
	Psalm XXIII	39
	From Psalm CIII	363
Davidson, John	In Romney Marsh	339
Davies, Mary Carolyn	The Door	232
Davies, William H.	Ale	104
	Leisure	305
	Sadness and Joy	348
	Songs of Joy	370
Dickinson, Emily	I'm Nobody!	137
	Morning	169
	My Nosegays Are for Captives	330
	Simplicity	306
Dobson, Austin	Don Quixote	26
	"With Pipe and Flute"	332
Dodd, Lee Wilson	The Escape	324
	More Life . . . More!	95
Driscoll, Louise	God's Pity	230
Emerson, Ralph Waldo	Days	142
	Each and All	156
	The Mountain and the Squirrel	148
Erskine, John	Dedication	240
Evans, Florence Wilkinson	The Flower Factory	217

AUTHOR'S INDEX

Ficke, Arthur Davison	Portrait of an Old Woman 231
Field, Eugene	Little Boy Blue 213
	Wynken, Blynken and Nod 127
Firkins, Chester	On a Subway Express 320
Fitzgerald, Edward	From the Paraphrase of The Rubáiyát of Omár Khayyám 292
Fitzgerald, Edward	From The Rubáiyát of Omár Khayyám 146
Flecker, James Elroy	The Old Ships 171
Fletcher, John	Care-Charming Sleep 123
	Sleep 131
Frost, Robert	The Tuft of Flowers 242
Gale, Norman	The Second Coming 239
	To Sleep (Extract) 124
Garland, Hamlin	Do You Fear the Wind? 21
Garrison, Theodosia	Compensation 162
	One Fight More 47
Gates, Ellen M. Huntington	Sleep Sweet 133
Gay, John	From Lines on a Lap Dog 205
Gilbert, W. S.	Ferdinando and Elvira 55
	The Heavy Dragoon 82
Guiney, Louise Imogen	Doves 16
	The Kings 4
	The Wild Ride 270
Guiterman, Arthur	Strictly Germ-Proof 60
Hagedorn, Hermann	Discovery 322
	Flood Tide 330
	Ladders Through the Blue 155
Harvey, F. W.	From Ducks 84
Helton, Roy	The Song of Dark Waters 232
	A Street Car Symphony 175
Henley, William Ernest	Invictus 367
Herbert, George	From The Collar 109
Herford, Oliver	The Chimpanzee 54
Heyward, DuBose	Epitaph for a Poet 27
Hodgson, Ralph	The Bells of Heaven 205

AUTHOR'S INDEX

Author	Title	Page
Hodgson, William Noel	Before Action	32
Hood, Thomas	The Bridge of Sighs	221
Hovey, Richard	Comrades	256
	At the End of the Day	3
	From The Death Song of Taliesin	360
	Vagabondia	89
Howe, M. A. DeWolfe	At the Heart	160
	The Helmsman	14
	A Treasure House	277
Hunt, Leigh	Abou Ben Adhem	228
	Jenny Kissed Me	358
Jeffers, Robinson	A California Vignette	316
	Not Our Good Luck	158
	Salmon Fishing	209
	Suicide's Stone	35
	From Tamar	107
	To the Stone Cutters	138
Jewett, Sophie	Communion	359
	Sleep	119
	The Soldier	35
Kaupman, George	Advice to Worriers	83
Keats, John	From The Eve of Saint Agnes	297
	Fancy	198
	From To Homer	36
	Ode to a Grecian Urn	299
	Ode to a Nightingale	285
	To Sleep	117
	Sonnet	342
Kingsley, Charles	Clear and Cool	309
Lampman, Archibald	Midsummer Night	125
Landor, Walter Savage	Finis	161
Lang, Andrew	Ballade to Theocritus, in Winter	308
	The Odyssey	264
Lanier, Sidney	A Ballad of Trees and the Master	327
	The Marshes of Glynn	310
Lear, Edward	The Jumblies	62

AUTHOR'S INDEX

Loines, Russell Hillard	On a Magazine Sonnet	80
Long, Haniel	Dead Men Tell No Tales	179
Longfellow, Henry Wadsworth	The Arrow and the Song	278
Longley, Snow	Sonnet	161
Lovelace, Richard	To Althea, from Prison	41
de la Mare, Walter	Tartary	188
Markham, Edwin	The Man with the Hoe	237
	Outwitted	242
	Victory in Defeat	370
Marquis, Don	Spring Ode	53
	Unrest	266
Masefield, John	Laugh and Be Merry	347
Matthews, Brander	The Ballade of Adaptation	64
Meeker, Marjorie	Walls	323
Middleton, Scudder	A Woman	229
Millay, Edna St. Vincent	First Fig	89
Miller, Joaquin	Byron	245
	From Columbus	46
	For Those Who Fail	38
Milton, John	From Il Penseroso	291
	From Il Penseroso	184
	From Il Penseroso	123
	From L'Allegro	355
	From Lycidas	291
	On His Blindness	276
	To Cyriack Skinner	94
	To Mr. Lawrence	93
Moody, William Vaughn	Pandora's Song	376
Moore, Hamilton	A Fine New Ballad of Cawsand Bay	68
Moore, Virginia	Courage	28
Morgan, Angela	Grief	22
Morley, Christopher	Epitaph for Any New Yorker	61
	From Sleep	121
	Verification	201
Myers, F. W. H.	From Saint Paul	280

AUTHOR'S INDEX

Neihardt, John G.	Let Me Live Out My Years	41
Newman, Cardinal John Henry	The Pillar of Cloud	34
O'Sheel, Shaemas	Exultation	267
Parker, Dorothy	Song of the Open Country	322
Patmore, Coventry	Fool and Wise	160
	The Kiss	76
	Magna est Veritas	281
	The Toys	214
Patton, Margaret French	Comfort	373
Perry, Lilla Cabot	Death, Life, Fear	19
	Horseman Springing from the Dark: A Dream	43
Phillips, Stephen	From Herod	196
Poe, Edgar Allan	To Helen	288
Pulsifer, Harold Trowbridge	Ecstasy	95
	The Riderless Horse	42
Raleigh, Sir Walter	His Pilgrimage	182
Reese, Lizette Woodworth	Heroism	46
	A Little Song of Life	362
	Tears	375
Rittenhouse, Jessie B.	My Wage	141
	The Secret	354
Roberts, Charles G. D.	All Night the Lone Cicada	25
Robinson, Edwin Arlington	From Captain Craig	29
Rorty, James	The Bell	96
	Escape	328
Rossetti, Christina	Come, Blessed Sleep	119
	If So Tomorrow Saves	367
	Let Me Sleep	131
Rossetti, Dante Gabriel	The Blessed Damozel	190
Sandburg, Carl	They Will Say	219
	Joy	161
Savage-Armstrong, George Francis	One in the Infinite	139
Schauffler, Robert Haven	Harvest	229

AUTHOR'S INDEX

Schauffler, Robert Haven	Homesick in England	332
	"Scum o' the Earth"	233
Scott, Duncan Campbell	An August Mood	147
	Be Strong!	15
	Idle to Grieve	372
	A Road Song	100
Shakespeare, William	King Henry before Harfleur	265
	Mercy	240
	Moonlight Music	298
	Queen Mab	171
	Sonnet	288
	Such Stuff as Dreams	298
	Where Is Fancy Bred?	198
Shelley, Percy Bysshe	Closing Lines of Prometheus Unbound	49
	The Invitation	318
	My Soul Is an Enchanted Boat	128
	From Ode to the West Wind	48
	Ozymandias	137
	The Poet's Dream	197
	To ——	289
	To Sleep	121
Sidney, Sir Philip	After Blenheim	143
Southey, Robert	From The Faerie Queene	130
Spenser, Edmund	From The Faerie Queene	122
	The Idle Lake	96
	The Ministering Spirits	374
Speyer, Leonora	Duet	372
	From "Of Mountains"	19
	Measure Me, Sky!	153
	Protest in Passing	42
Stephen, James Kenneth	A Sonnet	79
Sterling, George	The Balance	368
Stevenson, Robert Louis	The Celestial Surgeon	108
	If This Were Faith	44
Stringer, Arthur	Life-Drunk	105

AUTHOR'S INDEX

Author	Title	Page
Stringer, Arthur	There Is Strength in the Soil	326
Strong, L. A. G.	The Madman	196
	Rufus Prays	220
Tabb, John B.	The Difference	61
	Sleep	132
Teasdale, Sara	In the Wood	317
	Lessons	14
Tennyson, Alfred	The Brook	335
	The Charge of the Light Brigade	258
	Flower in the Crannied Wall	158
	From The Lotus-Eaters	122
	Sweet and Low	126
	Tears, Idle Tears	296
	From Ulysses	17
Thomas, Edith M.	From Sursum Corda	268
Thompson, Francis	To My Godchild	216
Thorley, Wilfrid	Buttercups	170
Tomson, Graham R.	The Optimist	361
Torrence, Ridgely	From The House of a Hundred Lights	140
Towne, Charles Hanson	A Prayer for the Old Courage	33
Trebor, Nevah	Illusion	369
Turner, Nancy Byrd	Concerning Brownie	206
	Going up to London	185
	To a Staring Baby in a Perambulator	145
Unknown	The Amateur Bard on Woman	74
	Found on an English Sun Dial	278
	Golden Hands	351
	Jonnë Armstrong	7
	Ode to Discord	66
	The White Paternoster	120
	From Psalm XLVI	15

Unknown	Psalm XCI	49
	From Psalm XCV	351
	Psalm CXXI	31
Untermeyer, Jean Starr	Nature Cure	307
Untermeyer, Louis	Prayer	24
	Spratt vs. Spratt	80
	Voices	338
Van Dyke, Henry	The Wind of Sorrow	369
Vaughan, Henry	From A Vision	155
Vinal, Harold	To One with Hands of Sleep	130
Ward, May Williams	My House	138
Watson, William	To a Friend	280
	Ode in May	98
	Courage, Mon Ami!	107
	Creeds	153
Wells, Carolyn	A Penitential Week	65
Wharton, Edith	A Lyrical Epigram	205
White, Grace Hoffman	Unvanquished	38
Whitman, Walt	The Beasts	139
	From Passage to India	237
	From Passage to India	112
	A Selection from The Poem of Joys	110
	From The Poem of Joys	21
	A Selection from Song of the Open Road	101
	What Is the Grass?	181
Wickham, Anna	The Recompense	279
Widdemer, Margaret	The Factories	218
Wilcox, Ella Wheeler	The World's Need	245
Wilkinson, Marguerite	Before Dawn in the Wood	328
Wordsworth, William	From Character of the Happy Warrior	45
	The Daffodils	340
	England and Switzerland, 1802	317
	From Lines above Tintern Abbey	341
	Mutability	299

Wordsworth, William	To Sleep	133
	A Translation from Michael Angelo	131
	Up! Up! My Friend	325
	The World	305
Wylie, Elinor	Bells in the Rain	129
Yeats, William Butler	Into the Twilight	94
	The Lake Isle of Innisfree	343
	An Old Song Resung	110
	To a Friend Whose Work Has Come to Nothing	349
	To His Heart, Bidding It Have No Fear	6
	When You Are Old	360

TITLE INDEX

Abou Ben Adhem	Leigh Hunt	228
Advice to Worriers	George Kaupman	83
After Blenheim	Robert Southey	143
Air of Coolness Plays upon His Face, An	Sarah N. Cleghorn	154
Ale	William H. Davies	104
All Night the Lone Cicada	Charles G. D. Roberts	25
Amateur Bard on Woman, The	Unknown	74
Angler	Isabel Fiske Conant	353
Anodyne, The	Sarah N. Cleghorn	163
From Apparent Failure	Robert Browning	24
Arrow and the Song, The	Henry Wadsworth Longfellow	278
At the End of the Day	Richard Hovey	3
At the Heart	M. A. DeWolfe Howe	160
August Mood, An	Duncan Campbell Scott	147
Auld Lang Syne	Robert Burns	241
Balance, The	George Sterling	368
Ballad	Charles Stuart Calverley	77
Ballade of Adaptation, The	Brander Matthews	64
Ballade to Theocritus, in Winter	Andrew Lang	308
Ballad of Trees and the Master, A	Sidney Lanier	327
Beasts, The	Walt Whitman	139
Before Action	William Noel Hodgson	32
Before Dawn in the Wood	Marguerite Wilkinson	328
Bell, The	James Rorty	96
Bells in the Rain	Elinor Wylie	129
Bells of Heaven, The	Ralph Hodgson	205
Be Strong	Duncan Campbell Scott	15
Blackbird Suddenly, A	Joseph Auslander	353
Blessed Damozel, The	Dante Gabriel Rossetti	190

TITLE INDEX

Bridge of Sighs, The	Thomas Hood	221
Brook, The	Alfred Tennyson	335
Buttercups	Wilfrid Thorley	170
Byron	Joaquin Miller	245
California Vignette, A	Robinson Jeffers	316
From Captain Craig	Edwin Arlington Robinson	29
Care-Charming Sleep	John Fletcher	123
Celestial Surgeon, The	Robert Louis Stevenson	108
From Character of the Happy Warrior	William Wordsworth	45
Charge of the Light Brigade, The	Alfred Tennyson	258
Child's Song Overheard, A	Grace Hazard Conkling	169
Chimpanzee, The	Oliver Herford	54
Clear and Cool	Charles Kingsley	309
Closing Lines of Prometheus Unbound	Percy Bysshe Shelley	49
From Collar, The	George Herbert	109
From Columbus	Joaquin Miller	46
Come, Blessed Sleep	Christina Rossetti	119
Comfort	Margaret French Patton	373
Communion	Sophie Jewett	359
Compensation	Theodosia Garrison	162
Comrades	Richard Hovey	256
Concerning Brownie	Nancy Byrd Turner	206
Couplet	William Blake	338
Courage	Karle Wilson Baker	37
Courage	Virginia Moore	28
Courage, Mon Ami!	Willard Wattles	98
Creed of the Wood, The	Katharine Lee Bates	331
Creeds	Willard Wattles	153
Crew Poem, A	Edward Augustus Blount, Jr.	82
Daffodils, The	William Wordsworth	340
Days	Ralph Waldo Emerson	142
Dead Men Tell No Tales	Haniel Long	179
Death, Life, Fear	Lilla Cabot Perry	19
From Death Song in Taliesin, The	Richard Hovey	360

TITLE INDEX

Dedication	John Erskine	240
From Deep, The	Gladys Cromwell	337
Difference, The	John B. Tabb	61
Discovery	Hermann Hagedorn	322
Don Quixote	Austin Dobson	26
Door, The	Mary Carolyn Davies	232
Doves	Louise Imogen Guiney	16
Do You Fear the Wind?	Hamlin Garland	21
From Ducks	F. W. Harvey	84
Duet	Leonora Speyer	372
Each and All	Ralph Waldo Emerson	156
Ecstasy	Harold Trowbridge Pulsifer	95
Enamoured Architect of Airy Rhyme	Thomas Bailey Aldrich	26
England and Switzerland, 1802	William Wordsworth	317
Envoy	Bliss Carman	276
Epilogue to Asolando	Robert Browning	12
Epitaph for Any New Yorker	Christopher Morley	61
Epitaph for a Poet	DuBose Heyward	27
Escape, The	Lee Wilson Dodd	324
Escape	James Rorty	328
From Eve of Saint Agnes, The	John Keats	297
Exultation	Shaemas O'Sheel	267
Factories, The	Margaret Widdemer	218
From Faerie Queene, The	Edmund Spenser	130
From Faerie Queene, The	Edmund Spenser	122
Falconer of God, The	William Rose Benét	174
Fancy	John Keats	198
Father William	Lewis Carroll	85
Ferdinando and Elvira	W. S. Gilbert	55
Fine New Ballad of Cawsand Bay, A	Hamilton Moore	68
Finis	Walter Savage Landor	161
First Fig	Edna St. Vincent Millay	89
Flood Tide	Hermann Hagedorn	330
Flower Factory, The	Florence Wilkinson Evans	217

TITLE INDEX

Title	Author	Page
Flower in the Crannied Wall	Alfred Tennyson	158
Fool and Wise	Coventry Patmore	160
For Mercy, Courage, Kindness, Mirth	Lawrence Binyon	245
For Sleep When Overtired or Worried	Sarah N. Cleghorn	118
For Those Who Fail	Joaquin Miller	38
Found on an English Sun Dial	From the Latin	278
Give a Rouse	Robert Browning	257
Gladness	Anna Hempstead Branch	349
God's Pity	Louise Driscoll	230
Going up to London	Nancy Byrd Turner	185
Golden Hands	Unknown	351
Grief	Angela Morgan	22
Harvest	Robert Haven Schauffler	229
Heavy Dragoon, The	W. S. Gilbert	82
Helmsman, The	M. A. DeWolfe Howe	14
From Herod	Stephen Phillips	196
Heroism	Lizette Woodworth Reese	46
Hill-Born, The	Maxwell Struthers Burt	334
His Ally	William Rose Benét	36
His Pilgrimage	Sir Walter Raleigh	182
Homesick in England	Robert Haven Schauffler	332
Hope in Failure	A. E.	13
Horseman Springing from the Dark: A Dream	Lilla Cabot Perry	43
From House of a Hundred Lights, The	Ridgely Torrence	140
"How They Brought the Good News from Ghent to Aix"	Robert Browning	261
Idle Lake, The	Edmund Spenser	96
Idle to Grieve	Duncan Campbell Scott	372
If So Tomorrow Saves	Christina Rossetti	367
If This Were Faith	Robert Louis Stevenson	44
Illusion	Nevah Trebor	369
I Love the Friendly Faces of Old Sorrows	Karle Wilson Baker	374

TITLE INDEX

From Il Penseroso	John Milton	291
From Il Penseroso	John Milton	184
From Il Penseroso	John Milton	123
Immortality	Matthew Arnold	40
I'm Nobody	Emily Dickinson	137
In Romney Marsh	John Davidson	339
In the Wood	Sara Teasdale	317
Into the Twilight	William Butler Yeats	94
Invictus	William Ernest Henley	367
Invitation, The	Percy Bysshe Shelley	318
Jenny Kissed Me	Leigh Hunt	358
Jonnë Armstrong	Old Ballad	7
Joy	Hilda Conkling	354
Joy	Carl Sandburg	161
Jumblies, The	Edward Lear	62
Kind Sleep	Isabel Fiske Conant	117
King Henry before Harfleur	William Shakespeare	265
Kings, The	Louise Imogen Guiney	4
Kiss, The	Coventry Patmore	76
Kubla Khan	Samuel Taylor Coleridge	167
Ladders Through the Blue	Hermann Hagedorn	155
Lake Isle of Innisfree, The	William Butler Yeats	343
From L'Allegro	John Milton	355
Last Lines	Emily Brontë	10
Laugh and Be Merry	John Masefield	347
Leisure	William H. Davies	305
Lepanto	Gilbert K. Chesterton	249
Lessons	Sara Teasdale	14
Let Me Live Out My Years	John G. Neihardt	41
Let Me Sleep	Christina Rossetti	131
Life-Drunk	Arthur Stringer	105
From Lines above Tintern Abbey	William Wordsworth	341
From Lines on a Lap Dog	John Gay	205
Little Boy Blue	Eugene Field	213
Little Song of Life, A	Lizette Woodworth Reese	362
From Lotus-Eaters, The	Alfred Tennyson	122

TITLE INDEX

From Lycidas	John Milton	291
Lyrical Epigram, A	Edith Wharton	205
Madman, The	L. A. G. Strong	196
Magna Est Veritas	Coventry Patmore	281
Man with the Hoe, The	Edwin Markham	237
Marshes of Glynn, The	Sidney Lanier	310
Measure Me, Sky!	Leonora Speyer	153
Mercy	William Shakespeare	240
Midsummer Night	Archibald Lampman	125
Ministering Spirits, The	Edmund Spenser	374
Moonlight Music	William Shakespeare	298
More Life . . . More!	Lee Wilson Dodd	95
Morning	Emily Dickinson	169
Mountain and the Squirrel, The	Ralph Waldo Emerson	148
Mutability	William Wordsworth	299
My Garden	Thomas Edward Brown	337
My House	May Williams Ward	138
My Nosegays Are for Captives	Emily Dickinson	330
My Soul Is an Enchanted Boat	Percy Bysshe Shelley	128
My Star	Robert Browning	180
My Wage	Jessie B. Rittenhouse	141
Nature Cure	Jean Starr Untermeyer	307
Night, The	Hilaire Belloc	120
Not Our Good Luck	Robinson Jeffers	158
O Altitudo!	Sarah N. Cleghorn	6
Ode in May	William Watson	98
Ode to a Grecian Urn	John Keats	299
Ode to a Nightingale	John Keats	285
Ode to Discord	Unknown	66
From Ode to the West Wind	Percy Bysshe Shelley	48
Odyssey, The	Andrew Lang	264
From "Of Mountains"	Leonora Speyer	19
Old Ships, The	James Elroy Flecker	171
Old Song Resung, An	William Butler Yeats	110
Old Stoic, The	Emily Brontë	39
On a Magazine Sonnet	Russell Hillard Loines	80

TITLE INDEX

On a Subway Express	Chester Firkins	320
On His Blindness	John Milton	270
On One Ignorant and Arrogant	William Cowper	147
On the Death of a Favourite Canary	Matthew Arnold	210
One Fight More	Theodosia Garrison	47
One in the Infinite	George Francis Savage-Armstrong	139
Optimist, The	Graham R. Tomson	361
Outwitted	Edwin Markham	242
Over the Shoulders and Slopes of the Dune	Bliss Carman	350
Ozymandias	Percy Bysshe Shelley	137
Pandora's Song	William Vaughn Moody	376
From Passage to India	Walt Whitman	237
From Passage to India	Walt Whitman	112
Penitential Week, A	Carolyn Wells	65
Pillar of Cloud, The	John Henry, Cardinal Newman	34
Pippa's Song	Robert Browning	371
Pitcher of Mignonette, A	Henry Cuyler Bunner	220
Place of Rest, The	A. E.	352
A Selection from Poem of Joys, The	Walt Whitman	110
From Poem of Joys, The	Walt Whitman	21
Poeta Fit, Non Nascitur	Lewis Carroll	70
Poet's Dream, The	Percy Bysshe Shelley	197
Pool of Sleep, The	Arlo Bates	132
Portrait of a Boy	Stephen Vincent Benét	173
Portrait of an Old Woman	Arthur Davison Ficke	231
Prayer	E. F. Benson	22
Prayer	Louis Untermeyer	24
Prayer for the Old Courage, A	Charles Hanson Towne	33
Prospice	Robert Browning	9
Protest in Passing	Leonora Speyer	42
From Psalm XIX	David	140
Psalm XXIII	David	39

TITLE INDEX

From Psalm XLVI	Unknown	15
Psalm XCI	Unknown	49
From Psalm XCV	Unknown	351
From Psalm CIII	David	363
Psalm CXXI	Unknown	31
Queen Mab	William Shakespeare	171
Recompense, The	Anna Wickham	279
Rich Man, The	Franklin P. Adams	76
Riderless Horse, The	Harold Trowbridge Pulsifer	42
From Rime of the Ancient Mariner, The	Samuel Taylor Coleridge	212
Road Song, A	Duncan Campbell Scott	100
From Rubáiyát of Omár Khayyám, The	Edward Fitzgerald	146
From the Paraphrase of Rubáiyát of Omár Khayyám, The	Edward Fitzgerald	292
Rufus Prays	L. A. G. Strong	220
Sadness and Joy	William H. Davies	348
From Saint Paul	F. W. H. Myers	280
Salmon Fishing	Robinson Jeffers	209
Say Not the Struggle Naught Availeth	Arthur Hugh Clough	28
"Scum o' the Earth"	Robert Haven Schauffler	233
Second Coming, The	Norman Gale	239
Secret, The	Jessie B. Rittenhouse	354
Simplicity	Emily Dickinson	306
Sleep	John Fletcher	131
Sleep	Sophie Jewett	119
From Sleep	Christopher Morley	121
Sleep	John B. Tabb	132
Sleep Sweet	Ellen M. Huntington Gates	133
So I May Feel the Hands of God	Anna Hempstead Branch	208
Soldier, The	Sophie Jewett	35
Solitude	William Allingham	324
Song	Robert Burns	290
Song of Dark Waters, The	Roy Helton	232
Song of the Open Country	Dorothy Parker	322

TITLE INDEX

A Selection from SONG OF THE OPEN ROAD	Walt Whitman	10
SONGS OF JOY	William H. Davies	370
SONNET	John Keats	342
SONNET	Snow Longley	16
SONNET	William Shakespeare	288
SONNET, A	James Kenneth Stephen	79
SPARK, THE	Helen Gray Cone	207
SPRATT VS. SPRATT	Louis Untermeyer	80
SPRING ODE	Don Marquis	53
STREET CAR SYMPHONY, A	Roy Helton	175
STRICTLY GERM-PROOF	Arthur Guiterman	60
"SUCH STUFF AS DREAMS"	Franklin P. Adams	78
SUCH STUFF AS DREAMS	William Shakespeare	298
SUICIDE'S STONE	Robinson Jeffers	35
From SUMMER NIGHT, A	Matthew Arnold	154
From SURSUM CORDA	Edith M. Thomas	268
SWEET AND LOW	Alfred Tennyson	126
From TAMAR	Robinson Jeffers	107
TARTARY	Walter de la Mare	188
TEARS	Elizabeth Barrett Browning	375
TEARS	Lizette Woodworth Reese	375
TEARS, IDLE TEARS	Alfred Tennyson	296
THERE IS STRENGTH IN THE SOIL	Arthur Stringer	326
THEY WILL SAY	Carl Sandburg	219
TIGER, THE	William Blake	183
TO ——	Percy Bysshe Shelley	289
TO ALTHEA, FROM PRISON	Richard Lovelace	41
TO CYRIACK SKINNER	John Milton	94
TO A FRIEND	William Watson	280
TO A FRIEND WHOSE WORK HAS COME TO NOTHING	William Butler Yeats	349
TO HELEN	Edgar Allan Poe	288
TO HIS HEART, BIDDING IT HAVE NO FEAR	William Butler Yeats	6
From TO HOMER	John Keats	36
TO MR. LAWRENCE	John Milton	93

TITLE INDEX

To My Godchild	Francis Thompson	216
To One With Hands of Sleep	Harold Vinal	130
To Safeguard the Heart from Hardness	Sarah N. Cleghorn	213
To a Staring Baby in a Perambulator	Nancy Byrd Turner	145
To Sleep (Extract)	Norman Gale	124
To Sleep	John Keats	117
To Sleep	Sir Philip Sidney	121
To Sleep	William Wordsworth	133
To the Stone Cutters	Robinson Jeffers	138
From Town Pictures	Ernest Crosby	225
Toys, The	Coventry Patmore	214
Translation from Michael Angelo, A	William Wordsworth	131
Treasure House, A	M. A. DeWolfe Howe	277
Tuft of Flowers, The	Robert Frost	242
From Ulysses	Alfred Tennyson	17
Unrest	Don Marquis	266
Up! Up! My Friend	William Wordsworth	325
Unvanquished	Grace Hoffman White	38
Vagabondia	Richard Hovey	89
Verification	Christopher Morley	201
Victory in Defeat	Edwin Markham	370
Villanelle, with Stevenson's Assistance	Franklin P. Adams	358
From Vision, A	Henry Vaughan	155
Voices	Louis Untermeyer	338
Waiting	John Burroughs	275
Walls	Marjorie Meeker	323
We	Hervey Allen	106
What Is the Grass?	Walt Whitman	181
When You Are Old	William Butler Yeats	360
Where Is Fancy Bred?	William Shakespeare	198
Where None Intrudes	Lord Byron	310
White Paternoster, The	Old Rhyme	120
Wild Joys of Living, The	Robert Browning	263
Wild Ride, The	Louise Imogen Guiney	270

TITLE INDEX

Wind of Sorrow, The	Henry Van Dyke	36
"With Pipe and Flute"	Austin Dobson	33
"With Whom Is No Variableness, Neither Shadow of Turning"	Arthur Hugh Clough	280
Woman, A	Scudder Middleton	229
From Word at St. Kavin's, The	Bliss Carman	279
Work	Elizabeth Barrett Browning	277
World, The	William Wordsworth	305
World's Need, The	Ella Wheeler Wilcox	245
Wynken, Blynken and Nod	Eugene Field	127

FIRST LINE INDEX

A book of verses underneath the bough,	Edward Fitzgerald	292
A casement high and triple-arched there was,	John Keats	297
A child said, *What is the grass?* fetching it to me with full hands;	Walt Whitman	181
A fierce unrest seethes at the core	Don Marquis	266
A flock of sheep that leisurely pass by,	William Wordsworth	133
A garden is a lovesome thing, God wot!	Thomas Edward Brown	337
A man said unto his angel:	Louise Imogen Guiney	4
A pitcher of mignonette	Henry Cuyler Bunner	220
A whiff of forest scent,	Katharine Lee Bates	331
Abou Ben Adhem (may his tribe increase!)	Leigh Hunt	228
Afoot and light-hearted, I take to the open road,	Walt Whitman	101
After the whipping, he crawled into bed;	Stephen Vincent Benét	173
Ah, if man's boast, and man's advance be vain,	Louise Imogen Guiney	16
Ah! leave the smoke, the wealth, the roar	Andrew Lang	308
Alas! What boots it with uncessant care	John Milton	291
All day with anxious heart and wondering ear	Louis Untermeyer	338
All honor to him who shall win the prize,	Joaquin Miller	38
All night the lone cicada	Charles G. D. Roberts	25
All that I know	Robert Browning	180

399

FIRST LINE INDEX

And fast beside there trickled softly downe	Edmund Spenser	130
And more to lulle him in his slumber soft,	Edmund Spenser	122
And when, immortal mortal, droops your head	Francis Thompson	216
As I went down to Dymchurch Wall,	John Davidson	339
As I went up to London,	Nancy Byrd Turner	185
As one that for a weary space has lain	Andrew Lang	264
Ask me why I peer	Marjorie Meeker	323
At a pleasant evening party I had taken down to supper	W. S. Gilbert	55
At the gate of the West I stand,	Robert Haven Schauffler	233
At the midnight in the silence of the sleep-time,	Robert Browning	12
Aye, on the shores of darkness there is light,	John Keats	36
Because I coveted courage	Virginia Moore	28
Because I craved a gift too great	Theodosia Garrison	162
Behind him lay the great Azores,	Joaquin Miller	46
Behind thy pasteboard, on thy battered hack,	Austin Dobson	26
Best and brightest, come away	Percy Bysshe Shelley	318
Be strong O warring soul! For very sooth	Duncan Campbell Scott	15
Be you still, be you still, trembling heart;	William Butler Yeats	6
Bless the Lord, O my soul:	David	363
Bowed by the weight of centuries he leans	Edwin Markham	237
But let my due feet never fail,	John Milton	291
But thou, O Sleep, bend down and give	Norman Gale	124

FIRST LINE INDEX

By all the glories of the day	William Noel Hodgson	32
Care-charming Sleep, thou easer of all woes,	John Fletcher	123
Cares and anxieties,	Sarah N. Cleghorn	118
Child, I surrender—and hereby declare	Nancy Byrd Turner	145
Children, behold the Chimpanzee:	Oliver Herford	54
Clear and cool, clear and cool,	Charles Kingsley	309
Close ranks and ride on!	Harold Trowbridge Pulsifer	42
Come, blessed Sleep, most full, most perfect, come	Christina Rossetti	119
Come, gentle Sleep, Death's image tho' thou art,	William Wordsworth	131
Come, Sleep, and with thy sweet deceiving	John Fletcher	131
Come, Sleep, O Sleep, the certain knot of peace,	Sir Philip Sidney	121
Comrades, pour the wine tonight	Richard Hovey	256
Courage is armor	Karle Wilson Baker	37
Cyriack, whose Grandsire on the Royal Bench	John Milton	94
Daughters of Time, the hypocritic Days,	Ralph Waldo Emerson	142
Dear gray-eyed Angel, wilt thou come to-night?	Sophie Jewett	119
Defeat may serve as well as victory	Edwin Markham	370
Down by the salley gardens my love and I did meet;	William Butler Yeats	110
Do you fear the force of the wind,	Hamlin Garland	21
Dusk of a lowering evening,	Sophie Jewett	359
Enamoured architect of airy rhyme	Thomas Bailey Aldrich	26
Endow the fool with sun and moon,	Coventry Patmore	160
Ever let the Fancy roam,	John Keats	198

FIRST LINE INDEX

Fear death?—to feel the fog in my throat,	Robert Browning	9
Fill me with sassafras, nurse,	Don Marquis	53
Flower in the crannied wall,	Alfred Tennyson	158
Foil'd by our fellowmen, depress'd, outworn,	Matthew Arnold	40
. . . For I have learned	William Wordsworth	341
For Mercy, Courage, Kindness, Mirth,	Lawrence Binyon	245
From low to high doth dissolution climb,	William Wordsworth	299
Give me my scallop-shell of quiet,	Sir Walter Raleigh	182
Glad that I live am I;	Lizette Woodworth Reese	362
Glooms of the live-oaks, beautiful-braided and woven	Sidney Lanier	310
God, if this were enough,	Robert Louis Stevenson	44
God is our refuge and strength,	Unknown	15
God pity all the brave who go	Louise Driscoll	230
God, though this life is but a wraith,	Louis Untermeyer	24
God who, whatever frenzy of our fretting,	F. W. H. Myers	280
Golden hands,	Unknown	351
Great things are done when men and mountains meet;	William Blake	338
Half a league, half a league,	Alfred Tennyson	258
Haste thee nymph, and bring with thee	John Milton	355
Have little care that Life is brief,	Bliss Carman	276
Heaven is in my hand, and I	Joseph Auslander	353
Heaven overarches earth and sea,	Christina Rossetti	367
He drew a circle that shut me out—	Edwin Markham	242
Heed not the folk who sing or say	Graham R. Tomson	361

FIRST LINE INDEX 403

He fought for his soul, and the stubborn fighting	William Rose Benét	36
Helen, thy beauty is to me	Edgar Allan Poe	288
Hence loathed Melody, whose name recalls	Unknown	66
Here, in this little Bay,	Coventry Patmore	281
Here lies a spendthrift who believed	DuBose Heyward	27
Here Shock, the pride of all his kind, is laid,	John Gay	205
He that dwelleth in the secret place of the Most High	Unknown	49
Horseman, springing from the dark,	Lilla Cabot Perry	43
How happy is the little stone	Emily Dickinson	306
How oft do they their silver bowers leave	Edmund Spenser	374
How pitiful are little folk—	Willard Wattles	153
How shall I be a poet?	Lewis Carroll	70
How sweet the moonlight sleeps upon this bank!	William Shakespeare	298
How swiftly, once, on silvery feet	Anna Hempstead Branch	208
I bargained with Life for a penny.	Jessie B. Rittenhouse	141
I come from haunts of coot and hern,	Alfred Tennyson	335
I dragged my body to the pool of sleep,	Arlo Bates	132
I dreamed last night I stood with God on high,	Snow Longley	161
I dreamed last night of a dome of beaten gold	Stephen Phillips	196
I flung my soul to the air like a falcon flying.	William Rose Benét	174
I go a-fishing	Isabel Fiske Conant	353
I go in vesture spun by hands	Jessie B. Rittenhouse	354
"I had a dream last night:"	Edwin Arlington Robinson	29

FIRST LINE INDEX

I have climbed ladders through the blue!	Hermann Hagedorn	155
I have come far for this cleansing;	James Rorty	328
I have seen old ships sail like swans asleep	James Elroy Flecker	171
I have shut my little sister in from life and light,	Margaret Widdemer	218
I heard the waterfall rejoice,	Sara Teasdale	317
I heard the wind among the trees,	Harold Trowbridge Pulsifer	95
I heard you singing, singing alone	Grace Hazard Conkling	169
I hear in my heart, I hear in its ominous pulses,	Louise Imogen Guiney	270
I love the friendly faces of old Sorrows;	Karle Wilson Baker	374
I love the glamour of English towns,	Robert Haven Schauffler	332
I met a traveller from an antique land	Percy Bysshe Shelley	137
I pray you, Sadness, leave me soon,	William H. Davies	348
I saw Eternity the other night,	Henry Vaughan	155
I saw you take his kiss! 'Tis true.	Coventry Patmore	76
I shot an arrow into the air,	Henry Wadsworth Longfellow	278
I sprang to the stirrup, and Joris, and he;	Robert Browning	261
I steadfastly will,	Sarah N. Cleghorn	213
I strove with none, for none was worth my strife.	Walter Savage Landor	161
I struck the board and cry'd, "No more;	George Herbert	109
I think I could turn and live with animals,	Walt Whitman	139

FIRST LINE INDEX 405

I think I'll do a fearful deed	L. A. G. Strong	196
I wandered lonely as a cloud	William Wordsworth	340
I went to turn the grass once after one	Robert Frost	242
I, who all my life had hurried,	Christopher Morley	61
I, who have lost the stars, the sod,	Chester Firkins	320
I will arise and go now, and go to Innisfree,	William Butler Yeats	343
I will confront Death smiling, and no tremor	Lilla Cabot Perry	19
I will lift up mine eyes unto the hills,	Unknown	31
Idle to grieve when the stars are clear above me,	Duncan Campbell Scott	372
If grief should come to me	Margaret French Patton	373
If I have faltered more or less	Robert Louis Stevenson	108
If I were Lord of Tartary,	Walter de la Mare	188
If you want a receipt for that popular mystery,	W. S. Gilbert	82
I'm nobody! Who are you?	Emily Dickinson	137
In Cawsand Bay lying,	Hamilton Moore	68
In men whom men condemn as ill	Joaquin Miller	245
In the darkening church	L. A. G. Strong	220
In the late evening, when the house is still,	Sarah N. Cleghorn	163
In this imperfect, gloomy scene	Unknown	74
In this wide Inland sea, that hight by name	Edmund Spenser	96
Into the loud surf,	Sarah N. Cleghorn	6
Into the woods my Master went,	Sidney Lanier	327
In Xanadu did Kubla Khan	Samuel Taylor Coleridge	167
I'se de niggah, I'se de niggah;	Roy Helton	232
It fortifies my soul to know	Arthur Hugh Clough	280
It is an August evening in a free roof-garden built for the		

FIRST LINE INDEX

people on a pier over the river.	Ernest Crosby	225
It was a summer evening,	Robert Southey	143
Jenny kiss'd me in a dream;	Franklin P. Adams	78
Jenny kissed me when we met,	Leigh Hunt	358
Joy is not a thing you can see.	Hilda Conkling	354
King Charles, and who'll do him right now?	Robert Browning	257
Laugh and be merry; remember better the world with a song,	John Masefield	347
Lawrence of vertuous Father vertuous Son,	John Milton	93
Lead, kindly light, amid the encircling gloom,	John Henry, Cardinal Newman	34
Let a joy keep you.	Carl Sandburg	161
Let me go forth, and share	William Watson	98
Let me live out my years in heat of blood!	John G. Neihardt	41
Let scoffers doubt it if they will—	Nancy Byrd Turner	206
Let us be just with life. Although it bear	George Sterling	368
Lisabetta, Marianna, Fiametta, Teresina,	Florence Wilkinson Evans	217
Little thinks, in the field, yon red-cloaked clown	Ralph Waldo Emerson	156
Man from the blindness attaining the succor of sight,	Richard Hovey	360
Matthew, Mark, Luke and John,	Unknown	120
Measure me, sky!	Leonora Speyer	153
Most Holy Night, that still dost keep	Hilaire Belloc	120
Mother of balms and soothings manifold,	Archibald Lampman	125
My candle burns at both ends;	Edna St. Vincent Millay	89

FIRST LINE INDEX

407

My heart aches, and a drowsy numbness pains	John Keats	285
My house is small,	May Williams Ward	138
My little dog:	Edith Wharton	205
My little Son, who look'd from thoughtful eyes	Coventry Patmore	214
My nosegays are for captives;	Emily Dickinson	330
My own hope is, a sun will pierce	Robert Browning	24
My soul is an enchanted boat,	Percy Bysshe Shelley	128
No coward soul is mine,	Emily Brontë	10
Not our good luck nor the instant peak and fulfillment of time	Robinson Jeffers	158
Now all the truth is out,	William Butler Yeats	349
Now do I hear thee weep and groan,	William H. Davies	104
Now, think you, Life, I am defeated quite?	Theodosia Garrison	47
O come, let us sing unto the Lord:	Unknown	351
O happy living things! no tongue	Samuel Taylor Coleridge	212
O joy of suffering!	Walt Whitman	21
O my Luve's like a red, red rose	Robert Burns	290
O soft embalmer of the still midnight!	John Keats	117
. . . O the joy of my spirit! it is uncaged! it darts like lightning!	Walt Whitman	110
Of all of the gruesome attempts at a twosome	Louis Untermeyer	80
Of every step I took in pain	Anna Wickham	279
Of my city the worst that men will ever say is this:	Carl Sandburg	219
Of wounds and sore defeat	William Vaughn Moody	376
Off with the fetters	Richard Hovey	89

FIRST LINE INDEX

Oft on a Plat of rising ground,	John Milton	184
Oh, it is good to camp with the spirit,	Willard Wattles	107
Oh lift me as a wave, a leaf, a cloud!	Percy Bysshe Shelley	48
Oh, the wild joys of living! the leaping from rock up to rock,	Robert Browning	263
Old cypresses	Robinson Jeffers	316
On a Poet's lips I slept	Percy Bysshe Shelley	197
On opal Aprilian mornings like this	Arthur Stringer	105
On the day when I stopped begging at the heels of Life,	James Rorty	96
Once more into the breach, dear friends, once more;	William Shakespeare	265
One more Unfortunate,	Thomas Hood	221
One word is too often profaned	Percy Bysshe Shelley	289
Out from the whirl of factional unrest,	Lee Wilson Dodd	324
Out of my sorrow	Leonora Speyer	372
Out of the Eden of my love,	Hermann Hagedorn	322
Out of the four and twenty hours,	Sarah N. Cleghorn	154
Out of the night that covers me,	William Ernest Henley	367
Out-worn Heart, in a time outworn,	William Butler Yeats	94
Over the shoulders and slopes of the dune	Bliss Carman	350
Passage to India!	Walt Whitman	237
Passage to more than India!	Walt Whitman	112
Peace is the heir of dead desire,	Robinson Jeffers	35
Plainness and clearness without shadow of stain!	Matthew Arnold	154
Poor Matthias! Wouldst thou have	Matthew Arnold	210

FIRST LINE INDEX

My heart aches, and a drowsy numbness pains	John Keats	285
My house is small,	May Williams Ward	138
My little dog:	Edith Wharton	205
My little Son, who look'd from thoughtful eyes	Coventry Patmore	214
My nosegays are for captives;	Emily Dickinson	330
My own hope is, a sun will pierce	Robert Browning	24
My soul is an enchanted boat,	Percy Bysshe Shelley	128
No coward soul is mine,	Emily Brontë	10
Not our good luck nor the instant peak and fulfillment of time	Robinson Jeffers	158
Now all the truth is out,	William Butler Yeats	349
Now do I hear thee weep and groan,	William H. Davies	104
Now, think you, Life, I am defeated quite?	Theodosia Garrison	47
O come, let us sing unto the Lord:	Unknown	351
O happy living things! no tongue	Samuel Taylor Coleridge	212
O joy of suffering!	Walt Whitman	21
O my Luve's like a red, red rose	Robert Burns	290
O soft embalmer of the still midnight!	John Keats	117
. . . O the joy of my spirit! it is uncaged! it darts like lightning!	Walt Whitman	110
Of all of the gruesome attempts at a twosome	Louis Untermeyer	80
Of every step I took in pain	Anna Wickham	279
Of my city the worst that men will ever say is this:	Carl Sandburg	219
Of wounds and sore defeat	William Vaughn Moody	376
Off with the fetters	Richard Hovey	89

FIRST LINE INDEX

Oft on a Plat of rising ground,	John Milton	184
Oh, it is good to camp with the spirit,	Willard Wattles	107
Oh lift me as a wave, a leaf, a cloud!	Percy Bysshe Shelley	48
Oh, the wild joys of living! the leaping from rock up to rock,	Robert Browning	263
Old cypresses	Robinson Jeffers	316
On a Poet's lips I slept	Percy Bysshe Shelley	197
On opal Aprilian mornings like this	Arthur Stringer	105
On the day when I stopped begging at the heels of Life,	James Rorty	96
Once more into the breach, dear friends, once more;	William Shakespeare	265
One more Unfortunate,	Thomas Hood	221
One word is too often profaned	Percy Bysshe Shelley	289
Out from the whirl of factional unrest,	Lee Wilson Dodd	324
Out of my sorrow	Leonora Speyer	372
Out of the Eden of my love,	Hermann Hagedorn	322
Out of the four and twenty hours,	Sarah N. Cleghorn	154
Out of the night that covers me,	William Ernest Henley	367
Out-worn Heart, in a time outworn,	William Butler Yeats	94
Over the shoulders and slopes of the dune	Bliss Carman	350
Passage to India!	Walt Whitman	237
Passage to more than India!	Walt Whitman	112
Peace is the heir of dead desire,	Robinson Jeffers	35
Plainness and clearness without shadow of stain!	Matthew Arnold	154
Poor Matthias! Wouldst thou have	Matthew Arnold	210

# FIRST LINE INDEX

Pray list to me a modest while;	George Kaupman	83
The quality of mercy is not strain'd	William Shakespeare	240
Ravaged of faith I fled,	Grace Hoffman White	38
Readers of riddles dark,	Helen Gray Cone	207
Riches I hold in light esteem,	Emily Brontë	39
Roll on, and with thy rolling crust	George Francis Savage-Armstrong	139
Rumble along, over the water	Roy Helton	175
Say not the struggle naught availeth,	Arthur Hugh Clough	28
Scorn not the sonnet, though its strength be sapped,	Russell Hillard Loines	80
Serene, I fold my hands and wait,	John Burroughs	275
Set me over the main again,	Lee Wilson Dodd	95
She answered, standing dark against the west	Robinson Jeffers	107
She had an understanding with the years;	Scudder Middleton	229
She is the fairies' midwife, and she comes	William Shakespeare	171
She limps with halting painful pace	Arthur Davison Ficke	231
She moves as other women move	Harold Vinal	130
Should auld acquaintance be forgot,	Robert Burns	241
Sing out, my Soul, thy songs of joy;	William H. Davies	370
Sleep falls, with limpid drops of rain,	Elinor Wylie	129
Sleep, let me sleep, for I am sick of care;	Christina Rossetti	131
Sleep sweet within this quiet room,	Ellen M. Huntington Gates	133
Slip into sleep as easy as a gown	Isabel Fiske Conant	117

FIRST LINE INDEX

So happy were Columbia's eight,	Edward Augustus Blount, Jr.	82
Solitude is very sad,	William Allingham	324
So many gods, so many creeds,	Ella Wheeler Wilcox	245
Soon may the edict lapse, that on you lays	William Watson	280
Still let us go the way of beauty; go	Charles Hanson Towne	33
Stone-cutters fighting time with marble, you foredefeated	Robinson Jeffers	138
Stone walls do not a prison make,	Richard Lovelace	41
Such quiet gray and green! Such peaceful farms!	Hermann Hagedorn	330
Sundown is but the mortal eye's confusion,	Nevah Trebor	369
Sweet and low, sweet and low	Alfred Tennyson	126
Tears, idle tears, I know not what they mean,	Alfred Tennyson	296
Tell it again in stronger tones	Jean Starr Untermeyer	307
Tell me where is Fancy bred,	William Shakespeare	198
Thank God, bless God, all ye who suffer not	Elizabeth Barrett Browning	375
The Antiseptic Baby and the Prophylactic Pup	Arthur Guiterman	60
The auld wife sat at her ivied door,	Charles Stuart Calverley	77
The blessed Damozel lean'd out	Dante Gabriel Rossetti	190
The dawn of the everlasting day	E. F. Benson	22
The days shorten, the south blows wide for showers now,	Robinson Jeffers	209
The fire of love was burning, yet so low	Henry Van Dyke	369
The half-dream crumbles and falls through:	Christopher Morley	201

FIRST LINE INDEX

The heart is but a narrow space	M. A. DeWolfe Howe	160
The heavens declare the glory of God;	David	140
The littlest door, the inner door,	Mary Carolyn Davies	232
The little toy dog is covered with dust,	Eugene Field	213
The Lord is my shepherd;	David	39
The Mountain and the Squirrel	Ralph Waldo Emerson	148
The native drama's sick and dying,	Brander Matthews	64
The poet's song, the painter's art,	M. A. DeWolfe Howe	277
The quality of mercy is not strain'd	William Shakespeare	240
The rich man has his motor-car	Franklin P. Adams	76
The Saviour came. With trembling lips	Norman Gale	239
The soldier fought his battle silently.	Sophie Jewett	35
The week had gloomily begun	Carolyn Wells	65
The world has brought not anything	Anna Hempstead Branch	349
The world is so full of a number of things	Franklin P. Adams	358
The world is too much with us; late and soon,	William Wordsworth	305
The year's at the spring,	Robert Browning	371
There dwelt a man in faire Westmerland,	Unknown	7
Therefore, my friends, I say	Bliss Carman	279
There in close covert by some brook	John Milton	123
There is no escape by the river,	Richard Hovey	3
There is a pleasure in the pathless woods,	Lord Byron	310

FIRST LINE INDEX

There is strength in the soil;	Arthur Stringer	326
There is sweet music here that softer falls	Alfred Tennyson	122
There lies the port; the vessel puffs her sail:	Alfred Tennyson	17
There must be fairy miners	Wilfrid Thorley	170
These our actors,	William Shakespeare	298
They heard that she was dying, and they came,	Robert Haven Schauffler	229
They say that dead men tell no tales!	Haniel Long	179
They went to sea in a sieve, they did;	Edward Lear	62
This house of flesh was never loved of me,	Leonora Speyer	42
Though now thou hast failed and art fallen, despair not because of defeat,	A. E.	13
Thou mayst of double ignorance boast,	William Cowper	147
Thou still unravished bride of quietness!	John Keats	299
Tiger, Tiger, burning bright	William Blake	183
Time flies,	Unknown	278
To one who has been long in city pent	John Keats	342
To suffer woes which Hope thinks infinite;	Percy Bysshe Shelley	49
'Twould ring the bells of Heaven	Ralph Hodgson	205
Two voices are there; one is of the deep;	James Kenneth Stephen	79
Two voices are there; one is of the Sea,	William Wordsworth	317
Unc' Si, de Holy Bible say,	John B. Tabb	61
Unless I learn to ask no help	Sara Teasdale	14
Unto the deep the deep heart goes,	A. E.	352

FIRST LINE INDEX

Up and rejoice, and know thou hast matter for revel, my heart!	Edith M. Thomas	268
Up heart, away heart,	Duncan Campbell Scott	100
Upon our eyelids, dear, the dew will lie,	Marguerite Wilkinson	328
Upon this trouble shall I whet my life	Angela Morgan	22
Up! up! my friend, and quit your books,	William Wordsworth	325
What are we set on earth for? Say, to toil;	Elizabeth Barrett Browning	277
What art thou, balmy sleep?	John B. Tabb	132
What! doubt the Master Workman's hand		
What is this life if, full of care,	Ridgely Torrence	140
What shall I ask for the voyage I must sail to the end alone?	William H. Davies	305
We are no other than a moving row	M. A. DeWolfe Howe	14
We who have come back from the war,	Edward Fitzgerald	146
When God had finished the stars and whirl of coloured suns	Hervey Allen	106
When I consider how my light is spent,	F. W. Harvey	84
When I consider Life and its few years—	John Milton	276
When imperturbable the gentle moon	Lizette Woodworth Reese	375
When, in disgrace with Fortune and men's eyes,	John Erskine	240
When lights are low, and the day has died,	William Shakespeare	288
When the full-bosomed and free-limbed Spring	Dorothy Parker	322
	Shaemas O'Sheel	267

When you are old and gray and full of sleep	William Butler Yeats	360
Where floating shapes of stars and leaves	Gladys Cromwell	337
Where the pines have fallen on the hillside	Duncan Campbell Scott	147
Whether we climb, whether we plod,	Lizette Woodworth Reese	46
White founts falling in the Courts of the sun,	Gilbert K. Chesterton	249
Who is the pioneer?	Leonora Speyer	19
Whose powers shed round him in the common strife,	William Wordsworth	45
Will there really be a morning?	Emily Dickinson	169
With pipe and flute the rustic Pan	Austin Dobson	332
The world has brought not anything	Anna Hempstead Branch	349
The world is so full of a number of things	Franklin P. Adams	358
Wynken, Blynken, and Nod one night	Eugene Field	127
Yet, in the end, you take us all, dear Sleep—	Christopher Morley	121
"You are old, Father William," the young man said,	Lewis Carroll	85
You who are born of the hills,	Maxwell Struthers Burt	334